CHRISTIAN
NEIGHBOR-LOVE

CHRISTIAN NEIGHBOR-LOVE
An Assessment of Six Rival Versions

GARTH L. HALLETT

Georgetown University Press
Washington, D.C.

Library of Congress Cataloging-in-Publication Data

Hallett, Garth L., 1927-
    Christian neighbor-love : an assessment of six rival versions /
Garth L. Hallett.
        p.   cm.
    Bibliography: p.
    Includes index.
    ISBN 0-87840-479-1   ISBN 0-87840-480-5 (pbk.)
    1. Love—Religious aspects—Christianity.   2. God—Worship and
love.   I. Title.
BV4639.H23 1989
241.5—dc19   88-29182
                                                                        CIP

CONTENTS

PREFACE

"It is plain," it has been said, "that the idea of love occupies a—not to say the—central place in Christianity, both from a religious and an ethical point of view."[1] Yet at the heart of this central notion a crucial obscurity persists. "Agape" calls for love of neighbor as well as love of God, and for love of God shown through love of neighbor. How, though, is this neighbor-love to be conceived? As chapter 1 documents, Christians past and present have understood agape's call to service of others in half a dozen different, incompatible ways. To date, however, these conflicting conceptions have not been identified and listed, nor have they been systematically compared and assessed, so as to discern their implications and determine their respective credentials. Each of the six variants has had its adherents. Each has been argued for in preference to some other. But none has been validated through a systematic sifting of all six rival positions. Thus, strange as this assertion may sound after nearly two millenia of Christian emphasis on agape, the Christian norm of neighbor-love offers relatively virgin territory for inquiry.

The present exploration of this territory, in the manner suggested, will be both theological and philosophical, and hence should interest both Christians and non-Christians. After reaching a tentative Christian solution on the basis of Scripture and tradition, I shall examine the views of philosophers, since they have come at the issue more analytically than theologians have. However, even philosophical literature contains no treatment as comprehensive as that forced on me by Christians' rich and varied thinking through the centuries. My hope is that readers will find the scrutiny of this richness and variety intellectually stimulating, practically significant, and spiritually challenging, as I have.

The study's structure is simple: Three brief introductory chapters prepare three longer chapters of inquiry, and a final chapter assesses the significance of the verdict reached.

I am grateful to Daniel Harrington and Walter Hayes for assistance in scriptural and patristic research; to Gerard Hughes, Robert O'Toole, Martin Palmer, James Pollock, Jules Toner, and S. Youree Watson for comments and criticism; and to Jeannette Batz for stylistic polishing. The work has profited greatly from their generous help.

Saint Louis, Missouri

1

A Neglected Question

In the view of many Christians, the gospel command of neighbor-love lacks neither clarity nor force, however much our thinking may dim or dilute it. "It is somehow hard to grasp and to hold firmly," Paul Furfey for instance observes, "the simple truth that love is the Christian's sole moral obligation. For some obscure reason, writers constantly tend to redefine Christian morality in other and more complex terms." For Furfey, "the familiar texts in which Jesus Christ stated categorically and in the clearest possible language the primacy of love" offer ample guidance.[1] "The Christian's obligation to act against the problem of racial injustice or the problem of poverty or any other social problem is quite easily solved under the Authentic Code. One simply applies to a specific situation the general obligation. 'You shall love your neighbor as yourself'."[2] Citing person-to-person problems rather than social concerns, Rudolf Bultmann writes with equal firmness: "The demand for love needs no formulated stipulations; the example of the merciful Samaritan shows that a man can know and must know what he has to do when he sees his neighbor in need of his help. The little words 'as yourself' in the love-commandment pre-indicate both the boundlessness and the direction of loving conduct."[3]

Assertions like Furfey's and Bultmann's contain much truth if rightly understood; yet in one significant respect they are misleading. It may be true that the injunction to love one's neighbor as oneself sufficiently indicates the answer to many a social problem, but the reason is not that the injunction states love's primacy "in the clearest possible language." It may be true that often, as in the gospel parable, a Christian can know straightaway what he or she should do for a needy neighbor; but the reason is not that "the demand for love needs no formulated stipulations." Indeed, Bultmann adds his own implicit stipulations when he interprets the commandment as indicating "both the boundlessness and the direction of loving conduct." And the stipulations he divines in the commandment of neighbor-love are ones most contemporary exegetes do not find there.

The controversy surrounding this particular scriptural formula (Mt 22:39; Mk 12:33; Lk 10:27) is part of a larger disagreement that has long obscured the heart of Christian ethics. According to one traditional reading, the phrase *as yourself* "does not mean 'as much as yourself,' for this would be against the order of charity."[4] Rather, from the very words *as yourself* it can be inferred "that a man must love himself more than his neighbour."[5] According to a second common reading, the commandment enjoins equality rather than self-preference: "It is required of those who would love God that they put the welfare of their neighbor on a par with their own."[6] They are to love others "with the same conviction, the same energy, the same determination as one gives to defending and furthering his own life, his own convictions, his own possessions."[7] According to a third, equally strong tradition, "by this commandment 'as yourself' man is not commanded to love himself but he is shown the wicked love with which in fact he loves himself; in other words, it says to him: You are wholly bent in on yourself and versed in self-love, and you will not be straightened out and made upright unless you cease entirely to love yourself and, forgetting yourself, love only your neighbor."[8] "The command turns the lock of the stronghold of self-love as with a master key and casts self-love out."[9]

This is but a sampling. Christian disagreement extends still further, both with regard to this scriptural injunction and with regard to neighbor-love in general. It has for instance been urged, in contrast with the preceding readings of Scripture, that "the words 'as yourself' do not indicate how much love, or for that matter that any amount of love, may be withheld; instead, they describe the sort of love Christians should give to others."[10] Indeed, "whether it is right for us to love ourselves, whether it is right for us to wish that others should do good to us, are questions neither raised nor answered. It is simply taken for granted that men are not indifferent to their own welfare."[11] If, however, we do raise such questions and ask, for example, how a Christian should balance benefit to self and benefit to others, we discover still more varied verdicts than those suggested by interpretations of the saying "You shall love your neighbor as yourself."

Six Rival Norms

Nine main competing rules of preference, apportioning benefit to self and to others, are theoretically conceivable. Ranging from complete egoism to total altruism, their content may be suggested by the labels: Other-Denial, Other-Forgetfulness, Other-Subordination, Self-Preference, Parity, Other-Preference, Self-Subordination, Self-Forgetfulness, and Self-Denial. The last six of these, which I shall now characterize more fully, are represented—more or less extensively, more or less explicitly—in the history of Christian thought. The names I attach to them I capitalize, both here and hereafter, as a reminder of the special sense accorded to each expression. Experience suggests the need to emphasize this reminder and thereby forestall misunderstandings; so let me repeat: The following six capitalized expressions all have special senses, throughout this study, and the senses they have are the ones I shall now indicate.

1. Self-Preference

According to this norm, *in deciding between alternative lines of action, a person should take account of others' good but should give more weight to his or her own good than to the equal good, collective or individual, of others.* Where I, the agent, must choose between benefit to myself and equal benefit to another, I should choose to benefit myself. Where I must choose between harm to myself and equal harm to another, I should spare myself and let the other person suffer. Only when others seem likely to benefit much more, collectively or individually, from one option than I would from some other alternative, more favorable to myself, should I give precedence to their interests. Just how much greater their prospective benefit would have to be to tip the scales the other way, the norm of Self-Preference does not indicate.

This position was long dominant in Catholic moral theology. "It is according to the order of charity," wrote Aquinas, "that a man love himself less than God and more than his neighbor."[12] "One's own good," Durandus concurred, "is to be loved and sought more than another's."[13] Suarez saw no reason to doubt that, "other things being equal, according to the order of charity it is better to assist oneself than to assist others."[14] Through the centuries, a host of manualists have spelled out further details (my spiritual good over another's spiritual good, my temporal good over another's temporal good, my life over another's life, and so forth). In chapter 5 I trace and evaluate this tradition.

2. Parity

In this view, *equal benefit, whether to oneself or another, should receive equal weight, and unequal benefit unequal weight, without preference either way.* If, with two options facing me, it appears that I would benefit equally in both and my neighbor would benefit more in the second, I should choose the second. If I would benefit more in the first and my neighbor equally in both, I should prefer the first. If I would benefit more in the first and my neighbor would benefit still more in the second, I should opt for the second. If each of several neighbors would benefit as much or more from the second as I would from the first, in that case, too, I should opt for the second. And so forth.

When John Stuart Mill enjoined the strictest impartiality between one's own happiness and others', he alleged Christian backing for his view.[15] And indeed from earliest times, Parity too has had its Christian spokesmen (Justin,[16] Origen,[17] Basil,[18] Augustine,[19] Maximus,[20] William of St. Thierry,[21] Bellarmine,[22] Bossuet,[23] Niebuhr,[24] Wiebering,[25] . . .) and continues to have them: "Affectively and effectively, a Christian should love his neighbor 'as himself,' without making any difference between love of self and love of neighbor."[26] "We are to be of the same mind to all men and not to love anyone more or less than another."[27] "It is necessary to learn more and more to put self and the neighbour on the same plane, so that we may gradually come to take as much account of the neighbour's wishes as of our own."[28]

3. Other-Preference

Reversing Self-Preference, Other-Preference dictates that *in deciding between alternative courses of action, a person should take account of his or her own good but should give more weight to the equal good, collective or individual, of others.* According to this position, a person may sometimes legitimately prefer an option less favorable to others, but only if their loss means a much greater gain for himself. How much greater the gain would have to be to legitimize such a choice, the norm of Other-Preference does not say.

Among the innumerable sayings of Christian ethicians, preachers, and spiritual writers that tilt the balance in favor of one's neighbor, many indicate nothing more than Other-Preference. "Christian love," it may be said without further stipulation, "must also be characterized by an attitude of service, that is, putting the neighbor and his or her concerns first."[29] With regard to earthly goods, "it is in itself permissible, indeed generous and advisable, to give the neighbor precedence."[30] Thus, according to St. Nilus, "in buying or selling necessary commodities, we should not bargain to the disadvantage of our brother, but should prefer to suffer a loss ourselves."[31] In like vein, St. Leo the Great praised "the holy widow of Sarepta . . . who offered the blessed Elias in the time of famine one day's food, which was all she had, and putting the prophet's hunger before her own needs, ungrudgingly gave up a handful of corn and a little oil."[32] Again, "When St. Paulinus, bishop of Nola, had used up all he had for the redemption of captives and the necessities of the needy, he finally became a slave himself so as to free another from slavery. And we read that this deed of his was not blamed, but rather highly praised by St. Gregory."[33]

4. Self-Subordination

In this understanding of neighbor-love, *one may and should give independent consideration to one's own benefit, but only on the condition that maximum benefit to others is first assured (whether directly or indirectly, through benefit to oneself).* Thus, according to St. Ambrose, "the upright man must never think of depriving another of anything, nor must he ever wish to increase his own advantage to the disadvantage of another."[34] This says more than Other-Preference; one's own good must not compete with others'. Yet no further limitation is placed on benefit to self, as it is in more stringent forms of altruism enjoining self-forgetfulness or self-denial. Occasionally, the absence of any restriction not related to others' good is stated quite explicitly: "Love of my neighbor does not exclude the possibility that I incidentally seek my own which can be allied with it [sic]";[35] "agape does not rule out acting for one's own benefit in situations where the consequences to others would be indifferent."[36] "In Paul, too," insists Karl Barth, "the Christian's dying and being dead and buried with Christ has nothing whatever to do with an unrelated self-negation and asceticism that is of value only in itself. When Paul describes himself as exhausted and wasted and spent like capital, he adds: 'For your souls' (2 Cor. 12:15)."[37]

5. Self-Forgetfulness

Here, *in choosing a course of action, a person should consider his or her own benefit only in relation to others'; it should not be given any independent weight.* Aelred of Rievaulx appears to envisage such a norm when he writes that, ideally, "my love for God, with all my heart, soul, and strength, would have no place for my own interests, but only for those of Christ. And before the warmth of my love for my fellow men all self-centredness would melt away, so that my every thought and aim would be focused on them."[38] For Jürgen Moltmann, "love is the acceptance of the other without regard to one's own well-being."[39] "From Cassian to Saint John of the Cross or Saint Ignatius of Loyola, as from Plotinus to Saint Francis of Sales, the same theme reappears"—the blessedness of indifference to self and self's concerns.[40]

6. *Self-Denial*

In this most extreme understanding of Christian altruism, *a person should never seek his or her own good save as a means to others' good; so far as maximum benefit to others permits, self-service should be minimized.*

Self-Forgetfulness merges easily with Self-Denial, and it is sometimes difficult to tell which norm is intended. Is "selfless" love, for example, a love that merely *takes no thought for* self, or one that goes further and *denies* self? The ambiguity lessens when reference is made to the "selfless love revealed in Jesus, the man completely for others,"[41] and disappears entirely when the love proclaimed is "a completely self-denying love."[42] Similar-sounding sayings can be found in every period—in patristic times (for example, Ambrose,[43] Augustine,[44] Basil,[45] Benedict,[46] Chrysostom,[47] Leo the Great[48]), medieval (à Kempis,[49] Albert,[50] Bernard,[51] Catherine of Siena,[52] Eckhart,[53] Hugh of St. Victor,[54] Ruysbroeck,[55] Scotus,[56] Suso,[57] Tauler,[58] William of Auvergne,[59] the *Book of the Poor in Spirit*[60]), modern (Bossuet,[61] Bucer,[62] Calvin,[63] Loyola,[64] John of the Cross,[65] Luther,[66] Vincent de Paul[67]), and contemporary (Arndt,[68] Birngruber,[69] Brunner,[70] Bultmann,[71] Doherty,[72] DuRoy,[73] Guardini,[74] Hammarskjöld,[75] Henry,[76] Knox,[77] Lecky,[78] Lütgert,[79] Nygren,[80] Thomas,[81] and others).

Since these six rival norms constitute the backbone of the present inquiry, I shall make a few preliminary analytic observations concerning them, then dwell on certain points at greater length in later chapters. First, numbers 2, 4, 5, and 6 draw sharp boundaries, whereas 1 and 3 do not, since they fail to indicate how much more heavily one's own good should weigh in the scales than another's, or vice versa.[82] Second, all six norms, nonetheless, may on occasion fail to indicate what course of action to prefer; for all six may sometimes yield a tied verdict between competing alternatives (as may any conceivable formulation of egoism or altruism). Third, all the norms except Parity may dictate incompatible actions for self and other (for instance, may dictate that both take a specific desirable or undesirable seat), but none yields contradictory verdicts (for example, that the same person both take and not take a specific seat).[83] Fourth, since the norms, as listed, progressively shift the emphasis from self to others, any service to others required by one of the norms is required by all that follow it, and any self-service allowed by one is allowed by all that precede it. Fifth, the norms at both extremes look less extreme in practice than in abstract formulation, for care of self may call for much service of others and service of others may call for much care of self.

The Norms' Implications

Despite this rapprochement, it makes a difference which rule one favors and follows; and the difference may be notable, either cumulatively or on some single occasion. To illustrate:

Self-Preference versus Parity

As his huge construction crane began to tip, its too-massive load swinging out of control nearly twenty stories up, Tom O'Brien tensed to leap through his cabin door to safety. Every nerve in his body screamed: *Jump!* But an image flashed before his mind of shattered buildings avalanching into the street, crushing pedestrians, flattening autos and buses, killing scores of people. By staying at the controls, he might, just might, be able to prevent such carnage. And he did. When the crane's boom, cab, and monster tractor-treads followed the 53,000-pound load into the excavation where O'Brien had managed to guide it, he was the only person hurt.[84]

Even the weakest form of Christian altruism would advise this man to do as he did. Even Self-Preference, if kept within sane limits, would rate the lives of scores over the life or safety of a single individual. However, consider a case like that of Maximilian Kolbe, who offered himself in place of one other man when the camp commandant picked ten prisoners to die.[85] The man Kolbe replaced in the starvation bunker had a wife and children, whereas Kolbe, a Franciscan monk, did not. True, Kolbe's fellow religious would miss him, but not as sorely as the man's wife and children would miss him. So Parity would suggest that he do as he did and die in the other's place. Self-Preference, however, would be less demanding. The greater weight it accorded Kolbe's life would balance the added benefit to the other man's wife and children. In such an assessment of relative benefits (which is here, of course, just illustrative and therefore perfunctory), any form of Self-Preference that departed more than minimally from equal consideration for self and neighbor would countenance Kolbe's staying in his place and letting the other man die, whereas perfect Parity would not.

Not only may Self-Preference permit self-regarding conduct; it may forbid other-regarding conduct. For example, "It is generally and reasonably allowed to be legitimate," writes Alan Donagan, "to give a bodily organ such as an eye or a kidney for transplantation, in order to save a faculty, or the life, of another. Yet this must not be at the cost of that faculty in the giver, or of his life. One may not blind oneself to save another from blindness."[86] Parity would permit either option; Self-Preference would not, save for special reasons over and above the exchange of life for life or of sight for sight.[87]

Options like O'Brien's and Kolbe's are exceptional, but they could easily be replaced by everyday illustrations. Such examples would have the advantage of showing that even Self-Preference and Parity, the least altruistic of the six norms, call for continual sacrifice of self. The more heroic examples have the different advantage of showing that the sacrifice required by even these relatively undemanding norms may sometimes be extreme. However, either type of illustration—the everyday or the extraordinary—can be used to make the present point that the implications of Self-Preference and Parity do not perfectly coincide. Sometimes their verdicts agree; sometimes they do not. And when they do not, the difference may be one of life or death.

Parity versus Other-Preference

Immediately after the crash of Air Florida's Flight 90 in January, 1982, an unforgettable scene played itself out in the dark, icy waters of the Potomac River. Twice a balding, middle-aged man (whom strong evidence identifies as a passenger named Arland Williams) had a chance to save himself; twice he chose instead to pass the lifeline to another and await his turn. When the other survivors had been rescued and his turn finally arrived, the man had disappeared beneath the ice.[88]

I pick this incident because of the stark simplicity of the comparisons Williams was able to make. He knew nothing of the four survivors with whom he found himself. He knew nothing of their characters, occupations, life expectancies, dependents, or potential contributions to society. He knew only that they were human beings as he was. Each time the lifeline came to him, it was life versus life, and Williams in each instance gave preference to another's life over his own. This the norm of Other-Preference would clearly ask of him whereas the norm of Parity would not.

Here, once again, more mundane illustrations might be substituted to suggest the frequency of such options. If no dividing or distributing is possible, but either I or somebody else gets the lifeline, the promotion, the job, the house, the wife, the seat, or the last chop on the plate, Other-Preference recommends that I do without. Where benefits can be shared, it suggests that I take the lesser portion. My welfare and happiness are to be considered too, but less than another's. Parity, on the contrary, makes no such demands.

Other-Preference versus Self-Subordination

A man asks his hostess, "Do you mind if I smoke?" She does, in fact, mind a great deal. If the discomfort she anticipates, to eyes, throat, and lungs, looks sufficiently great relative to his likely pleasure from smoking, Other-Preference may countenance the reply, "Yes, I'm afraid I do," whereas (other things being equal) Self-Subordination would not.

"Retired couple hit lottery jackpot" the headline proclaims. What will they do with the money? A girl has received a box of chocolates. How will she distribute them? Other-Preference might advise her: "Hand them around liberally to your playmates, three or four apiece, but keep one or two for yourself." Self-Subordination would go further (other things being equal) and suggest: "Keep none for yourself, but give that extra pleasure to the others." Subject to the same proviso, Other-Preference would tell the retired couple to be generous in their good fortune but to keep something for themselves, whereas Self-Subordination would advise that they distribute all their winnings and continue to live as before. In small matters and in large, the two norms may dictate different verdicts.[89]

Self-Subordination versus Self-Forgetfulness and Self-Denial

When, in 1931, Reinhold Niebuhr contemplated marriage, it was with a mixture of joy and pain. His mother let him know that she could not bear to leave his home; his fiancee, Ursula Keppel-Compton, would be wretched if he refused her. In some respects marriage might help his ministry; in other respects it might hinder it. As far as others were concerned, the scales may have seemed evenly balanced. Yet Niebuhr himself wanted very much to marry.[90] In such a situation, Self-Subordination, Self-Forgetfulness, and Self-Denial give different answers. For Self-Subordination his personal inclinations would count in favor of marriage; for Self-Forgetfulness they would not; for Self-Denial they would point in the opposite direction and, with no clear advantage either way to others, would decide against the marriage rather than in favor of it.

Less momentous illustrations occur daily, even hourly. You are driving to the office, for example, and follow a scenic route; you are working at home and sit outside to enjoy the spring day; you are eating in a restaurant and order your favorite dish. The scenic route may not be shorter or quicker, but it is more pleasant. The work could be done as efficiently indoors, but not as enjoyably. The favorite dish is not more nourishing, digestible, or reasonably priced, but it is more agreeable. In each such instance, given equal benefit to others, Self-Subordination would approve your choice. The scenery, the weather, the favorite dish are all good things; enjoy them, and be thankful. Self-Forgetfulness, on the contrary, would have you take no thought for your personal enjoyment, and Self-Denial would tell you to avoid it. Given equal benefit to others, it would advise that you choose a less inviting route, order a less tasty dish, and work indoors, away from the loveliness of spring.

Of course, benefit to others may not balance out equally. By boosting your spirits, the pleasure derived from the scenic route, the spring day, or the tasty dish may energize your work and thus indirectly benefit those your work serves. However, countervailing benefits to others, direct or indirect, may readily obtain, case by case. The uglier route may be slightly shorter or less time-consuming. Out in the balmy weather, you may not reach the phone in time. Your favorite dish may be less nourishing, digestible, or reasonably priced than alternative choices. And so forth. Often, such detailed comparison of pros and cons may not be feasible or realistic; but when it is, the result may be as I have hypothesized, with benefits to others roughly balancing out. And in that case, Self-Subordination will yield a different judgment than either Self-Forgetfulness or Self-Denial.

Since Self-Forgetfulness says neither yea nor nay to self-benefit when others are equally served either way, it may seem more a psychological prescription than a rule of action. However, a norm that *permits* what Self-Subordination *enjoins* and Self-Denial *forbids* differs in its directives from these more decisive norms. And to judge from their words, Christian ethicians have sometimes favored this in-between position.

Inadequate Analyses

The sixfold scheme just presented, with its distinctions and analyses, reveals the inadequacy of many familiar characterizations of Christian altruism. It hardly suffices, for example, to describe charity as "active helpfulness."[91] All six norms prescribe active helpfulness, even to the extent of risking one's life, as Tom O'Brien did. Again (as Charles Harris notes), "if love means only 'continuous regard for the welfare of others,' it rules out only ethical egoism."[92] The weakest form of Christian altruism enjoins no less; the choice between the six altruistic norms still confronts us.

Equally indeterminate are traditional exhortations to aid our neighbor as we are "able,"[93] "according to our means,"[94] or "according to our strength."[95] Physically and legally, we are capable of distributing all we possess; but should we? Somewhat more definitely, "some of the Fathers say that a man who does not give at least a tenth part of his honest income to charity is covetous."[96] Does it make no difference, though, how large the man's income is and how great are his needs, or how pressing, by comparison, are the needs of those to be assisted? Once again, where should the preference go, how strongly: to oneself or to others? In identical situations, Self-Preference might conceivably prescribe: "Keep all you have!" while Self-Denial advised: "Give it all away!"

St. Alphonsus Liguori attended somewhat to such differences when he cited the majority view of his day that it probably suffices for the "rich" to give two percent of their income to the "ordinary poor" (*pauperes communes*), but not if their riches are superabundant.[97] However, this stipulation is still unsatisfactory. If the amount that should be given varies with the two factors mentioned—the giver's wealth and the receiver's need—and both factors vary continuously, so does the percentage of one's wealth that should be given in alms. It does not make good sense to state specific percentages in abstraction from specific needs and specific riches.

Scholastic manualists showed some recognition of this fact, but not enough. Distinguishing between "extreme need," "serious need," and "ordinary need," they then prescribed, for example, that when another is in "serious" need there is a grave obligation to give him something from one's "superfluity."[98] Often they stated precisely what percentage the "something" had to be (see chapter 3). Such prescriptions may appear to improve on the vaguer deliverances of a preference-rule, such as the six listed above, but the opposite is in fact the case. Accurate assessment of how much one is "obliged" to give, and how seriously (the manualists' typical questions), requires assessment of how serious is the "serious" need and how superfluous the "superfluity." The phrase *serious need* is doubly indefinite: it covers the whole spectrum between "extreme need" and "ordinary need," and no clear border separates it from either.[99] An expression like *superfluity* is equally vague, covering anything from ten dollars to ten million beyond what is needed to maintain—or attain[100]—a peasant's life-style or a Rothschild's. In combination with a preference-rule, such concrete data (ten dollars or ten million, a peasant's life-style or a millionaire's) provide clearer guidance than do prescriptions that state need and wealth in broad, indefinite terms.

In answer to the question "How much should we give?" John Wesley offered a startlingly different response. "One of his frequently repeated sermons was on Mt. 6:19-23 ('Lay not up for yourselves treasures upon earth . . . '). Christians should give away all but 'the plain necessaries of life'—that is, plain, wholesome food, clean clothes and enough to carry on one's business. One should earn what one can, justly and honestly. But all income should be given to the poor after one satisfies bare necessities."[101] Wesley practiced what he preached. "Sales of his books often earned him £1,400 annually, but he spent only £28 on himself. The rest he gave away. He always wore inexpensive clothes and dined on simple food. 'If I leave behind me ten pounds,' he once wrote, 'you and all mankind bear witness against me that I lived and died a thief and a robber'."[102]

Such radical generosity sounds like genuine gospel living. No finagling about percentages; just ask what you really *need*, and give the rest away. However, although Wesley's example is surely admirable and may approximate more closely what Christian charity requires, his response suffers from certain shortcomings. For one thing, like the Scholastics' abstract percentages, it casts scant light on O'Brien's, Kolbe's, or Arland Williams's cases, or on most of the others I have cited. What general norm is implicit in Wesley's specific instructions? Furthermore, even a preference-rule that backed Wesley's solution on most occasions, might not on all. Do honesty and justice suffice in business dealings? Would any preference-rule say without further stipulation: "Earn what you can?" And how are "necessaries" to be judged? Jesus sometimes dined with the rich.

When Francis Xavier visited the Daimyo of Yamaguchi, he went in style. On the other hand, should even "bare necessities" always be clung to? Kolbe chose to starve to death; Williams passed up the lifeline and drowned.

Despite its greater generality, Charles Harris's analysis reveals similar shortcomings. He first proposes the following scheme:

> If we let "O" stand for the object or recipient of love and "S" for the subject of love or the agapist himself and if we consider the consequences of actions as either favorable, unfavorable or indifferent, then a series of cases arises. A given action can have consequences which are:
>
> (a) Favorable to both O and S.
> (b) Favorable to O and unfavorable to S.
> (c) Favorable to O and indifferent to S.
> (d) Unfavorable to O and favorable to S.
> (e) Unfavorable to O and unfavorable to S.
> (f) Unfavorable to O and indifferent to S.
> (g) Indifferent to O and favorable to S.
> (h) Indifferent to O and unfavorable to S.
> (i) Indifferent to O and indifferent to S.[103]

Concerning the strongly altruistic tradition deriving from Luther, Calvin, and still earlier representatives, Harris then observes: "According to Nygren's and Bultmann's understanding of *agape,* an action with the consequences described in (b) should be performed, and actions with the consequences described in (c)-(f) should not be performed." In fact, no familiar version of Christian altruism would give such a verdict. Even Self-Forgetfulness and Self-Denial, as typically understood, would want to know *how* favorable to the recipient (a), (b), and (c) are. And if only alternatives (d), (e), and (f) were available, they would want to know *how* unfavorable to the recipient each alternative was. The chief concern of these norms is service, not self-denial. Accordingly, if either (a) or (c) promised greater benefit to O than (b) did, or if (d) promised less harm to O than (e) or (f) did, that is the option the norms would prefer, regardless of how S was affected.

Some formulations, it is true, might suggest a different emphasis, on self-denial rather than on service. "The *Agape* of Christ," writes Reinhold Niebuhr, "which is the norm of Christian selfhood, is always finally defined as sacrificial love, as the love of the cross. ('And walk in love.even as Christ loved you and gave himself for you.')"[104] Doubtless the word *sacrificial* should be read in the light of the closing words, *for you.* Stress is on the positive more than on the negative. Even so, agape is not thus "finally defined." Niebuhr, like many, failed to recognize that emphasis on self-sacrifice clarifies nothing. Self-sacrificing love is not of itself "the highest liberality,"[105] "the highest proof of true piety,"[106] or distinctive of

Christian agape.[107] Nor do the two words *sacrifice* and *service* adequately denote "the Christian method of seeking the answer to the Lord's prayer, 'Thy kingdom come'."[108] *Any* form of altruism, even the least demanding, entails continual self-sacrifice, even on occasion the sacrifice of life itself.

This may appear a paradox. But consider Jesus' case. "It is expedient for you," Caiphas declared, "that one man should die for the people, and that the whole nation should not perish" (Jn 11:50). "He did not say this of his own accord," John explains, "but being high priest that year he prophesied that Jesus should die for the nation, and not for the nation only, but to gather into one the children of God who are scattered abroad." If, then, as we have seen, Self-Preference would require that Tom O'Brien risk his single life to save the lives of scores, surely it would prescribe that Jesus surrender his single physical life for the spiritual life of multitudes. Love's least altruistic formulation would call for this greatest sacrifice. Doubtless "it is impossible to give a greater proof of love than to sacrifice one's most precious possession—life itself—for another."[109] Yet the most self-regarding reading of agape may prescribe this greatest gift.

Similar remarks apply to the tale of the Good Samaritan. For Bultmann, as we have seen, this parable exemplifies the "boundlessness" of Christian charity. For David Freedman, it "points to the extraordinary quality of the Samaritan's love for his unfortunate fellow-creature."[110] Yet even the norm of Self-Preference would call for nothing less. The Samaritan expended some time and money; the wounded man risked losing his life. Their prospective losses were nowhere near equal. Accordingly, any version of agape, from Self-Denial to Self-Preference, would render the same verdict: Stop and take care of him. Dress his wounds, place him on your mount, put him up at an inn.

If every norm of the six I have listed would give the same answer—if all without distinction would tell Tom O'Brien to risk his life, Jesus to sacrifice his, and the Samaritan to put himself out—it may appear inconsequential which of the six a person prefers and follows. This impression contains much truth, as well as much falsehood. And a virtue of the preceding analysis is that it brings out both the truth and the falsehood.

First, the truth. The adoption of one form of agape rather than another does indeed make little difference in comparison with the choice for agape rather than pure egoism. There lies the great divide. For if even self-preferring altruism were put into practice, our personal and social lives would change beyond recognition. All travelers along the road of life would do as the Samaritan did, as Tom O'Brien did, as Jesus did (supposing there were still robbers to provide victims or Romans to furnish crosses). The extraordinary would become ordinary.

Traditional talk of "self-sacrificing love" obscures this fact. Describing such love as "extraordinary," "the highest liberality," or "distinctively Christian" makes it appear beyond the bounds of reason or possible obligation. In comparison, putting one's neighbor on a par with oneself may look more reasonable and feasible, while self-preferential love may seem positively self-indulgent. Yet on reflection, the amount of sacrifice these less demanding loves enjoin may prove astonishing. For the agent, being only one, may often be outnumbered, as O'Brien was. His or her benefit or need may easily be outweighed by another's, as the Samaritan's was. And others' greater need and greater numbers may frequently combine, as they did in Jesus' case, and call for sacrifice as extreme as that required by even the most rigorously altruistic preference-rules.

As other illustrations I have cited make clear, however, there is also much falsehood in the impression that it makes little difference which norm of neighbor-love one adopts. The sacrifice of Kolbe, called for by Parity but not by Self-Preference, and that of Arland Williams, required by Other-Preference but not by Parity, indicate how great the difference may occasionally be. And less momentous options, like those in the restaurant, at home, and on the way to work, demonstrate how great may be the cumulative effect of adopting one rule rather than another. For most people, no day passes without presenting numerous options which would be decided differently by different versions of Christian neighbor-love.

It is therefore cause for surprise that, despite countless discussions of Christian charity, the conflicting norms just cited have never before been identified and listed, much less been compared and evaluated so as to determine, if possible, which of the rival versions Christians should prefer.[111] The reasons for this neglect merit examination; for, as the next chapter shows, they have more than purely historical interest.

2

Obstacles to Inquiry

The surprisingly limited consideration given the Christian norm relating self and others first came to my attention when I was writing a book entitled *Christian Moral Reasoning*. Having asked what criterion of right and wrong Christians should favor if they wish to remain consistent in their thinking yet true to their varied Christian heritage, and having concluded that value-maximization alone satisfies this prescription, I was led to inquire: *Whose* good should be maximized? Should mine? Should my neighbor's? Or should there be parity between us?[1] This further issue was inescapable once the more general norm of morality was identified. But no general criterion of right and wrong had previously been elicited from the wealth of Christian tradition, much less this specific, value-maximizing one;[2] hence the subsidiary issue of agape's norm for self and others had not previously come into clear, prominent focus. This suggests one likely reason for the neglect the issue has suffered.

It may be objected that agape is the Christian criterion of right and wrong, and that Christians have always known it is. However, if offered as an alternative to the norm of value-maximization, such a suggestion would reveal slight awareness of how varied and often ill-defined Christians' conceptions have been when they spoke of "agape," "charity," or "love." Fifty years ago, Nygren could lament the little effort that had been made to fathom the Christian idea of love; "it is treated," he complained, "as if it hardly needed explanation."[3] In the intervening years, little has been done to clarify agape as a norm of conduct. In particular, the question of mine and thine has remained basically where it stood during preceding centuries.

What, then, is the source of this long-standing neglect? With reflection, many likely contributing factors come to mind, besides the one just mentioned. Since the same factors—the same explicit reasons or subtle, unstated influences—are still operative today and may obscure the need for the present inquiry, I shall cite and comment on a number of the more likely ones.

"Thought Is Inimical to Love"

"The process of thought," it has been said, "ever denies love. It is thought that has emotional complications, not love. Thought is the greatest hindrance to love.... Thought does not lead to love, thought does not cultivate love."[4] So has judged the East, and so has often judged the Christian West. The words of Jean Baptiste Massillon testify eloquently to the sort of misgivings agapistic calculations may arouse:

> I know that charity hath its order and its measure; that in its practice it ought to use a proper distinction; that justice requires a preference to certain wants: but I would not have that methodical charity (if I may thus speak) which to a point knows where to stop—which has its days, its places, its persons, and its limits—which, beyond these, is cruel, and can settle with itself to be affected only in certain times and by certain wants. Ah! are we thus masters of our hearts when we truly love our brethren? Can we at our will mark out to ourselves the moments of warmth and indifference? Charity, that holy love, is it so regular when it truly inflames the heart? Has it not, if I may so say, its transports and its excesses? And do not occasions sometimes occur so truly affecting, that, did but a single spark of charity exist in your heart, it would show itself, and in the instant would open your bowels of compassion and your riches to your brethren?[5]

This common antipathy to calculation or exact discrimination exemplifies a more general syndrome. As Frank Sheed remarks, "To many, the idea of bringing the intellect fully into action in religion seems almost repellent. The intellect seems so cold and measured and measuring, and the will so warm and glowing. Indeed the joy of the will is always figured in terms of warmth—such words as ardor, fervor and the like come from Latin words for a fire burning: there is a fear that intellect can only damp down the fire."[6] However, some people are on fire with love, others with lust, others with ambition, others with desire for revenge. Some hunger and thirst for justice, others for justice as they see it. The most varied longings and emotions stir the human heart, and it is not guaranteed, by the mere fact that we are Christians, that our desires are holy ones. Love must be discerning.

"Love Knows Best"

"Many again," Sheed continues, "who do not find the use of the intellect in religion actually repellent, regard it as at least unnecessary—at any rate for the layman—and possibly dangerous. One can, they say, love God without any very great study of doctrine."[7] The like is thought to hold for love of neighbor. "Love, and do as you will," Augustine observed long ago;[8] and his words have echoed through the centuries. "If you possess charity," wrote Caesarius of Arles, "even though you have much wealth, she will know what to do with it. Charity knows best to whom to extend alms and what amount, what to give and what to hold back."[9] "Love alone," John Robinson concurs, "because, as it were, it has a built-in moral compass, enabling it to 'home' intuitively upon the deepest need of the other, can allow itself to be directed completely by the situation."[10]

Evidently, when Augustine, Caesarius, Robinson, and others[11] speak thus about "charity" or "love," they have the one true form in mind, to which we may safely entrust our decisions. But which form is that, and how do we know that we have it? No doubt a true compass will point north. But what if one compass points north, another northwest, a third northeast, and others in still other directions; which one shall we take as our guide? The compasses themselves cannot tell us.

"Love Does Not Calculate"

Agape, it is said, refers "to a quality of response to people and situations which cannot be pinned down in precise rules."[12] "All true love is without calculation."[13] "Justice among men, especially commutative justice, distributive and legal justice, can somehow be defined and enforced. But pure love ... is simply a liberating event and attitude that generates a freedom that goes far beyond the human definitions of justice. Love can never be measured quantitatively."[14]

But actions can be, and are, thus measured. A person gives, shares, does, or sacrifices more or less. And which is the preferable amount? If "pure love," being indefinite, has nothing to say on such questions, it appears irrelevant to action, which is always definite. However, this objection tends to merge with the next; so let us pass on.

"Love Knows No Limits"

"Christian love," we read, "has always been understood, not as a legal obligation, but as a movement by which persons never rest satisfied with any given expression of love, but always seek further to give themselves more thoroughly."[15] "It is spontaneous, uncalculating, adventurous, sacrificial love, giving itself freely and without limit for others."[16] "Love will go as far as the neighbour needs it. It has no limits."[17]

Sometimes, indeed frequently, such sayings should not be taken too literally. Having been told that love is selfless and excludes all self-seeking, we may then learn to our surprise that we are duty-bound to love ourselves, that "this is a law of nature, of reason, and of grace. . . . We instinctively seek our good, and avoid everything which may harm us."[18] On one page we may read that "the inward and essential nature of love is to give of self to the utmost,"[19] yet a few pages later restrictions may appear: "Love wills to impart itself up to the limit of the maintenance of its own worth of being, but no further . . . The ethical limit of self-impartation is always to be found in the ethical necessity of self-affirmation."[20] Doubtless, too, "limitless" giving should not be understood as giving that incapacitates the giver for greater service; the neighbor's future needs should also be considered. Thus, "limitless" love does indeed recognize a limit; "uncalculating" love does at least some calculating. And even if a strongly altruistic stance is intended, what precise stance is it: Self-Subordination? Self-Forgetfulness? Self-Denial? Which of these alternatives is deemed preferable, and why? Mere assertion of an answer to a question, as though no other answers existed, is no substitute for defense and elucidation of the favored solution.

No Mine or Thine

It may be felt that to envisage conflicting interests that have to be adjudicated is to presuppose the absence of community. The Christian ideal, some might say, is not an ideal norm but a mutual relationship that has no need of norms. "Perfect love knows no giving. What is there to give? All mine is thine, all thine is mine. Together we share, not give. But as we detach ourselves little by little, the old separate self comes back and we hand something across the chasm. How sad when exuberant love thus declines into intentional giving."[21] Doubtless there is truth in this objection. Perhaps, indeed, it is not good that charity be too calculating. But its giving or sharing will take one form or another, in agreement with this or that rule; and which form is preferable? How are the words "All mine is thine, all thine is mine" to be translated into practice? Do they implicitly reject the first two or three interpretations of Christian charity—Self-Preference, Parity, and perhaps Other-Preference—in favor of some stronger version? But again: in favor of which version, and why?

Fear of Legalism

To many, Catholic casuistry has seemed a regression to the pharisaic dotting of i's which Jesus resisted to the death and Paul rejected in favor of Christian liberty. And the attempt to determine more precisely the demands of Christian love may appear to resemble such casuistry. "How can one reduce this general obligation of helping one's neighbor to practical rules here and now?" Furfey asks. "Legalistically minded moral theologians have tried to answer this question by distinguishing various degrees of need, 'extreme' need, 'quasi-extreme' need, 'grave' need, and 'common' need. They have talked about the obligation of giving away one's 'superfluous' goods. The more one reads these theologians, the more muddied the problem becomes."[22]

It is obscured, I have suggested, through inattention to basic principles. The casuists' .hedging, like the Pharisees' rigor, betrays unclarity concerning love's requirements. Once a general rule of preference is determined and embraced, much can be left to the individual conscience. Then and only then does love provide a "built-in moral compass" permitting us to judge what is best.

Emphasis on Self

Broader and deeper than the widespread assumption that self comes first in conflict situations is the assumption that self comes first in ethics generally. It is likely that this assumption, too, has helped to deflect Christians from careful consideration of agape's norm and the apportioning of benefits to self and others. For Christian thought has been strongly influenced by Greek thought, and specifically by the way in which the philosophers of ancient Greece conceived the central ethical problem.

> For them the question "how should I live?" took what to us seems a fundamentally prudential or self-regarding form. It amounted for them to an inquiry as to how a man could secure *his own* happiness, fulfilment or perfection. Benevolence, altruism, philanthropy, a concern for the happiness of others occupied a secondary, and even marginal, position in their ethical recommendations. It was not conceived as an end in itself but rather as a means to, or a condition of, the self-realisation of the individual.[23]

It may be, as the same author then remarks, that "Christianity . . . first established an essential connection between morality and the happiness or well-being of humanity at large."[24] Nonetheless, Greek influence entered early and readily upon ground prepared by many a scriptural saying; it did not have to await Aquinas's classically eudaemonistic formulations. Thus we read for instance in St. Gregory Nazianzen's eulogy on St. Basil: "Basil rendered service freely, relieving the dearth of food without drawing any profit therefrom. He had in view only one object: to win mercy by being merciful, and to acquire heavenly blessings by his distribution of grain here below."[25] It would appear from such a saying that the service Basil rendered and the people he helped held only instrumental interest for him. I shall not dwell, here at the start, on the merits or demerits of such a viewpoint, but shall just point out that it diverts attention from the service rendered and the optimum norm for rendering it. The emphasis falls elsewhere.

Focus on the Transcendent

In Christendom, this concentration on self, diverting attention from others, their needs, and the extent to which their needs should be met, has coincided with a focus beyond and above the self, which has appeared to legitimize such self-preoccupation. To seek happiness is to seek God, our Alpha and our Omega. "Only God," Augustine characteristically declared, "is to be loved for himself, while this world, that is, all sensible things, are to be spurned."[26] Accordingly, "when he elaborates the content of neighbor-love, Augustine does not give much prominence to the natural needs of body or soul which we may suppose the neighbor to have. In practical terms, love of the neighbor is evangelism. He is a man, and men find their blessedness in God. The only service of lasting significance that we can render him is to lead him to that blessedness."[27] To haggle over thine and mine or concern oneself with the proper balance of earthly benefits would distract us from the one thing necessary. "An intelligent man, who thinks about communion and life with God, will never cling to anything low and earthly," St. Anthony advises, "but will direct his mind towards the heavenly and the eternal."[28] "The goods of this life," Pomerius agrees, "are but an impediment to lovers of the blessings to come."[29] We should pay them no heed.

Yet we do heed them and must, as Christians. According to Matthew 25, the test by which we shall be judged—the test of the Son who "went about doing good," the test of the Father who makes his sun to shine and his rain to fall on the just and unjust alike—is our manner of distributing this world's goods: How much have we done for hungry, thirsty, lonely, ailing human beings? So the query recurs, inescapably: How much *should* we do for them? What norm does Christian love, rightly understood, propose?

Focus on Obligation

Proponents of Parity or of some more strongly altruistic norm might judge that Kolbe did a splendid, Christian deed when he stepped forward from the ranks and offered himself for another, but they might hesitate to affirm that he was obliged to act as he did. They might judge that Arland Williams, too, did the better, more Christian thing when he passed the lifeline to others, yet might be reluctant to say that he would have sinned had he acted less heroically. Thus, for whatever reason, the ideal or supererogatory is frequently distinguished from the mandatory; and emphasis falls on the latter when moralists ply their trade. Duty has been far more carefully defined than counsel. Often, it is true, Christians have reminded other Christians that charity commands and does not merely advise. But the need for such a reminder is significant. It suggests a further reason why agape's norm has been neglected.

There are not two acceptable norms of charity, one minimalist and the other maximalist. Hence to conceive the realm of morality in terms of precepts, and precepts in terms of charity's minimal requirements, is to relegate examination of agape's one, full norm to a separate realm of reflection. And in that realm close analysis or the formulation of norms may appear neither needful nor appropriate. "This morality of charity aspires to the most perfect by counsel and not by obligation; it rigorously excludes only sin; in the realm of what is good, it assures full freedom."[30] According to this viewpoint, if, for instance, a young man sees that one career will permit him to do far more good than some other, he is not obliged to choose it. After all, alternative careers also offer occasions for good, to others or oneself, and may be embraced for that reason. Such is the reasoning I have read and such is the reasoning I have heard, from a professor who stressed the "primacy of charity in moral theology" but clung to the counsel-precept distinction as traditionally understood.

Self-Preference, Parity, Other-Preference, Self-Subordination, Self-Forgetfulness, Self-Denial—all seek to do good, to oneself and to others. But the mix varies widely from one extreme to the other, and so do the consequences. Hence more guidance is needed than the assurance that no sin results from choosing one way or the other, and that a person may choose as inspired. St. Paul spoke of a "better way," the way of charity. Which of these rival ways is it?

The Divine Model

"Be imitators of God," says Ephesians, "as beloved children. And walk in love, as Christ loved us and gave himself up for us, a fragrant offering and sacrifice to God" (5:1-2). From this and similar injunctions (for instance, Mt 5:43-48, 18:15-35) it has been inferred that "essentially . . . the call to holiness means nothing else but the call to compassionate, sympathetic and active love of one's neighbor in accord with the ideal and the example of God."[31] More specifically, since God's love "is not an acquisitive love, but a love that gives,"[32] it has seemed that the love to which we are called is "a self-giving in service approaching the freedom from self-interest with which God himself loves all his creatures."[33] However, no clear conclusion can be drawn from the Creator's love, one way or the other, with regard to benefits for self versus benefits for others. For God's good does not compete with ours, as our temporal good competes with that of other human beings. In this respect, then, God cannot serve as a model. We cannot observe his response to our problem, then do likewise; for our problem is not his. It is no cause for wonder, then, that Christians who have sought to emulate the Father's love have not thereby reached clarity concerning agape's norm.[34]

The like may be said of the imitation of Christ. True, the overall picture of Jesus that emerges from the gospels is of a man for others, not of a self-preferrer or practicer of Parity. Yet hardly a gospel incident tells clearly for or against any one of the six rival norms. Even the sacrifice of Calvary, as assessed in John 11:52, would conform to all six norms (see chapter 1). Thus, strange as it may sound, there is no contradiction (though there may be error) in saying: "We should give the preference to ourselves, yet sacrifice ourselves for others as Jesus did." So here, too, the proposed paradigm does not yield a ready verdict, and it is not surprising that Christians who have sought to model themselves on Jesus' love have not thereby achieved clarity concerning agape's norm. In their perusal of Scripture, not even the list of alternative formulations would readily occur to them.

On this topic as on others, I have found that a strong theological current, long followed without question,[35] cannot be countered effectively by just a few words, no matter how clear or a propos they may be. A commentator who had read the preceding remarks was nonetheless able to write: "In the New Testament, loving your neighbor as yourself does not stand alone, and I believe that, for example, the implications of God as trinitarian [are] an essential factor in human self-understanding as fundamentally communitarian and other-oriented; thus, there is not really a dichotomy or such a clear, unrelated choice between love of self and love of neighbor, since they are both grounded in our understanding of God and the human person as created in God's image. Since you feel that methodologically you may rely on the Christian dimensions of human life in an explicit way, I think you must include some of these basic elements in your approach. Without them, among other things, I think your argument becomes more deontological in a curious way. Even the maximalization of value becomes secondary to a quest for a norm that has lost its basic human and Christian roots."

What God as one cannot make manifest, God as triune may. But how? How might the mysterious modes of exchange between the divine persons clarify the familiar modes of exchange between human persons? How might a relationship in which there is no loss or gain serve as paradigm for the apportionment of loss and gain? Granted, the divine mutuality may suggest a life of sharing; but in all six norms there is sharing—indeed, constant sharing, sacrificial sharing, sharing as extreme as Tom O'Brien's or Maximilian Kolbe's. What most closely approximates the divine mutuality, it seems, is the exchange of noncompeting goods such as knowledge and affection. And these goods and their exchange lie outside the scope of this inquiry. For they occasion no problem. As chapter 3 explains more fully, the benefits in question in this study are competing goods, that is, goods for which, at least on occasion, my having more may mean your having less, or vice versa. Should Jesus die so that many others may live, spiritually? Should O'Brien risk dying so that many others may survive, physically? Should Arland Williams risk dying, that one other person may survive? And so forth. Such are the options that confront human persons and call for clarification. No such options confront the divine persons. It is therefore not surprising that those who have sought light from the life of the Holy Trinity have failed to illumine the human problem. To insist, even now, that enlightenment be sought from such a source is to assure continued darkness concerning agape's norm.

Coincidence of Answers

I have noted that all six articulations of Christian altruism might agree in commending Jesus' or O'Brien's sacrifice of self. Bishop Butler goes further and suggests that all six norms are equivalent in practice.

> I must however remind you that though benevolence and self-love are different; though the former tends most directly to public good, and the latter to private: yet they are so perfectly coincident, that the greatest satisfactions to ourselves depend upon our having benevolence in a due degree; and that self-love is one chief security of our right behaviour towards society. It may be added, that their mutual coinciding, so that we can scarce promote one without the other, is equally a proof that we were made for both.[36]

Hence to Butler my query about agape might well seem otiose. "It is needless," he wrote, "to compare the respect [conscience] has to private good, with the respect it has to public; since it plainly tends as much to the latter as to the former."[37]

Butler corroborates this optimistic estimate by appealing to a future life, to the comforts and pangs of conscience, and to others' praise and blame. In this present life, however, it is far from clear that one's own good—Jesus', Kolbe's, Williams's, O'Brien's—coincides with others'. And though the comfort of a good conscience may offset many an evil— perhaps even the evil of starving to death in a bunker—the question remains what sacrifices or refusals of sacrifice a Christian conscience should draw comfort from or should instead regret. Which ones should others commend and which ones should they condemn, thereby causing pleasure or pain to the doer? No doubt if everyone agreed on the one true norm, public praise or censure would conspire with private to render virtue pleasant and vice uncomfortable. But what *is* the one true norm; and why suppose that all people know and accept it, despite the apparent diversity of their views?

That Butler did, in fact, suppose such moral agreement appears from his further, equally pertinent remarks:

> The inquiries which have been made by men of leisure after some general rule, the conformity to, or disagreement from which, should denominate our actions good or evil, are in many respects of great service. Yet let any plain honest man, before he engages in any course of action, ask himself, Is this I am going about right, or is it wrong? Is it good, or is it evil? I do not in the least doubt, but that this question would be answered agreeably to truth and virtue, by almost any fair man in almost any circumstance. Neither do there appear any cases which look like exceptions to this; but those of superstition, and of partiality to ourselves.[38]

Who, for instance, would find fault with Arland Williams's heroic generosity, there in the freezing waters of the Potomac? Would any Christian?

Yes, to judge from explicit statements already quoted, many would. Charity, they would say, should begin at home. Furthermore, such disagreement is not rare, as Butler's claims might suggest. A. C. Ewing, for instance, writes:

> While the obligation to contribute something to charity if one can afford it is generally recognized, only a very small minority of people have felt it their duty to curtail their comforts and luxuries very seriously on that account, and still less the comforts and luxuries of those dependent on them. Yet there can hardly be any doubt that, even if we allow for any indirect evil effects which might accrue, in most cases money given to any even tolerably well managed charity will do much more good by relieving the suffering of those in distress than would be done by using the same money to increase the pleasure of a person who is at all tolerably comfortable by enabling him to have a more pleasant house, better furniture, more tobacco, more holiday travel, etc.[39]

No doubt this "small minority" and the large majority both contain Christians. Thus Butler's confidence is ill-founded not only with respect to people and morality in general but specifically with regard to Christians and agape's norm. It would appear from Ewing's remarks that in many of their concrete moral judgments many Christians do not accept *any* version of agape. Discussion of its requirements is therefore far from idle.

"*An Inadequate Norm*"

Butler would say that we have small need of agape's norm, first because benefit to others and benefit to self coincide, second because the dictates of conscience are immediately, intuitively clear. Others doubt the norm's value for a different reason. André Godin writes: "Would it be possible to make charity play the role of a 'criterion' which could assist the adult conscience to recognize the good action from the bad, to discern appetence or repugnance with regard to his deepseated will? Can it be a criterion, either to ensure personal conduct, or for the appreciation of others' behaviour, or, finally, as a basis for the broad lines of a morality which would be founded on this criterion?"[40] Godin thinks not. "This criterion is insufficient."[41] F. Hürth concurs: "The principle of charity is too indeterminate for it regularly to suffice for judgment, for the faithful or even for theologians."[42] Although this claim contains some truth, it may be largely self-verifying. Accept agape as nebulous, and it may indeed offer little guidance. Attempt no verdict between vying formulations, and concrete moral judgment may indeed prove difficult. But I have already indicated how mistaken it is to suggest, as Godin does, that a specific rule of preference cannot assist in the judgment of conduct. Each of agape's six versions has different, distinct implications.

Emphasis on the Subject

If the Christian norm of neighbor-love has remained indefinite, the single most important reason, I suspect, is the stress placed on persons rather than actions and on attitudes rather than norms. "It is sometimes suggested," William Frankena notes, "that an ethics of virtue is preferable to one of duty—that morality should center on character, dispositions, virtues and vices, rather than on external conduct, rules, and oughts or ought nots."[43] However, virtue is as virtue does; dispositions cannot be judged or understood apart from conduct. Which form of agape should win our inner approbation? Which should we be disposed to follow?

Surely this is a legitimate, important question; and it cannot be illumined by considering feelings, motives, personal convictions, and the like. A study of objective morality may and should prescind from subjective morality—from moral sentiments, dispositions, attitudes, and intentions.[44] Yet I have found, to my surprise, that any effort to focus abstractively on agape's objective requirements meets strong resistance.

One reason is a misunderstanding triggered by the word *objective*. "I know that you claim to be prescinding from sentiments, dispositions, etc. in a quest for objectivity," one reader objects, "but I think that true objectivity must include these 'subjective' dimensions." Here the word *objectivity* is the tip-off. Evidently, the quest for an objective norm, in the sense of one governing observable behavior rather than interior acts or attitudes, has been mistaken for the pursuit of an objective norm in the sense of one reliably arrived at without undue influence from the inquirer's personal "sentiments, dispositions, etc." To be sure, I would like my final verdict to be objective in this latter sense; but that has nothing to do with the choice of an objective rather than a subjective focus. Were I concerned with agape's subjective norm rather than its objective norm, I would wish no less that my verdict be duly objective. In neither case, though, would I be directly concerned about the verdict's objectivity. The inquiry here proposed is ethical, not epistemological.

A second misunderstanding may also generate resistance to an objective focus. It may be thought, mistakenly, that to focus on just a behavioral norm is to prescind from all but behavior. This would indeed be illegitimate. An adequate estimate of human action must attend to the human beings involved and how they are affected, whether externally (in their possessions, occupations, personal relations, and so forth) or internally (in their dispositions, attitudes, feelings, and so on). To abstract from the subjective moral aspects of an agent (right intention, virtuous disposition, adequate reflection, etc.) is not to abstract from the subjective implications of the agent's action, whether for the agent or for others. Only the former abstraction is here contemplated.

However, any such abstraction, even if rightly understood, is likely to be resisted. A chief reason is the error Aquinas noted long ago: to abstract, it is thought, is to falsify. One has snipped the seamless garment of reality. Elsewhere, such objections would hardly arise. No distortion of reality would be feared, for example, from considering just the acreage of a farm and not its produce, or from describing just the farm and omitting all mention of the county, state, region, continent, planet, solar system, galaxy, or universe to which the farm belongs. It would be judged neither fallacious nor misleading to describe a woman's appearance and say nothing about her personality, or to mention her family but pass over her club, neighborhood, church, profession, nation, race, species, genus, filum, and order. In instances like these, the absurdity of anti-abstractive objections is fairly evident; in ethics, however, it is better veiled.

The veiling is effected in part by essentialistic thinking and its common assumptions about the uses of words. Thus one well-known work declares:

> Contemporary theologians are once again insisting that any attempt to evaluate the moral object of an action apart from motive and circumstances is necessarily incomplete and inadequate. It is the whole action including circumstances and intention that constitutes the basis for ethical judgment. This is not to say that the concrete act is not an important consideration. It is simply to insist that the genuine moral meaning of particular individual acts is most accurately discerned not solely from an abstract analysis of the

biology of the act but necessarily including [sic] the circumstances as well as intention that surround the action.[45]

Here there is no acknowledgment of varying types of discussion and their respective viewpoints—objective or subjective, prospective or retrospective—nor of corresponding shifts in the meaning of terms like *ethical* and *moral*. If, however, it is English we are speaking, with its ordinary, varied meanings, we cannot truly assert, universally and without qualification: "It is the whole action including circumstances and intention that constitutes the basis for ethical judgment." More often than not, judgments of right and wrong legitimately abstract from questions of motive or intention; and such judgments, too, count as "ethical" or "moral." Even were they not so labeled, this fact of usage would carry no such implications as the quoted words proclaim. Anyone who decides to do what is right for the objective reasons that make it right is subjectively in order, though he give not a thought to himself or his intentions. Anyone who studies the reasons that make actions objectively right or wrong may be theoretically in order, though he give not a thought to the motives, intentions, attitudes, or feelings with which the actions are performed. Abstraction need not falsify.

The Impression of Irrelevance

A similarly anti-abstractive thrust appears in another objection to the present inquiry. A reader writes: "We cannot or should not in Christian moral thought deal with the notion of agape or the question of giving priority to self or others apart from the perspective of the Incarnation & mystical Christ. Certainly the glory of God in Christ is *the* priority in Christian thought; and if what we do or neglect to do for others or for self is done or not done for Christ in us, then the question whether I or my neighbor gets priority is in every concrete situation a question of what would be more for the glory of God in this situation. In fact I think it can be shown that whatever is more for the glory of God is more for everyone's good, and the whole question as a *general* question of whether I should favor myself or my neighbor is irrelevant."

This impression of irrelevance and the reasoning on which it rests call for a distinction (stressed in chapter 3) between derivative, second-order questions and basic, first-order questions. Granted, we should in every situation choose what is to God's greater glory; but what gives God greater glory? Doubtless Christian conduct does, but what counts as Christian conduct? Does Self-Preference, or Parity, or Other-Preference, Self-Subordination, Self-Forgetfulness, Self-Denial? This is the first-order question; the other is derivative. Thus the objection appears no more damaging than the assertion, "We need only determine what is the right (better, Christian, more perfect) thing to do; we need not concern ourselves about mine and thine." This remonstrance reverses epistemological priorities. We cannot determine what, specifically, is the right, better, or Christian thing to do—what gives God greater glory or is more according to his will—without first reaching a verdict on the preference-rule relating self and others.

Generalizations Unhelpful

Emphasis on the particularity of persons and their situations may also call in question the utility of rules like those in chapter 1. Thus, with regard to the more other-regarding norms in the list, Joel Kupperman warns: "If Bloggs gives most of his disposable income above the poverty line to the poor, but keeps some, there is a strong risk that, instead of feeling a glow of self-acceptance as a result, he will feel guilty and inadequate (for not doing more), while at the same time feeling a natural envy and resentment of those who are doing less (and who thus allow themselves more of the common gratifications). The net result of this could well be an increased sourness rather than sweetness of character, as well as the eventual abandonment of the altruistic demands he makes on himself."[46]

> Thus what we should recommend in such matters always must be hypothetical ("If thou wilt be perfect . . . "), and ideally the "If" clause should include specifications of psychological strength, likely psychological reactions, likely effects on the network of personal relationships, etc. We might say to Bloggs, "If you can give most of your disposable income above the poverty line to the poor without (a) damaging your closest personal relationships, (b) retaining an immoderate sense of what you should be doing which interferes with your self-acceptance and peace of mind, (c) coming to feel cheated of the common gratifications that you will be giving up, or envious of those who do not give up such gratifications, or (d) destroying the sources of energy in your life, then you should do so." Even this hypothetical recommendation is very probably too general and schematic: there is a case for saying that there should be as many different recommendations of what should be done as there are people to whom they are to be addressed. We are far from the demands of morality here, and far from any territory in which generalisation is very useful.[47]

To be sure, the general is not the particular, and does not provide the particular, and does not suffice, by itself, without the particular. However, strictures like the above apply chiefly to specific behavioral norms, not to abstract rules of preference like those in chapter 1. The latter do not say to give more or keep less or divide wealth equally. They state recipes for determining right actions, in view of pertinent circumstances like those listed under (a), (b), (c), and (d). Not even Self-Denial would recommend "destroying the sources of energy in your life."

The Better the Enemy of the Good

I would rather feel compunction for my sins, the well-known saying of the *Imitation of Christ* declares, than know the definition of compunction.[48] Reading such a statement, one may safely surmise that no definition will be forthcoming. What is judged less important will receive less attention; what is judged more important will receive more. This practical conclusion does not follow logically, but historically and actually it very often has. Attention has usually centered on what seemed more important. And subjective love has appeared more important than objective love. Loving persons have been rated over loving acts.

Even granting the correctness of this comparative evaluation, objective charity might still have sufficient importance to merit prolonged reflection. And such scrutiny of agape in action might prove more revealing than the scrutiny of agape in agents. As we shall see, value primacy does not correlate with conceptual or epistemological primacy. It does not generally, and it does not in the present instance. By their fruits you shall know the goodness of the trees, not the goodness of the fruits from the trees.

Antithetical Thinking

Christian thinkers have fancied sharp dichotomies. Commenting on 1 Cor 13:3, Karl Barth declares: "It is love alone that counts—not acts of love as such, however great."[49] "*Neither individual nor social utility determines the worth of Christian charity,*" declares Franz Keller, "*but the right disposition from which it proceeds.*"[50] For Leslie Stephen, morality is internal, not external; hence "the moral law . . . has to be expressed in the form, 'be this,' not in the form, 'do this'."[51] In like vein, John Sheets asserts: "We can see that the notion of service is coextensive with the meaning of the Christian. It is not something that he does. It first of all is something he is."[52] One might suppose that if it is first of all something he is, then at least secondarily it is something he does. But to say "It is not only or primarily something that he does" would weaken the antithesis. And a long tradition has preferred to keep secondary values in their places.[53] Hence close attention to mere works of charity, or their norm, becomes less likely if the charity that begets them is deemed "infinitely superior."[54]

Taken at face value, such dichotomies are false. Consider Barth's. If works of virtue are worthless, so is the desire or disposition to do them. If, for instance, it makes no difference whether the hungry are fed, the naked are clothed, the sick are tended, the lonely are visited, the ignorant are instructed, or the homeless are sheltered, then it makes no difference whether people are inclined to such behavior. But if neither the behavior nor the corresponding inclination matters, a passage like Matthew 25 becomes incomprehensible. Although rhetoric has its attractions, especially in parenesis, truth and understanding are better served by careful reflection and accurate expression. In pairings like those cited, "both-and" should replace "either-or."

Summing Up

The preceding collection makes no claim to completeness. No one of the reasons listed, nor even the whole set, adequately explains the meager attention the norm of neighbor-love has received. Despite some Christians' misgivings about thought or fears of legalism; despite frequent emphasis on self, on the transcendent, on obligation, on personal love as superior to loving acts; despite these and all the other factors cited, Catholic moralists have nonetheless spelled out many a detail concerning the "order of charity," with God first, self second, and neighbor third. How is it that these same moralists, inclined as they were to close analysis, did not attend to alternative versions of agape? How is it that, as we shall see, they so largely ignored contrary currents in Christian thinking, and were in turn ignored by them? Here still other factors would have to be cited. Mention would have to be made, for example, of attitudes toward Scripture and of its traditional treatment; of reverence for authoritative teachers (for example, Augustine, Lombard, Aquinas); and of essentialistic, nonhistorical, nonlinguistic modes of thought.

To a greater or less extent, all the factors I have listed are still operative in Christian thinking, and were mentioned for that reason; they are not mere clues to a historical conundrum. As my references and quotations attest, people still look askance at thought, still believe that love knows best, that it does not calculate, that it knows no limits, that it recognizes no mine or thine. They still fear legalism; still focus on the self, the subject, the transcendent, the obligatory; still consult a divine model; still reverse epistemological priorities; still think in dichotomies; still tend to extol the higher at the expense of the lower. It was therefore necessary to respond point by point in defense of the neglected question which I intend, at last, to pursue. It is legitimate and important, I maintain, to inquire which of Christian charity's six rival formulations merits acceptance.

In urging this conclusion I have had to strike a compromise between brevity and prolixity. To most readers the majority of the objections I have canvased may look as unconvincing as they do to me. So, not wishing to flog a whole herd of dead horses, I have been succinct in my responses. On the other hand, perhaps a majority of readers will feel that one or the other objection has some merit; and even one, if left unanswered, might turn them away from the inquiry to come. So I have felt obliged to mention and respond to each potential obstacle, if only briefly. The length of the series and the inclusion of a chapter containing it are explained by the surmise that, for reasons like those cited, most prospective readers of this study may find its question as problematic as its answer.

3

Preliminary Clarifications

More pronouncedly of late than in the past, it seems, Christian thinkers have taken a dim view of attempts at analytic precision. When a focused inquiry is proposed, the objection of narrowness is sure to be raised. Several illustrations of this tendency appeared in the last chapter. "Contemporary theologians," one citation admonishes, "are once again insisting that any attempt to evaluate the moral object of an action apart from motive and circumstances is necessarily incomplete and inadequate." The insistence that any treatment of agape's norm take account of Christological and trinitarian doctrine reveals the same antipathy to sharply focused inquiry. A further illustration is a reader's response to the suggestion I make in the present chapter, that attention center on self-versus-other and prescind from the related issue of nearest-versus-neediest. "It seems to me," he writes, "that you run the risk of losing the social dimension altogether. ... Today, I think you must confront more directly the 'preferential option for the poor'." It apparently makes little difference to such a critic whether the preference-rule relating self and others casts any light on the option for the poor, or vice versa. The book treats of agape in act; agape in act includes a preference for the poor; therefore this preference, too, must be emphasized.

I can appreciate the appeal of holistic thinking. *If* objective morality could be inferred from subjective morality and vice versa, *if* agape's objective norm could be derived from credal truths, *if* all preference-rules could be illumined simultaneously—the result would be profoundly satisfying. Would that truth were a single whole and we could grasp it in its entirety! However, wishing that one's flashlight were a searchlight or one's searchlight were the sun, does not make it so. It is legitimate and necessary, then, to specify the direction of a proposed investigation and to do so with all requisite precision. Thereafter, any time the inclination arises to resist the resultant narrowing, the response must be: Will a broader focus illuminate the chosen area of inquiry, or will it only perpetuate past obscurity and confusion? One reason, I believe, why unclarity still reigns with regard to agape's preference-rule for self and others is the antipathy of many Christian thinkers to abstractive, analytic thought and their consequent reluctance to bring the issue into sharp focus.

Chapter 1 has explained what single question I here intend to pursue. Both chapters 1 and 2 have explained why I consider it worth pursuing. The present chapter now defines the question more exactly and concludes with comments on the procedure to be followed. If the coming investigation is to be understood and its results accepted, it is necessary to specify precisely, in advance, what falls within the inquiry's ambit, what does not, and why.

Questions Bypassed

First, the study's focus may be stated negatively by means of the following contrasts:

Conduct, not Esteem

As has already been noted, the study to be undertaken concerns the evaluation of actions, not of persons. Hence it sidesteps contemporary polemic concerning self-esteem. "The church and Christian theology," the modern critic is wont to complain, "have often given the impression of teaching that one should love God and one's fellow man but deprecate or despise oneself. This is an entirely senseless affirmation. In fact, it is pernicious."[1] The point may be granted, but does not concern us here; for it carries no evident implications for altruistic action. A sense of self-worth is compatible with any of the six norms enunciated in chapter 1. A person might think well of himself and therefore look out for number one, or might instead think well of himself because he ignores number one.

The Ideal, not Just the Precept

Confined to conduct, the proposed inquiry covers the whole of conduct; for, bypassing a venerable and influential doctrine, it draws no distinction between counsel and precept. Hence the rules of chapter 1 must be rightly understood. The fact that they contain the word *should* might suggest that they always impose a moral obligation; that on all occasions a person is duty-bound to do as the norm prescribes. This would be a misreading. As I have explained elsewhere, moral terms like *duty* and *obligation* "are, as it were, heavy artillery, reserved for larger targets and severer criticism."[2] Slight deviations from an altruistic norm may be mere "imperfections," not "sins"; minor observances of the norm may be "preferable," "better," or "more perfect" but not "obligatory."[3]

This aspect of standard linguistic usage, to which I shall conform, is reflected in many a passage and many a work, for instance in Law's *Call*:

> Further, as all things that are lawful are not therefore expedient, so there are some things lawful in the use of liquors and apparel, which by abstaining from them for pious ends may be made means of great perfection.
>
> Thus, for instance, if a man should deny himself such use of liquors as is lawful; if he should refrain from such expense in his drink as might be allowed without sin; if he should do this, not only for the sake of a more pious self-denial, but that he might be able to relieve and refresh the helpless, poor, and sick . . . [he] might be said to do that which was highly suitable to the true spirit, though not absolutely required by the letter of the law of Christ.[4]

Why not "absolutely required"? Is not charity the law of Christ? Did not Dives sin? Yes, but Dives had an abundance, whereas the man Law envisages does not. Hence Christian altruism, however formulated, would require greater giving from Dives, and his failure to give departed farther from the ideal. Hence Law refrains from saying that the man would sin if he failed to relieve "the helpless, poor, and sick" by denying himself small pleasures. He would deviate from the norm, but less seriously than high-living Dives did.

Contrast this perspective with Kurt Baier's:

> We are morally required to do good only to those who are actually in need of our assistance. The view that we always ought to do the optimific act, or whenever we have no more stringent duty to perform, would have the absurd result that we are doing wrong whenever we are relaxing, since on those occasions there will always be opportunities to produce greater good than we can by relaxing. For the relief of suffering is always a greater good than mere enjoyment. Yet it is quite plain that the worker who, after a tiring day, puts on his slippers and listens to the wireless is not doing anything he ought not to, is not neglecting any of his duties, even though it may be perfectly true that there are things he might do which produce more good in the world, even for himself, than merely relaxing by the fireside.[5]

Not only does this passage have a very different sound from Law's, but several difficulties vitiate its reasoning. Supposedly the "relief of suffering" would be an instance of doing good "to those who are actually in need of our assistance"; hence the opening sentence receives no support from and is not illustrated by what follows. One may also doubt whether more good would be done in the world if workers never relaxed after a tiring day. Furthermore, if for a given worker on a given evening it is true that "there are things he might do which produce more good in the world, even for himself," then we might say that there are things it would be better for him to do, even if he is not obliged to do them. Baier recognizes no such distinction. Law does, and so do I. I have therefore deemed it necessary to explain the sense of the term *should,* as above, so as to indicate the full breadth of chapter 1's preference-rules. They cover matters of counsel as well as of precept.

It might seem that a clearer formulation of the six rules would obviate the need for such explanations. The use of *preferable* or *better* in place of *should* would indicate unmistakably that matters of counsel are included. However, the word *should* is in fact appropriate, for the six rival formulae all enunciate general obligations. Altruism, as specified by one or the other rule, is a Christian duty. Whether a given altruistic action is an objective duty depends on how notably alternative actions would depart from the Christian norm. Such a discrimination can be reached case by case, and only case by case, when and if it is called for.

Abstracting from the precept-counsel issue has several advantages. One is broader relevance. Whichever norm one opts for, it holds on both sides of the precept-counsel distinction. Provided no higher or complementary norm determines otherwise (see below), if the difference between alternative solutions is great, the preference-rule imposes an obligation. Subject to the same proviso, if the difference between alternatives is slight, the rule just indicates the better, more desirable thing to do. The degree of difference between alternatives—whether great or slight—might conceivably need to be determined, but exactly where the line between "great" and "slight," or "serious" and "not serious," should be drawn is seldom an important question.[6]

Neither is it a clear question, susceptible of a clear answer. Consider a typical discussion in the counsel-precept mode. In his once widely used compendium, Heribert Jone echoes the traditional position on almsgiving: "Whoever annually puts 2% of his superfluous income to this purpose does his duty by the poor."[7] "Note, however," he adds, "that only the extreme limits of sin are indicated here. Whoever leads a truly Christian life will certainly do more than this for those in ordinary need." I have already indicated the failure of such analyses to take due account of just how great the superfluity is, relative to what style of life, and how needy are the poor folk in question. I would now add that even were these factors all invariant, the figure 2% would still be matter for amazement. Not 3%, nor 1%, but precisely 2%! On one side of that sharp border lies sin, on the other lies mere imperfection; on one side lies duty, on the other lies mere counsel.[8] But how can this be known, or even be surmised?[9] How can a precise answer be given to such an imprecise query?[10] It is as though, in all seriousness, one theoretician were to draw the line between drizzle and downpour at five drops per second and another were to argue for ten. This game is not worth playing.

A further reason for this negative appraisal appears in the same example. Not only are such precise discriminations unnecessary; not only are they impossible; but careful calculation of what is and is not obligatory (2%? 5%? 7%? 14%?) is likely to foster a minimalist attitude. No doubt Jone's reminder about "a truly Christian life" is salutary, but the damage has already been done. Those who give just 2% have been absolved of any sin. They have "done their duty" by the poor. Of course, there are dangers from the other extreme as well; insistence on love as a law, without regard for distinctions, may burden consciences. However, the focus here adopted avoids this drawback, too. The sense of *should* in the rules to be considered is neither minimalist nor maximalist. It prescinds from the question of gravity.

When and if that question does arise, however, the question that concerns us (agape's objective norm) proves decisive. Whether in given circumstances a person errs notably in preferring his own good or in neglecting his good for that of another cannot be determined even approximately unless it is made clear who should be preferred, to what extent. What one preference-rule approves another may disapprove; what one mildly disapproves another may condemn as seriously wrong.

Self versus Others, not Nearest versus Neediest

The choice of a preference-rule from among the list of six may be an important—indeed the most important—clarification of the principle of beneficence; but it is not the only clarification that is necessary. Traditional discussion of the "order of charity" has examined, for example, whether preference should be given to God or to self, to self or to others, to soul or to body, to those nearest and dearest or to the neediest.[11] Once they are clearly understood, the first and third of these questions, concerning God and self and concerning soul and body, are relatively unproblematic. More perplexing and practically significant are the second, which compares self and others, and the fourth, which compares others who are nearest and others who are neediest. Though importantly related, these two queries are nonetheless distinct. Both issues are so large and complex that I shall focus on just one of them and leave the other for later study. Since the second question has still more frequent application than the fourth, and is logically prior to it, that is the one I have chosen for present scrutiny. I shall focus on just the balance between self and others.

The word *others* should be understood accordingly, as defined by this restriction. The rules of preference stated in chapter 1 are concerned with the neighbor as such, in abstraction from details that may also have moral relevance: whether the person in question is one's parent, one's child, one's ward, one's client, a person to whom one is bound by a promise, and so forth. The question at issue here may therefore be stated more fully as: "*Other things being equal,* who should be preferred: oneself, one's neighbor, or neither?"

The "self" and the "neighbor" in question are primarily individual, not collective. That is, the inquiry centers principally on the relation between single human beings and other human beings, and derivatively on the relation of single human beings to society as a whole. Only secondarily and in conclusion (though at considerable length) does it consider analogous relationships between agents in a larger, collective sense— groups, classes, nations, and the like—or between these and society as a whole. Christian Scripture and tradition have had much more to say about person-to-person relations, and clarity must therefore be sought at that level before inquiry passes, in chapter 7, to possible implications for collective altruism.

The Benefits to Be Balanced

Chapter 1's six norms speak in vague and general terms about preferring one's own good to another's or preferring another's good to one's own or putting one's own good on a par with another's, without further specification of the "good" in question. Yet in order to understand the issue resolved by the norms, and the sense of their respective claims, it is necessary to understand the nature and range of the benefits they apportion.

No Category Excluded

The benefits that call for a decision between self and others may be divisible, or they may be indivisible. Of a divisible estate I may get all or the other may get all, or we may divide it more or less evenly between us. Of a nondivisible job, either the other takes all or I take all; it cannot be shared. But whether divisible or indivisible, the benefits in question are always competing goods: we cannot both have the whole estate, or a given portion of it; we cannot both have the job; and so forth.

Goods of any and every variety—physical, artistic, intellectual, emotive, social, moral, or religious—may compete in this way. My health, wealth, education, contentment, reputation, virtue, or religious development may vie with another's. Or my health may vie with his wealth, her education with my artistic development, my ease with their friendship, their peace of mind with my good name. Or a single value on one side may compete with a varied collection on the other. Or a varied collection may vie with a varied collection. The possible configurations are many, as are the values.

One current theory recognizes all these varying possibilities of conflict but severely restricts the ability of preference-rules to deal with them. According to this view, comparative assessments of values within the same category make sense, whereas intercategory comparisons do not. Hence, if my health, wealth, education, contentment, reputation, virtue, or religious development vies with another's, there is no difficulty. Same-category value competes with same-category value, and their relative weight may be judged. The other's gain may be compared with mine, in health, wealth, education, or what have you. If, however, my health vies with another's wealth, my education with another's artistic development, my ease with others' friendship, their peace of mind with my good name, or the like, the first three preference-rules (Self-Preference, Parity, and Other-Preference), which require balancing my benefit against others', are no longer applicable. For according to this theory, intercategory comparisons are not possible. Indeed, were the theory correct, even the last three preference-rules (Self-Subordination, Self-Forgetfulness, and Self-Denial) would be inapplicable on the numerous occasions when varied benefits to others must be compared, to see which course of action would benefit them most, or when direct benefit to others vies with indirect benefit, through benefit to self, and these direct and indirect benefits belong to different categories. If, for example, my education vies with another's artistic development and my education promises social, intellectual, or financial benefits to others, then, according to the incommensurability thesis, there would be no way to determine which course of action is of greater benefit to others. Such varied benefits could not be comparatively assessed.

In a full critique of this doctrine, previously published, I argued that the alleged impossibility of intercategory comparisons "has no sound basis in argument, experience, intuition, or the meanings of words."[12] I shall therefore proceed on the assumption that all six preference-rules are applicable to all the varied kinds of conflict just enumerated. For the first three rules to apply, directly conflicting benefits to self and to others need not belong to the same value category. For the last three rules to apply, indirectly conflicting benefits (those conferred, on the one hand, and those promised or permitted by benefit to self, on the other) need not belong to the same category. For all six rules to apply, competing benefits to various third parties (this neighbor versus that) need not be of the same category.

Of equally broad significance is the question: Which benefits should be recognized as genuine values and therefore as weighing in the scales of decision? Christians may have misgivings when they read: "A common catalogue of goods includes: *health, wealth, happiness, fame* and *power*. Most desirable objects can be classified under one of these headings."[13] Health and happiness look acceptable, wealth more questionable, fame and power still more questionable, especially if they are proposed as inherently desirable.[14] However, to examine and adjudicate all species and subspecies of alleged values would take me too far from the scope of the present inquiry. In order to choose between alternate preference-rules, as I intend, I need not determine which of the benefits cited on various occasions are indeed benefits.

However, one or two types of value call for special comment. The value of autonomy or self-reliance, for example, has a general relevance that other values do not. What I confer, others cannot achieve; what I do for them, they cannot do for themselves. So benefits bestowed are not the only ones to consider. "It is of the essence of proper respect that we encourage others to be co-agents, and accept and welcome them as such."[15] "Even Jesus did not seek simply to give, but to induce in those to whom he gave a similar disposition."[16]

From this sample benefit—the desire to give—it can be seen that moral and spiritual values belong with those to be balanced when applying a preference-rule. It is true, as others have observed, that spiritual goods "cannot be selfishly monopolized, as can the material goods. . . . They are a spring at which we drink our fill, and no one can divert the spring for his own selfish profit."[17] It is also true that, "unlike material possessions, goodness is not diminished when it is shared, either momentarily or permanently, with others, but expands and, in fact, the more heartily each of the lovers of goodness enjoys the possession the more does the goodness grow."[18] Nonetheless, a person might for instance reflect: "If I stay in this office, working with Nan, the temptation to infidelity may be too great; if, on the other hand, I quit my job, my family may suffer financially." The man's moral welfare might conflict with his dependents' financial welfare. If so, it, too, would have to weigh in the scales of decision—the moral value versus the nonmoral; and its influence might well be decisive.

Contextual Restrictions

There is no incoherence in such balancing. Incoherence would arise only were it supposed that the morality of following a given preference-rule or the immorality of violating it might conflict with other values to be considered in applying the rule, and might affect the verdict. To base a verdict on itself would be to beg the question.[19]

Though such confusion is seldom blatant, there is often reason to suspect its presence. Consider, for example, Aquinas's repeated declaration that "to incur spiritual loss by committing sin is never lawful, even to save one's neighbor."[20] Only if there is a higher law than love of neighbor, and one that may conflict with love of neighbor, does this assertion make ready sense. If, however, the law of love is supreme and permits or enjoins saving one's neighbor, it is not possible to incur spiritual loss through the *sin* of saving one's neighbor. Thus, although spiritual benefits, even for oneself, must also be consulted in applying a preference-rule, the specific spiritual value of obeying or violating the rule cannot coherently figure among the competing values that indicate what the rule requires on any given occasion.

Neither, perhaps, can happiness. Sometimes the word *happiness* is synonymous with *gladness* or *joy*. So used, it designates a single, fairly definite value. ("Happiness," one writer declares, "isn't a mysterious condition that needs to be dissected carefully by wordologists or psychologists. It's your state of mind when you're experiencing something pleasurable; it's when you feel good."[21]) Frequently, however, and especially in ethical discussion, happiness is not some single value that may weigh in the scales against some other value—friendship, justice, pleasure, health, peace, or the like—but is instead an ill-defined congeries of values.

> We say, for instance, "Those were the happiest years of my life," or, "I was very happy at that school." Now what does this happiness consist in? Some constant or recurring feeling which we now recall having experienced during those years? Doesn't it amount to this: during that happy time I had many friends, did interesting things, was in good health, had few toothaches or quarrels, was praised for my work, and so on? That's what happiness amounts to, this variable weave in which the pleasant, exciting, interesting, friendly, and so on predominate, and the painful, boring, nasty, ugly and so on are infrequent and slight.[22]

To view happiness, in this common, comprehensive sense, as a rival value in competition with these, its varied constituents, would be incoherent.

However, even in this broader sense "happiness" is not all-inclusive, and problems like the following therefore arise and must be dealt with, if allusions to one's own and others' "welfare" are to have clear meaning: "Is my neighbour's welfare determined by what he wants, by what will make him happy, or by that which he ought to want (i.e. that, contentment with which would be admirable)? Do I love my neighbour if I do all I can to further his wishes, comfort, and aspirations, while remaining indifferent to the question whether their attainment makes him morally laudable? Alternatively do I love him if my zeal is only for his moral character without regard for his happiness?"[23] The answer of Christian tradition has been clear. It has not ignored people's happiness, here or hereafter, but it has disregarded preferences, whether others' or one's own, if it judged them to be mistaken or immoral. Augustine's attitude in the *Soliloquies* is typical:

> R. But, I ask you, why do you want the men you love to live or to dwell in your company?
> A. So that we can all at the same time and in unity of heart seek our souls and God. In this way the one who first makes the discovery easily leads the others thither without any toil.
> R. Suppose they do not want to seek such things?
> A. I will induce them to want to.[24]

Especially of late, this attitude has been criticized. In assisting others, it is said, we should consult their own desires and preferences, not their welfare as we conceive it. Otherwise we are guilty of value imperialism, paternalism, or some other vice.[25] Yet, consider a case like the following. In Irving Stone's *The Agony and the Ecstasy,* Pope Julius II asks young Michelangelo to carve his tomb. "He worked in a fever of exultation for several weeks, nourished by the unending flow of sketches that were born in his brain and brought to life in India ink."[26] What a magnificent conception! However, when shown the plans, his friend Jacopo Galli is less enthusiastic. "By the simplest arithmetic," he observes, "these forty figures on the tombs will take you between forty and a hundred years."[27] Jacopo does his best, as a good friend should, but Michelangelo will not listen. He takes his plans to Julius and accepts a commission that he cannot possibly complete and that becomes the bane of his existence for the next thirty years. If only Jacopo had managed to dissuade him, or change the pope's mind, or delay their meeting, or somehow save him from his folly! What a kindness it would have been to spare him such torment.

Granted, we must be doubly sure before passing from dissuasion to subversion of another's plans. And we should not impose our mere preferences on others. Often their desires determine and reveal what constitutes their genuine welfare. Yet Kierkegaard was right when he wrote, "If you can perceive what is best for him better than he himself, you shall not be excused because the harmful thing was his own desire, what he himself asked for."[28] This traditional position is the one I shall adopt, and the sense I shall suppose when I speak of relative benefits for oneself and for others. The benefits in question are not simply what we or they hanker for.

Similarly, in the scales of decision not all satisfactions count as pluses nor all dissatisfactions as minuses. There are inherently sinful satisfactions, born of hostility, malice, envy, jealousy, and the like. There are praiseworthy griefs, over one's past, others' sins, injustice in the world, and the like. The sinful satisfactions, whether one's own or others', never count in favor of a course of action; the praiseworthy griefs may.[29] "Blessed are they who mourn"; blessed are they who help them so to mourn.

This clarification leads to another, concerning the status of egoistic or altruistic affectivity. Suppose that the norm to be applied is Parity, and that, in a given situation, alternate decisions would bring equal good to oneself or to another. Suppose further that one finds self-seeking agreeable and self-sacrifice disagreeable. Does this fact decide the matter? Does this increment of personal satisfaction tip the scales in one's own favor? Should pleasure in giving, on the contrary, be permitted to tip the scales the other way, in favor of the neighbor? Or suppose that Self-Preference, not Parity, is a valid norm: Does the joy a person takes in giving tell in favor of self-denial? May the norm be turned against itself this way? If, on the contrary, the right norm is Self-Denial, and one takes pleasure in helping others, should one sacrifice that pleasure and cease to help others? May this norm, too, be used against itself?

The problem crops up repeatedly. I have joy in the Gospel, writes Karl Barth, if the act of self-giving is itself a cause of rejoicing to me. "I do not really perform it if I do so joylessly and unwillingly and grudgingly and with a thousand 'ifs' and 'buts.' And I will then find no joy in the Gospel, but prove only that so far I have not really heard the Gospel at all."[30] But if I find joy in giving, I please myself by pleasing others. My doing them good does me good. So it would appear that a norm of other-preference or self-denial no longer has any application in the life of one who wholeheartedly embraces it. Such a person serves self in serving others.

Something similar may hold for any person, whether egoistically or altruistically inclined. Christian writers have often stressed this paradox: "Whoever does not love himself, loves himself."[31] "Self-sacrifice and authentic self-development are as inseparable as were the cross and the resurrection."[32] "The possession of strong, deeply rooted interests in our fellows tends to enrich our own life and in so doing enhances greatly its joys and mitigates its inevitable sorrows."[33] "By using powers like trust, understanding, courage, responsibility, devotion, and honesty I grow also; and I am able to bring such powers into play because my interest is focused on the other."[34] So it might appear that no other-preferring rule ever calls for sacrifice of one's own genuine interests.[35] In practice, all six norms converge.

This inference is a confusion, and so is the whole type of reasoning I have been evoking. To be sure, if one or the other norm is preferable, that is the one to follow if we wish to grow as persons. But our growth through observance of the rule does not indicate what satisfies the rule; the rule does. Similarly, if one or the other norm is preferable, that is the one we should take pleasure in. But the pleasure we take in it does not count for or against an action; the norm does. Personal growth or personal pleasure may tell for or against an option, but not this derivative variety of pleasure or growth. Such reckoning would be incoherent and might falsify many a verdict.

It would be incoherent, for example, for a proponent of Self-

Preference to reflect: "This action conforms to the rule of Self-Preference, which is valid, and the action therefore gives me pleasure; this, then, is a reason for performing the action, since Self-Preference says I should consult my pleasure." It would be equally incoherent for a proponent of Self-Denial to reason: "This action conforms to the rule of Self-Denial, which is valid, and the action therefore gives me pleasure; this, then, is a reason against performing the action, since Self-Denial says I should not seek my pleasure." The pleasure of doing what I ought to do can have no say in determining what I ought to do. Neither, a fortiori, can the pleasure of conforming with an unacceptable rule, or the displeasure of conforming with an acceptable one. The coherent application of a preference-rule— whether Self-Preference, Self-Denial, or any other of the six—requires that all such derivative, second-order values or disvalues be excluded from consideration.

So, too, does the coherent determination of what preference-rule another person is applying or proposing. To illustrate. In chapter 5, I cite a passage from St. Ignatius Loyola which appears to favor Self-Denial. Against this interpretation it has been pointed out that elsewhere Ignatius speaks of seeking one's own salvation. For example, the *Spiritual Exercises'* "First Principle and Foundation" advises that we are created to praise, reverence, and serve God our Lord and by this means to save our souls. From such evidence it is inferred that Ignatius did not favor Self-Denial, in the strong sense defined in chapter 1, but Self-Subordination, which permits concern for self which does not conflict with concern for others. Indeed, the doubt is expressed whether any intelligent Christian has ever advocated Self-Denial as I have defined it, since none has ever denied that we might legitimately seek our own salvation. The reply to this objection is that it overlooks the focus fixed in this chapter and confuses first-order considerations with second-order ones. As the Ignatian principle notes, we are created to praise, reverence, and serve God and *thereby* to save our souls. But in what does God's praise and reverence consist? Is the divine majesty best served and praised by lives lived in accordance with Self-Preference, or Parity, or Other-Preference, or Self-Subordination, or Self-Forgetfulness, or Self-Denial? Our concern in the present study is this first-order question. Hence derivative, second-order, noncompeting values like the salvation of one's soul or the service and glory of God drop from direct consideration.

The Procedure to Be Followed

I imagine most Christians would agree that in order to answer a question like the one we have now defined, concerning a Christian preference-rule for serving self and others, it is necessary to consult Scripture, Christian tradition, one's own and others' experience, and reason. But just how this varied consultation should proceed is less evident. Where should one start, where should one end? How are these various sources to be related, and what authority should be accorded to each?

Commenting on Aristotle's *Ethics,* Henry Sidgwick wrote: "What he gave us there was the Common Sense Morality of Greece, reduced to consistency by careful comparison: given not as something external to him but as what 'we'—he and others—think, ascertained by reflection."[36] Christian ethicists have often adopted a similar approach. Trusting in the initial message received and in the continuing presence of the Spirit, they have had recourse, not to "common sense morality," but to the morality of Christendom, discoverable in Scripture and in Christian tradition, and have sought to "reduce it to consistency by careful comparison." With regard to this privileged source they have adopted an attitude analogous to the one Aristotle formulated: "Adhere generally, deviate and attempt reform only in exceptional cases in which . . . the argument against Common Sense is decisive."[37]

Such will be my approach in the present work, as it was in *Christian Moral Reasoning.* "Where else," I wrote, "might Christian norms be sought than in actual Christian thinking, current and past? No solution can be presented as the Christian solution, no approach as the Christian approach to morals, if it ignores the way Christ himself thought, or Christians after him."[38] Accordingly, the treatment was divided, much as it is here, between a historical part, furnishing samples from the distant and recent past, and an analytic, systematic part, reflecting on the materials thus provided. However, the fragmentation of Christian opinion concerning neighbor-love imposes one important difference of procedure.

"Our hope," I wrote in that earlier study, "will be to find a single main channel, that is, one criterion so dominant that it alone answers the question: If we wish to be both consistent and true to our Christian heritage, what criterion of right and wrong should we adopt?"[39] As chapter 1 has already made clear, it is vain to entertain any comparable ambition with regard to neighbor-love. On this issue, opinions have been too diffuse. However, I have discovered that Christian Scripture reveals less diversity; there a sharper focus does emerge. Accordingly, I have proceeded as follows. Chapter 4 elicits an answer from the New Testament. Chapter 5 examines the diverging views that grew up subsequently in Christendom, weighs the reasons for them, and finds the reasons wanting. Chapter 6 reviews varied objections from non-Christian sources, and finds them, too, unconvincing. The New Testament verdict stands. In conclusion, chapter 7 assesses the significance of this result.

This concise summary hardly suggests the difficulty of the enterprise. Angels might fear to venture where I have rushed in. The issue is dauntingly complex; the evidence varied, vast, and obscure. Most Christian discussions of charity do not touch on the issue that interests us; those that do, often reveal little awareness of plausible alternatives or pertinent distinctions. Repeatedly, authors who in one place appear to espouse one preference-rule seem elsewhere to endorse a different, competing one. A "paradox of analysis" therefore threatens: performing a necessary task of analysis, I may seem to attribute to Christendom a position more precise than any it has held. However, my task is more than mere reportage; it also involves much sifting and sorting. My query here, paralleling that in *Christian Moral Reasoning* and arising from it, is this: If Christians wish to be both consistent and true to their heritage, what preference-rule for mine and thine should they adopt?

4

The New Testament's Preference

"The Bible," it has been said, "seems less interested in making ethical judgments than the ethicist would like, and the ethical science seems to demand more precise measuring tools than the Bible affords."[1] Certainly much that the New Testament says about charity is not relevant for the ethical query that concerns us, and much that looks relevant turns out to be irrelevant. Furthermore, the passages which are in fact germane have been so variously interpreted as to discourage any hope of a uniform verdict. Some texts have been read as favoring Self-Preference, others as favoring Parity, others as favoring Other-Preference, Self-Subordination, Self-Forgetfulness, or Self-Denial, and still others as being opposed to any such balancing of benefit and harm.[2] However, not all readings have equal plausibility, and once the less likely interpretations are cleared away a focus does emerge.

Although it emerges both in the gospels and in the epistles and might be noted in one place then the other, I have preferred to review the total evidence a single time, as follows. At the start I shall clear the ground by setting aside much data that might appear pertinent but is in fact irrelevant. Then I shall sift the remaining texts for their significance, passing in review those that have been or might be cited in favor of each of the six alternative preference-rules. From this sifting, one of the six will emerge as the most strongly supported norm, with two others as its closest rivals.

In assessing each of the first four positions—Self-Preference, Parity, Other-Preference, and Self-Subordination—I shall weigh the evidence that appears favorable, note its limitations, then pass on. To avoid repetition, I shall not adduce as counterevidence all the texts that appear to back some more strongly altruistic norm, later in the series. Thus, I shall not cite against Self-Preference all the evidence for Parity, Other-Preference, Self-Subordination, Self-Forgetfulness, and Self-Denial, and against Parity all the evidence for Other-Preference, Self-Subordination, Self-Forgetfulness, and Self-Denial, and so forth, then run through all the same evidence a second, third, fourth, or fifth time, as favoring one of these later positions. This abstraction from the total evidence pro and con may offend the trained exegete's instincts; but all pertinent evidence will eventually receive due consideration—once.

Clearing the Ground

I remarked earlier that Jesus' acceptance of death so that "the whole nation might not perish" is compatible with any of the six preference-rules that relate the good of self and the good of others. Even Self-Preference would call for nothing less. Hence even the supreme Christian paradigm of self-sacrifice tells only for altruism and against egoism; it does not validate any single form of altruism. The same holds for the other manifestations of Jesus' charity in which the New Testament abounds:

> He came *propter nos homines;* He went about doing good (Acts 10:38); He loved us to the very end, delivering Himself (Gal. 2:20) up to death (Phil. 2:8) and even to the Eucharist (Jn. 13:1); solicitous lest He lose any of those entrusted to Him by His Father (Jn. 17:12-19) and wishing them to be with Him close to the Father (Jn. 17:24), He identified Himself with them as the vine with the branches (Jn. 15:5). Just as He thought of others during His life, being moved by human suffering (Lk. 7:11-13) even to tears (Jn. 11:35), He does not forget us when He is about to leave us: He recommends us to the goodness of the Father (Jn. 17:11), He promises not to leave us orphans (Jn. 14:18) but to send us another to befriend us (Jn. 14:16). And on the cross, before dying, He gives us His own mother (Jn. 19:26-27).[3]

We may feel that Jesus' love of others was stronger than that formulated by, for instance, the norm of Self-Preference or the principle of Parity; but none of the actions here cited suffices to show that he was. The six norms whose respective merits we are weighing are all altruistic norms; they all allow one's own good to be overridden either by another's greater need or by the needs of a greater number or by both together. All six norms can counsel or command the sacrifice of life itself. Indeed, all six might conceivably go farther still. Thus Martin Bucer writes:

> The minister . . . willingly stakes not only his body and sacrifices not only his material possessions but also his spiritual life and blessedness, if only his preaching the divine Word would lead others to a knowledge of God, to

blessedness, and thereby to praise and eternally to glorify the goodness of God. Moses was so minded. When the people of Israel had sinned, he begged God to forgive them, and said: "Lord, either forgive this sin of the people or erase me from the book which thou hast written" (Exodus 32:32). Likewise Paul writes: I tell the truth in Christ Jesus and I lie not, my conscience is my witness in the Holy Spirit, I have in my heart a great sadness and a restless affliction: I have desired to be banished from Christ for the sake of my brethren (Romans 9:1-3).[4]

For a single Jewish brother, Paul might not have felt the same sentiments. For his people as a whole, all six preference-rules would approve his readiness to sacrifice himself (were there any possibility of such an exchange). It is evident, then, that our consideration of evidence will have to be highly selective. Still, a great many scriptural sayings appear to have at least prima facie relevance for our question and have been cited in favor of one or the other norm.

Self-Preference

Eight times the New Testament enjoins love of neighbor "as oneself."[5] From this injunction an interpretation popularized by Aquinas has deduced the obligation to love oneself more than one's neighbor. "We see," reasons St. Thomas, "that a man's love for himself is, so to speak, the paradigm of his love for others. Now the paradigm is more than what takes after it. Therefore a man is bound in charity to love himself more than his neighbor."[6] As was noted earlier, others have read the command in just the opposite sense. According to Luther, "by this commandment 'as yourself' man is not commanded to love himself but he is shown the wicked love with which in fact he loves himself" and with which he should, instead, love his neighbor.[7] This interpretation, too, goes far beyond the text.[8] However, the very suggestion of patterning a good love of others on our bad love of self shows how groundless is the assumption that a paradigm automatically rates higher than what is patterned on it—or indeed that it rates at all. Thus the words *as yourself* neither enjoin self-love nor assign it primacy over neighbor-love.

From other New Testament data, Richard Völkl constructs a slightly more plausible case for self-preference:

The Christian, too, must hold fast to his Christian existence (Phil 3,16; 1 Cor 10,12), must guard his faith and his good conscience (1 Tim 1,19; 3,9; 2 Tim 3,14; 4,7). This duty can clash with that of love of neighbor. Indeed on occasion supernatural self-love appears to limit neighbor-love. With words drawn from the Old Testament Paul warns against mixing with things pagan: " . . . Come out from them, . . . Touch nothing unclean!" (2 Cor 6,17). The Romans are to avoid those who create dissensions and scandals (Rom

16,17), Titus is to shun the obdurate and look to himself (Tit 3,10f). Although a Christian would have to leave the world if he wished to avoid all contact with sinners, he should have no dealings with those who call themselves Christians and are not (1 Cor 5,9-11), for the danger of infection is great (1 Cor 5,6; cf. Eph 5,7). The priority of self-love revealed in this negative attitude becomes still clearer when Paul enjoins Timothy to attend to himself and his teaching so as to save himself and those entrusted to him (1 Tim 4,16), and urges the elders of Ephesus to take heed to themselves and the flock (Acts 20,28).[9]

Since in these final citations, concerning Timothy and the elders, there is no shadow of conflict between benefit to self and benefit to others, no inference can be drawn from them in favor of Self-Preference. And though the preceding negative injunctions may look harmful to those warned against, there is no indication that the authors of the injunctions so viewed them. On the contrary, in 1 Cor 7:16, Paul writes: "Wife, how do you know whether you will save your husband? Husband, how do you know whether you will save your wife?" And in 1 Cor 5:5, he explains: "You are to deliver this man to Satan for the destruction of the flesh, that his spirit may be saved in the day of the Lord Jesus."[10] Even had Paul been apprehensive that those avoided might be harmed, he surely believed that greater long-term harm would result, both for Christians and non-Christians, if Christians and non-Christians were affected in the ways he feared.[11] He may have been mistaken in his assessment of harms and benefits, but that is not relevant to the present issue.[12] The question is whether he, or the other authors cited, implicitly or explicitly recommended self-preferential love; and I see no reason to suppose that they did. In none of these instances did they say or imply: "True, those you shun will suffer, but you must put your own welfare ahead of theirs."

Parity

Many have read the command of neighbor-love as implicitly enjoining love of self ("It not only assumes a self-love but even takes it as the measure of neighbor love"[13]); and some have read the phrase *as yourself* as enjoining equal love of self and neighbor.[14] However, as Aelred of Rievaulx noted long ago, the scriptural injunction does not say "as much as yourself" but "as yourself."[15] "The words *as yourself*," Aquinas agreed, "touch on the manner of loving. They do not mean that a man must love his neighbour equally as himself, but in like manner as himself."[16] Descriptions of this manner have varied. A natural, straightforward reading is that of Chrysostom: "Do you wish to receive kindness? Be kind to another. Do you wish to receive mercy? Show mercy to your neighbor. Do you wish to be applauded? Applaud another. Do you wish to be loved? Exercise love.

Do you wish to enjoy the first rank? First concede that place to another."[17] Here there is no suggestion of balancing mine and thine; indeed, the final words may be read (despite a hint of reciprocity) as advising other-preference.

Interpretations like Chrysostom's suggest why the commandment of neighbor-love has often been equated with the "Golden Rule," to do unto others as you would have them do unto you (positive form) or to avoid doing to others what you would not wish done to you (negative form).[18] "The function of the Golden Rule," it is for instance said, "or of 'You shall love your neighbour as yourself' is not to provide a rule of thumb for all interpersonal relations, but rather to shatter the radical self-centredness which obscures our awareness of the needs or rights of others."[19] When an attempt is made to render the Golden Rule more precise, interpretation often takes a Kantian turn. The rule's force, suggests Alan Donagan, in agreement with Sidgwick, is "that of a principle of impartiality: in no system that incorporates it can it be permissible for A to treat B in a manner in which it would be impermissible for B to treat A 'merely on the ground that they are two different individuals, and without there being any difference between the natures or the circumstances of the two which can be stated as a reasonable ground for difference of treatment.'"[20] Whatever the merits of this reading, the main point to notice for present purposes is that this type of impartiality differs from that prescribed by Parity. Parity is no more universal than any of its rivals. All six preference-rules, from Self-Preference to Self-Denial, apply equally to all, so equally satisfy Donagan's stipulation. In none of them is it permissible "for A to treat B in a manner in which it would be impermissible for B to treat A."

Paul's advice concerning the collection for Jerusalem, in 2 Cor 8:13-15, is more pertinent as evidence for Parity. For the discussion there concerns the sharing of goods; and Paul explains: "I do not mean that others should be eased and you burdened, but that as a matter of equality your abundance at the present time should supply their want, so that their abundance may supply your want, that there may be equality." "It is not intended," Karl Schelkle comments, "that the gifts should aid the recipients, while the givers put such a strain on their resources that they themselves should be reduced to distress. All that is aimed at is an equality in the goods necessary to sustain life."[21] Parity, it appears, is the norm implicitly enjoined.[22]

In answer to this inference, two distinctions can be noted, both germane to the present inquiry. First, Paul expresses admiration for the Macedonians, who gave not only according to their means, but beyond their means (2 Cor 8:3); he is, however, unwilling to impose as an obligation what he admires as a generous ideal (2 Cor 8:8).[23] Second, his viewpoint as organizer of the effort must be distinguished from their viewpoint as participants. As an administrator of Christian charity, he is not partial to either side, the Corinthians who give or the Palestinians who receive. If the Corinthians gave too much, he might have to organize a second collection, to help the helpers.[24] Thus on close inspection, this evidence, too, appears weak. It does not support Parity as a personal preference-rule.

Other-Preference

The Macedonians' generosity evokes a higher paradigm: "For you know the grace of our Lord Jesus Christ, that though he was rich, yet for your sake he became poor, so that by his poverty you might become rich" (2 Cor 8:9).[25] The Christian ideal is something more than Parity; the welfare of others takes precedence over one's own. In Jesus' own words: "It is more blessed to give than to receive" (Acts 20:35). Texts like these (compare Lk 6:33-35, 14:12-14; Rom 12:10; 1 Jn 3:16) clearly go beyond Parity; but they do not clearly stop short of Self-Subordination, Self-Forgetfulness, or Self-Denial. They do not indicate that when interests conflict, one's own good should be given independent weight in competition with others'.

Phil 2:4 is sometimes translated in a way that more clearly suggests drawing the line at Other-Preference; for example: "Let each of you look not only to his own interests, but also to the interests of others" (Revised Standard Version). "'Also' must not be overlooked," remarks Paul Rees. "It gives perspective and balance to what Paul is urging. What is forbidden is the fixing of one's eye on one's own interests to the exclusion of the interests of others."[26] However, this reading, though common,[27] may be questioned on several grounds. For one thing, the Greek *kai* on which the word *also* is based is missing from some early manuscripts. Furthermore, even if retained, the *kai* need not be so interpreted.[28] In view of such texts as 1 Cor 10:33, of Paul's well-known penchant for sharp antitheses,[29] and of the immediate context,[30] it probably should not be. For reasons like these, less self-regarding translations[31] and interpretations of Phil 2:4 have been proposed. Spicq, for instance, remarks that Paul here "asks the Philippians to be concerned for the good of their brethren, without taking account of their personal interests."[32]

A further difficulty concerns the word "interests," with which translators have tried to capture the sense of the indefinite neuter expressions τὰ ἑαυτῶν and τὰ ἑτέρῶν. Some alternative interpretations of these expressions disconnect the verse from our question concerning active beneficence, and thereby eliminate it as evidence. Thus, Ralph Martin, following Ewald,[33] Bonnard,[34] and Collange,[35] suggests that Paul is advising his readers to be attentive, not to the interests of others, but to their "good points and qualities."[36] For Francis Beare, the interpretive choice is not between "qualities" and "interests" but between "qualities" and "rights."[37] For George Caird, there is "no serious doubt that the emphasis is on rights."[38] Surveying the wide range of possible interpretations, Pat

Harrell concludes that Paul "wished to be as general as possible."[39] If so, the verse reconnects with our question. However, this inclusive reading is far from certain.

Furthermore, it points up a final weakness of Phil 2:4 as evidence for Other-Preference rather than some still more altruistic norm. Being indefinite, the verse does not distinguish between self-service for one's own sake and self-service for others' sake. Our six preference-rules, including Other-Preference and its competitors, do so discriminate. They must: for even the purest moral egoist is duty-bound to show concern for others (for the egoist's sake), while the most extreme altruist is obliged to show concern for self (for others' sake). The question is whether one's concern for others should be related wholly, partly, or not at all to oneself, and whether one's concern for oneself should be related wholly, partly, or not at all to others. On this question Phil 2:4, even when taken in isolation from other scriptural evidence, sheds no clear light. And, of course, the verse should not be considered in isolation. Strong evidence, including the very next verses, points farther along the altruistic scale, to Self-Subordination, Self-Forgetfulness, or Self-Denial.

Self-Subordination

The label *Self-Subordination* elicits a favorite New Testament figure for Jesus and his followers—that of a servant or slave (in the sense of one devoted to service, without any connotation of "lack of freedom, unwilling service, cruel treatment, etc."[40]). "Whoever would be great among you must be your servant, and whoever would be first among you must be your slave; even as the Son of man came not to be served but to serve, and to give his life as a ransom for many" (Mt 20:26-28; cf. Mt 23:11; Mk 9:35; 10:42-45; 14:24; Lk 12:37).[41] "If I then, your Lord and Teacher, have washed your feet ["a service traditionally rendered by the lowest servant on the staff of house servants"[42]] you also ought to wash one another's feet" (Jn 13:14). "Have this mind among yourselves, which is yours in Christ Jesus, who, though he was in the form of God, did not count equality with God a thing to be grasped, but emptied himself, taking the form of a servant" (Phil 2:5-7). "Through love, be servants of one another" (Gal 5:13; cf. 1 Cor 9:19; 2 Cor 4:5).[43]

From texts like these, no strictly logical inference can be drawn to the norm of Self-Subordination (countenancing good to self only when it does not conflict with others' good). However, the texts do, on the one hand, clearly suggest a more purely altruistic norm than Other-Preference (which permits the agent's good to compete, if only minimally, with others'), but do not, on the other hand, suggest a more total self-denial, disconnected from service. To cite a nineteenth-century illustration of this self-subordinating balance, Sojourner Truth, who later became a well-known speaker and social activist, was in her youth an exemplary slave, who did more than was required of her; yet there was room in her life for dreaming, dancing, singing, chatting. Her own desires and preferences were allowed some scope, provided they did not conflict with her duties to her master.[44]

Thus Spicq's strongly self-denying interpretation of Gal 5:13-14 is not clearly justified: "It is evident that 'charity,' so understood, is a profound attachment that shows itself in works and that demands a total renunciation of oneself, similar to that of a slave who no longer belongs to himself but becomes his master's property."[45] On the other hand, Ernest Burton's reading appears too weak: "δουλεύω, generally meaning 'to yield obedience to,' 'to be in subjection to' . . . , is evidently here employed in a sense corresponding to that which δοῦλος sometimes has . . . , and meaning 'to render service to,' 'to do that which is for the advantage of.'"[46] As George Duncan notes, "when Paul speaks of 'serving one another' he means more than 'helping one another,' as would have been implied by the Greek verb *diakonein.* The verb which he uses is derived from *doulos,* a bondservant, a word which Paul so often uses of himself as a servant of Christ."[47] Being a slave or bond-servant is something more than rendering assistance[48] and something less than having no concern for oneself.

The Sermon on the Mount strikes a similar balance: "You have heard that it was said, 'An eye for an eye and a tooth for a tooth.' But I say to you, Do not resist one who is evil. But if any one strikes you on the right cheek, turn to him the other also; and if any one would sue you and take your coat, let him have your cloak as well; and if any one forces you to go one mile, go with him two miles. Give to him who begs from you, and do not refuse him who would borrow from you" (Mt 5:38-42; cf. Lk 6:29-30). For our purposes, it makes little difference whether these precepts are to be taken literally or, more plausibly, as "dramatic illustrations which exhibit and illuminate from various angles a consistent outlook on life."[49] On the one hand, they clearly go beyond any balancing of mine and thine; one's own interests are not to count in competition with others'.[50] On the other hand, the actions prescribed are all concessions made to others; there is no suggestion of self-denial unrelated to other people's needs or desires—no injunction to strip oneself of one's cloak if no one else receives it, no implication that one should go an inconvenient extra mile if no one else requests it. Other-Preference is surpassed; Self-Subordination is not.

It is true, as Robert Tannehill remarks, that "the commands are not based upon prudential considerations as to what will result in the greatest good for the other. Turning the other cheek is commanded because it is the opposite of what we naturally tend to do in the situation. In this way the command becomes as extreme as can readily be imagined. It stands in deliberate tension with the way in which men normally live and think."[51] It is also true that, as he adds, "no attempt is made to encompass a major area of human behavior under a general rule, or to cover such an area by systematic discussion of the legal and ethical problems of different classes of situations."[52] Yet in each prescription, I would agree, "the specific instance is indirectly suggestive for many other situations."[53] "The focal instance does not leave the decision maker without help. It helps not by giving a clear indication of what he is to do but by throwing a strong light on the situation from one direction, forcefully calling to his attention one factor in his situation. The command does not do the hearer's thinking for him; it starts him thinking in a definite direction."[54] The common focus, I would suggest, is self versus other; the consistent direction is Self-Subordination.

Karl Barth views the Pauline epistles from a similar perspective:

> It should be noted that in Paul, too, the Christian's dying and being dead and buried with Christ has nothing whatever to do with an unrelated self-negation and asceticism that is of value only in itself. When Paul describes himself as exhausted and wasted and spent like capital, he adds: "For your souls" (2 Cor 12:15). . . . He fills up what is lacking in the suffering of Christ in his own body "for the sake of his body, that is, the church" (Col. 1:24). It is thus said expressly by Paul that the necessary sacrifice of the Christian is as little unrelated as is Christ's own sacrifice. The humiliation which Christians undergo in fellowship with Christ as those who are baptized and reconciled to God through Christ, like the humiliation of Christ himself as described in Phil. 2:1-11, is not an end in itself. Not humility as such, not the virtue of humility, is commended in the exhortation to have the same mind among ourselves as is in Christ Jesus. What is commended is the humiliation or humility in which we all look to the interests of others and not just our own.[55]

Barth may be right in refusing to pass beyond Other-Preference or Self-Subordination to Self-Forgetfulness or Self-Denial, but I would hesitate to say that Paul expressly backs him in his refusal. And his survey of evidence is selective; other texts remain to be considered which might plausibly be interpreted as taking that further step.

Self-Forgetfulness or Self-Denial

I have proposed the figure of a servant or slave as suggesting Self-Subordination. Others have viewed it differently. It has been said, for example, that in Mt 20:26-27 "Jesus first speaks of the servant, the person who freely puts himself at the disposition of others, and then radicalizes his statement with the image of the slave, the non-person who has no rights or existence of his own, who exists *solely* for others."[56] If such was the image of a slave current in the first century, among both Romans and Jews, Christians and non-Christians, then, regardless of the varied reality of slavery (for example, Epictetus versus laborers in the mines), the gospel message may be more self-forgetting or self-denying than I have suggested.[57] However, it is clear that the author of the first gospel and his Christian readers did not so view slaves. And even had such been the universal perception, it still would not follow that such is the message of Mt 20:25-28. *Diakonos* and *doulos* may be synonyms,[58] chosen merely for variety.[59] Besides, self-forgetfulness or self-denial unrelated to others' welfare seems peripheral to the pericope's concerns.

The same holds, however, with regard to personal benefit such as Self-Subordination makes allowance for (that is, with regard to good for self which does not conflict with the service of others). That, too, is peripheral to the concerns of the passages cited at the start of the previous section. Thus, although these texts, which speak of Christ and Christian discipleship in terms of servitude or slavery, clearly go beyond mere Other-Preference, they do not as clearly exclude Self-Forgetfulness or Self-Denial.

Passages like Lk 6:35 and Lk 14:12-14 occasion similar uncertainty. "Love your enemies, and do good, and lend, expecting nothing in return." "When you give a feast, invite the poor, the maimed, the lame, the blind, and you will be blessed, because they cannot repay you." Were the impossibility of repayment the sole or principal reason for inviting the poor, this saying would suggest Self-Denial. In this supposition, the same amount of good would be done by inviting the rich or inviting the poor, but in the latter case no good would come to the giver; so that option should be preferred. However, there are obvious difficulties with this interpretation. Hence an equally plausible reading would be: "Let your concern for others be unaffected by any concern for self." That is, the implicit lesson may be Self-Subordination.[60]

Jesus' concern for the poor, the maimed, the lame, the blind, the confused and ignorant lost sheep of Israel was not motivated by the fact that they could not repay him. Yet the saying rings true that he was "a man for others," not "a man for others too." Peter Van Breemen develops this theme persuasively.

> Possibly one of the most characteristic qualities of Christ was this ability to live for others. In the words of Paul: "Christ did not think of himself" (Rom. 15:3): he was truly a man for others. And in this self-forgetfulness he was carrying out most completely his mission of being Emmanuel, finding himself because he had lost himself so fully, according to his own admonition: " . . . anyone who wants to save his life will lose it; but anyone who loses his life for my sake will find it" (Mt 16:25). It is this lack of concern about himself which is so typical of Christ, constituting, as it were, his very identity. It is the secret of his love for the people, his total availability to them in their need.[61]

Behind this portrayal stands a significant fact. In the lives of most people—ministers, priests, and religious included—it is easy to spot pleasures indulged, expenses incurred, and interests pursued which are only tenuously related to others' welfare, if at all. The same does not hold for Jesus, as portrayed by the gospels. Nowhere in their pages do we observe him serving his own good in a way unrelated to others' good: not when he rested by the well, nor when he drank his hosts' wine, nor when he accepted their invitations to dine, nor when he rode into Jerusalem instead of entering on foot. However, neither do we find him denying his own good in a way unrelated to others' good.[62] The gospels are concerned with Jesus' saving acts; hence they have little to say about the difference that separates Self-Subordination from Self-Forgetfulness or Self-Denial.

Accordingly, although Jesus' injunction to love one another "as I have loved you" (Jn 13:34; cf. Eph 5:1-2) may take us far—beyond Self-Preference or Parity or Other-Preference—it does not enable us to make this final discrimination, between Self-Subordination and still more strongly altruistic versions of agape. "Everyone agrees," writes Spicq, "in not taking the word 'as' (in 'as I have loved you') in the sense of degree or intensity of affection. . . . There is question of a love of the same nature and the same quality, of being attached to one's brethren and of devoting oneself to their service 'in the same way' as the Master."[63] The two incidents that precede the injunction in Jn 13:34 suggest what Jesus' way is. "'Love' consists in welcoming, in placing oneself at the service of others, so as to give them dignity and freedom through love (the washing of feet), and this without any limit or discrimination, with supreme respect for their freedom (the episode of Judas)."[64] Jesus' words "as I have loved you" also foreshadow what he is about to do. "Thus, disciples are to love 'to the very end' (13:1). There is to be no limit to the love of the disciples for one another; they are to love to the end of their lives, to the end of their strength, with the generosity of Jesus' love for sinners."[65] Hence, "the newness of the command now given by Jesus is that the love he requires of his disciples . . . will 'reverse the roles,' and bring the leader to serve as a slave, and the innocent to serve as the guilty, in the love that will bring peace to the world by its sacrificial quality. It will be a love that, like Christ's love for his own, does not ask questions about worthiness, but simply gives itself in humble service."[66] In all this, however, there is no question of sacrifice for sacrifice's sake. Concerning denial of self that has no relation to others the gospels do not speak, or at least do not speak clearly, either pro or con.

However, Paul's epistles may. In Phil 2:4, as we have seen, it is not sure whether the word *kai* is his, and if it is, what he meant by it. However, texts such as Rom 15:1, 1 Cor 10:24, 1 Cor 10:33, and 1 Cor 13:5 may speak less ambiguously, in favor of Self-Forgetfulness or Self-Denial.

The brevity of the pertinent phrase in 1 Cor 13:5 (οὐ ζητεῖ τὰ ἑαυτῆς) allows considerable freedom of interpretation, and translators make the most of it.[67] Some renderings suggest Self-Forgetfulness or Self-

Denial;[68] others are more clearly compatible with Self-Subordination;[69] many—indeed the majority—do not speak to the issue that concerns us.[70] However, to judge merely from translations, it might appear that the remaining three texts I have mentioned leave interpreters less liberty. We read, for instance, that we who are strong ought to bear with the failings of the weak "and not to please ourselves" (Revised Standard, Authorized Catholic, American Bible Society), "and not consider ourselves" (New English), "without thinking of ourselves" (Jerusalem). Translations of 1 Cor 10:24 and 10:33 cluster still more closely, and the majority give the same impression of enjoining Self-Forgetfulness or Self-Denial. For example, in the Revised Standard Version 1 Cor 10:24 advises: "Let no one seek his own good, but the good of his neighbor." The American Bible Society wording of 1 Cor 10:33 employs similar terminology: "I try to please everyone in all that I do, with no thought of my own good, but for the good of all, so they might be saved."

However, despite this similarity of translation, much diversity appears in exegetes' understanding of these passages. Not all commentators accept the verdict that Paul, at least, favored a more self-denying norm than Self-Subordination. On 1 Cor 10:24, Robertson and Plummer comment: "'Let no one seek his own good.' The prohibition is, of course, relative: seeking one's own good is not always wrong, but it is less important than seeking the good of others; and when the two conflict it is one's own good that must give way."[71] Concerning Rom 15:1, Cranfield affirms with equal sureness: "That it would be perverse to read into Paul's μὴ ἑαυτοῖς ἀρέσκειν any notion that everything which is delightful to one ought to be avoided simply because it is delightful (a notion which the ill-informed not infrequently ascribe to the Puritans and their heirs) should be obvious. What is meant here by not pleasing oneself is not pleasing oneself regardless of the effects which one's pleasing oneself would have on others."[72]

Although these authors may speak with too great assurance, there is much to be said for their interpretation, that is, for stopping short of Self-Forgetfulness or Self-Denial in our reading of these texts. To begin with, Paul's altruistic counsels here in Romans and in 1 Corinthians are occasioned by his concern about the welfare of brethren of weak faith, about dissensions and divisions among the Corinthians, and about the source of such problems, namely preoccupation with self. I see no reason to suppose that he was worried about a form of altruism which occasions no such problems, namely Self-Subordination, and wished to rule it out along with less purely altruistic stances. In addition, it seems unlikely that he adverted to the issue of good to self that makes no difference to others or recognized Self-Subordination as a compromise between self-seeking that conflicts with others' good and self-forgetfulness or self-denial that does not. (The plausibility of this surmise is confirmed by the fact that subsequent ethicists and exegetes have seldom noted or formulated this possible middle ground.) Finally, even had Paul adverted to and favored such a position, it is doubtful whether he would have indicated by careful distinctions that his criticisms did not exclude it, nor is it clear that he should have. To introduce such complications would have been neither rhetorically effective nor pedagogically wise. And I have already mentioned Paul's penchant for strong antitheses. It would hardly accord with his style to write: "Let no one seek his own good when it conflicts with others' good, but rather let him seek the good of his neighbor, unless seeking his own good makes no difference to his neighbor." Such an utterance he would have been loath to formulate, even had it stated his true thought more exactly.

The various reasons I have cited all suggest that, despite the literal sound of certain sayings in Romans and 1 Corinthians, Paul's preference may have been Self-Subordination rather than Self-Forgetfulness or Self-Denial. There are indications that such was in fact his position, and the position of the New Testament in general. Paul tells the Romans, for example, that he longs to visit them, "that I may impart to you some spiritual gift to strengthen you, that is, that we may be mutually encouraged by each other's faith" (Rom 1:11-12). He asks them to pray "so that by God's will I may come to you with joy and be refreshed in your company" (Rom 15:32). To the Corinthians he writes: "I made up my mind not to make you another painful visit. For if I cause you pain, who is there to make me glad but the one whom I have pained? And I wrote as I did, so that when I came I might not suffer pain from those who should have made me rejoice" (2 Cor 2:1-3). Such sayings are not what one would expect from an advocate of Self-Forgetfulness or Self-Denial. Neither, perhaps, is Paul's reminder: "He who sows bountifully will also reap bountifully" (2 Cor 9:6).

Elsewhere in the New Testament, 1 Tm 4:4 is fairly explicit: "For everything created by God is good, and nothing is to be rejected if it is received with thanksgiving." A New Testament illustration is wine—the wine Jesus drank, the wine he blessed at the Last Supper, the wine he provided in such abundance, and of such high quality, for the merrymakers of Cana. Jesus' very presence at a wedding *feast* seems problematic if the norm to be observed by all was Self-Forgetfulness or Self-Denial. Why, too, portray the hoped-for Kingdom as a festive gathering rather than as a beatific vision, centered on God alone? Should this symbolic representation (Mt 8:11, 22:2-3; Lk 14:15-24) be judged unfortunate?

Consider, also, Jesus' words to his apostles: "My soul is very sorrowful, even to death; remain here, and watch with me" (Mt 26:38). Was his request or subsequent complaint motivated solely by concern for their welfare? Was there no longing for their companionship in his dark hour? The implications of Jesus' prayer in the garden seem still clearer: "My Father, if it be possible, let this cup pass from me; nevertheless, not as I will, but as thou wilt" (Mt 26:39; cf. Lk 22:42). Such a plea strongly suggests that the cross is not desirable in itself, but only in relation to the Father's salvific will for others. Had Self-Denial been Jesus' norm, a more appropriate petition might have been: "Father, if it be possible let this chalice come to me; nevertheless, if you insist on my not suffering and dying, so be it: your will be done."

Similarly suggestive is Jesus' response to others' pleas, whether the pleas are for others or for themselves. "Jesus, Master, have mercy on us," the ten lepers call out, and they are healed (Lk 17:11-19). "Lord, if you will you can make me clean," the single leper pleads, and he is cleansed (Mt 8:1-4; Mark 1:40-45; Lk 5:12-15). "Master, let me receive my sight," Bartimaeus answers, and he sees (Mark 10:46-52; Lk. 18:35-43). "Lord, save me," Peter cries, and he is rescued from the waves (Mt. 14:28-32). The apostles turn to him in their fright, and they are saved (Mt. 8:23-27; Mk. 4:35-41; Lk. 8:22-25). The woman with a hemorrhage touches him, and she is cured (Mt: 9:20-23; Mk 5:25-34: Lk 8:43-48). "It is legitimate, then," suggests Éphrem Boularand, "to seek for oneself and for others health, freedom from the devil's vexations, deliverance from danger, and life itself—all the messianic values. Is it not in dispensing these things to people that Jesus revealed himself as the Christ (Mt. 11:2-6)?"[73]

Furthermore, it is difficult to reconcile intense concern for one's own eternal happiness and welfare with total unconcern for one's temporal happiness and welfare. Yet the New Testament makes constant appeals to and for the former (for example, 1 Tm 6:12; Phil 3:12-15, 20-21; 1 Cor 9:24-27, 13:12; 2 Cor 5:1-5; Gal 6:8; Rom 6:22; 2 Thes 1:5-10, 2:16).[74] It is often objected that "the highest result of an action can never be its desired result. It must be a by-product. If it is desired, the purity of the action is destroyed."[75] Granted, its purity is lost in the tautological sense that the action is now doubly, not singly, motivated. But the New Testament does not oppose such double motivation. It sees no "impurity" in desiring both service to one's neighbor and the happiness for oneself that results from such service. Provided that the one good does not become a mere means to the other, it is perfectly legitimate to love and desire them both.

The choice between Self-Subordination and Self-Denial is complicated by the fact that two distinct principles are invoked in favor of more thorough self-denial: one altruistic, the other ascetical; one horizontal, the other vertical; one relating self to others in a way that eliminates self from independent consideration, the other relating lower values to higher in a way that eliminates the lower from independent consideration. The ascetic principle, like the altruistic, has been traced to New Testament teaching. For instance, according to M. Lepin, "in order for the life of Jesus Christ to pass into us and penetrate us entirely, it is necessary first of all to crucify the flesh, mortify the spirit, destroy the old man, die to the life of nature."[76] This is true sacrifice, since one thus "destroys, immolates, slaughters, stifles desire and natural appetite, to the glory of God."[77] Such, he maintains, is the doctrine of Paul: "'You will live,' says the Apostle, 'if by the Spirit you put to death the deeds of the flesh' (Rom. 8:13); 'Those who belong to Christ Jesus have crucified the flesh with its passions and desires' (Gal. 5:24)."[78]

Contemporary exegetes take a different view of the "flesh" (*sarx*). "Flesh is man in hostility to God and represents that part of man which is not just physically but also morally weak and infirm."[79] "Flesh and spirit are completely opposed to one another, as sin and obedience to God, as selfishness and love, or as death and eternal life (Gal. 5:17)."[80] Thus,

> In the NT as in the OT the flesh must not be conceived as synonymous with the body, nor in any philosophical sense as the material component. The flesh is the psychophysical complex of man not in abstraction but in its concrete existent totality, historical man with his past and with his concupiscence and sin. To think of the flesh as merely the material component can lead and has led Christians to a false ascetical and mystical ideal which conceives that man is to be spiritualized by being dematerialized. A study of the ideas of flesh and spirit shows that this fragment of Platonism has no place in the NT scheme of salvation.[81]

The identification of "flesh" with human nature and its tendencies would be equally unfounded. *Fallen* nature, as such, should of course be resisted. But there is no suggestion, for example, that since humans have a natural preference for life Jesus should have preferred death, or that, since humans have a natural aversion to suffering, Jesus should have desired to suffer the agony of crucifixion, if only he could do so without detriment to others. If anything, the gospels suggest the contrary.

Final Verdict

Overall, it seems that when there is no question of conflict with God's call or others' good, the New Testament has no quarrel with benefit to self. If, then, texts like 1 Cor 10:24, 1 Cor 10:33, 1 Cor 13:5, and Rom 15:1 need not, and probably should not, be read as favoring Self-Forgetfulness or Self-Denial, they may be added to previous evidence in favor of Self-Subordination. For they do at least suggest that one's own good not be allowed to compete with others' good; and this Self-Subordination enjoins, whereas less altruistic norms do not. Similarly, although the image of a servant or a slave does not tell in favor of Self-Forgetfulness or Self-Denial and against Self-Subordination, it does suggest at least Self-Subordination rather than any less altruistic norm. The verdict of the New Testament would therefore seem to be that Christians, or people generally, should give precedence to others' good, and only seek their own when it does not conflict with others'.[82] This verdict is not so firm or evident that it could not be overridden by weighty considerations favoring some other norm; but, for those who accept the authority of the New Testament, the considerations would have to be especially weighty to warrant revision in a less altruistic direction rather than a more altruistic one. The closest New Testament rivals of Self-Subordination are Self-Forgetfulness and Self-Denial.

"If scripture were never clear," wrote Augustine, "it would not nourish you; if it were never obscure, it would not exercise you."[83] What is clear, I would say, is that the New Testament favors the latter half of the altruistic spectrum, that is, the last three of the six alternative rules of preference. What is less clear, and has exercised me most, is the choice within that half, between Self-Subordination on the one hand and Self-Forgetfulness or Self-Denial on the other. Yet a verdict can, I think, be given in favor of the former. However, as individual texts of the New Testament cannot be viewed in isolation, so the New Testament as a whole cannot be taken alone, but must be read in relation to subsequent life and thought, whether Christian or non-Christian.[84]

5

Christians' Varied Views

From chapter 1's listing we know that the single New Testament norm has diffracted into six rival norms, from Self-Preference at one extreme to Self-Denial at the other. How did the splintering occur, and why? What grounds have Christians had for shifting to other positions? Are the grounds valid?

I shall conclude that, although some are better than others, none are adequate. In arriving at this judgment I shall not ignore any of the five rivals to Self-Subordination. However, the chief tale to be told is that of two strong, antithetical traditions, one much more self-regarding than Self-Subordination and the other less so. Self-Preference, at one extreme, has vied with Self-Forgetfulness and Self-Denial, at the other.

In early Christian writings, Self-Preference could sometimes be read between the lines, for instance in instructions on almsgiving; later it surfaced quite explicitly. Insinuated in the *Sentences* of Peter Lombard, crystallized in the *Summa* of St. Thomas, it became the standard position of Catholic moralists far into the twentieth century. Not, however, of Catholic mystical and ascetical writers, who during the Middle Ages, echoing a still earlier viewpoint, urged complete forgetfulness of self. Protestants carried on this tradition, as did many Catholics, so that after the Reformation a double rift appeared, between Catholics and Protestants and between Catholics themselves. The Catholic ethical tradition and the Catholic spiritual tradition each went its own way, little troubled, it seems, by the need for dialog. The first was concerned with "obligation," the second with "counsel"; both sides' acceptance of this distinction veiled the important differences that separated them.

These developments I shall now recount in greater, though far from exhaustive, detail. My interest will center not so much on the historical fortunes of various positions as on the reasons cited in their support. I realize that arguments often surface as mere afterthoughts, adduced in behalf of doctrines held for other, unacknowledged, often unrecognized reasons. However, although the subtle historical influences that shape people's ways of thinking may explain their views, they seldom validate them. Hence I shall not engage in deep historical probing, or close textual analysis, of the sayings I cite. My interest is validity. The sole question that concerns me is this: Does any single argument, or any collection of arguments, proposed by Christians themselves warrant abandoning the preference for Self-Subordination suggested by the New Testament?

Self-Preference

As a mighty river, formed by many tributaries, can be traced at its beginning to some inauspicious trickle high in a mountain meadow, so the Catholic moral teaching of Self-Preference, though likewise derived from many sources, can be traced back to an innocent misreading, by Origen, Rufinus, and Jerome, of the Masoretic text of the Song of Songs, 2:4b, and to the Vulgate translation which resulted from the misreading: "Ordinavit in me caritatem."[1] So rendered, the half verse led Augustine to construct an "order of charity": "First love God, then yourself, then love your neighbor as yourself."[2] It was natural for this ordering to be read in the sense: Love God more than yourself and yourself more than your neighbor. And so it came to be interpreted.

In his systematic formulation of Augustine's thought, Peter Lombard hesitated—with good reason[3]—to give this interpretation. According to Augustine's *Christian Doctrine,* "there are four kinds of things that are to be loved—first, that which is above us; second, ourselves; third, that which is on a level with us; fourth, that which is beneath us."[4] Clearly, God, who is above us, should be loved more than ourselves, our neighbor, and our body. Clearly, too, both we and our neighbor, who is on a level with us, should be preferred to the body, which is beneath us. And Augustine said as much a few chapters later.[5] However, as Lombard recognized, neither this later passage nor the earlier one makes clear "whether we should love all people equally and as much as ourselves, or less."[6] After citing various views, he labeled as "not unlearned" the opinion that both affectively and effectively (*in exhibitione operis*) preference should be given to oneself.[7]

In Bonaventure's and Thomas's commentaries on the *Sentences,* all hesitancy disappeared. It is evident, Bonaventure wrote, that Augustine's listing does not follow a temporal order, but an order of excellence or dignity;[8] to place love of self before love of neighbor is to place love of self above love of neighbor. From a sermon of Augustine's, he plucked a passage which, if not scrutinized too closely, appeared to confirm this reading.[9] Aquinas, in his early commentary on the *Sentences,* cited the same passage from Augustine, but put more weight on his own independent arguments demonstrating that love of self should take precedence, both affectively and effectively,[10] over love of neighbor.[11] The *Summa* added further, fuller reasons in support of the same conclusion: "A man is bound in charity to love himself more than his neighbor."[12] Unlike Bonaventure[13] and others,[14] Thomas believed that this same order persists even in heaven.[15]

Through long centuries, Scholastic authors faithfully echoed Aquinas's position and arguments, as well as a crucial confusion. At the beginning of his treatment in the commentary on the *Sentences,* Thomas posed the objection: "Charity makes us give our bodily life for our brothers. Some nonbelievers, without any hope of life eternal, exposed themselves to death for love of their friends. So friendship and charity make us love our neighbors more than ourselves." To this objection he replied: "To give one's life for one's friend is a most perfect act of virtue; hence a virtuous person has a greater desire for this act than for his own bodily life. Accordingly, the fact that a person sacrifices his bodily life for his friend does not come from his loving his friend more than himself but from his loving the good of virtue more than his bodily good."[16] Self-Preference is not violated after all; perfect order is preserved. Many have repeated this explanation without noting its incoherence.[17] If the norm of Self-Preference holds, then it is not more virtuous to prefer one's neighbor; if it is more virtuous to prefer one's neighbor, then Self-Preference does not hold. Friendship might be a justifying factor, but not virtue—not if one really accepts the norm of Self-Preference.

In dealing with Thomas's objection, Scholastics were wont to say that friendship or virtue or some other special consideration may warrant one's sacrificing oneself for another but that, *other things being equal,* preference should go to oneself.[18] The neighbor *as neighbor* should take second place.[19] It was often made explicit that self-preference is not merely permissible but preferable; it is the better thing.[20] The same viewpoint emerges clearly from the arguments Scholastics and other Christians have proposed for Self-Preference. These make up in quantity for what they lack in quality. I shall start with several in Aquinas's commentary on the *Sentences,* then dwell on those in the *Summa,* which became standard, then add a few reasons that appear here and there in subsequent Christian writings.

1. In the commentary on the *Sentences,* the case for Self-Preference opens with the brief argument: "In proportion as a person loves someone's salvation, he avoids that person's sin. But a person should avoid his own sin more than another's. Therefore he should love his own salvation more than another's." The weakness of this inference is fairly evident. The

second premise is better explained by the fact that no one can make another's choices and thereby work out the other's salvation, whether in preference or in deference to his own.

2. The next reason reads: "What is natural is stronger than what is merely voluntary. But self-love is a natural inclination, whereas love of others rests merely on rational deliberation. Hence from charity a person should love himself more than others."[21] A first difficulty here concerns the jump from *is* in the premises to *should* in the conclusion. (Consider where such reasoning would lead if applied to the forgiveness of injuries or to love of one's enemies.) A second difficulty concerns the claim that people feel no natural sympathy for others.[22]

3. In the body of the same article, Thomas argues that a person's own good is found in God as its cause, in oneself as an effect, and in one's neighbor merely by way of similitude. But the reality itself is better than its mere likeness. Therefore one should love oneself more than one's neighbor. In this argument it is not clear, first of all, why one should take one's own good, not the neighbor's, as the point of reference, and treat the neighbor's good as the copy rather than one's own. Neither is it evident why similitude makes for inferiority. The explanation appears shortly afterward in the reply to an objection: "Although the good I have may be found more perfectly in my neighbor than in myself, still in me it is always more perfect as my own; for the other's good is not mine save through similitude." Here the *petitio principii* seems still more patent; one's own good is preferable because it is one's own. From preference for self there follows preference for self.[23]

4. In the *Summa* Aquinas returns to the question: "Ought a man in charity to love himself more than his neighbor?" His first argument for an affirmative reply is perhaps his best known: "We read in *Leviticus* and in *Matthew, You shall love your neighbour as yourself;* from which we see that a man's love for himself is, so to speak, the paradigm of his love for others. Now the paradigm is more than what takes after it. Therefore a man is bound in charity to love himself more than his neighbour."[24] The claim that the paradigm is "more than what takes after it" either makes a tautological assertion of epistemological primacy[25] or Platonically identifies epistemological primacy with valuational primacy.[26] The former interpretation makes the premise irrelevant; the latter makes it weak. No logical link requires that a model be superior in value to what is modeled on it, nor can such superiority be affirmed as de facto true in all cases, without including the instance here at issue and thereby begging the question. Whatever one may think of its truth, there is no incoherence in Luther's counterclaim, cited in chapter 1: "By this commandment 'as yourself' man is not commanded to love himself but he is shown the wicked love with which in fact he loves himself; in other words, it says to him: You are wholly bent on yourself and versed in self-love, and you will not be straightened out and made upright unless you cease entirely to love

yourself and, forgetting yourself, love only your neighbor." A model can serve in this way too.

5. Thomas's fullest argument occupies the body of the article:

> This is obvious from the very motive of our love. For, as we said above, we love God as the fount of that good which forms the basis of charity, then ourselves as sharing in it, and our neighbours as partners. But the motive for loving which this partnership provides implies a certain union with reference to God. Hence as unity is stronger than union, so the fact that a man himself participates in the divine good is a more powerful reason for loving than the fact that another is associated with him in this participation. Consequently a man ought in charity to love himself more than his neighbour.[27]

The meaning, relevance, and universal truth of "Unity is stronger than union" are all dubious, and would need elaboration to make this argument at all convincing. I cannot envision how such elaboration might succeed.[28] However, Thomas provides a few clues, and the clues suggest a further argument.

6. A little earlier, in II-II, q. 25, a. 4, he had written:

> Here we must concede that, strictly speaking, we do not have friendship for ourselves, but something more, because friendship implies a union of some kind, love being, as Dionysius puts it, a *unifying force,* whereas, with regard to himself, man possesses unity, which is something more than union. Accordingly, as unity is presupposed to union, so our love for ourselves is the model and root of friendship; for our friendship for others consists precisely in the fact that our attitude to them is the same as to ourselves. Aristotle remarks that *friendly feelings towards others flow from a man's own feelings towards himself.*[29]

So too, "All friendly actions which we do toward others are derived from the friendly actions which we do toward ourselves."[30]

Contemporary writers have stressed the dependence of love of others on initial love of oneself. However, a causal link is no more relevant than an epistemological; neither demonstrates the greater worth of self-love. 1 Jn 4:20 makes love of God dependent on love of self; yet love of self is not superior to love of God. Besides, even were it conceded that love of self is a precondition for love of others, and that love of self is therefore superior to love of others, no inference would follow concerning agape's norm. Thomas fails to distinguish between rating self-*love* over other-love and placing *self* ahead of others (in esteem, in service, or in both). The love might deserve higher rating but not the object of the love.

7. To the conclusion of his principal argument, Thomas appends a brief confirmation: "Consequently a man ought in charity to love himself more than his neighbour, as is indicated by the fact that, as sin is incompatible with eternal happiness, he may not incur such an evil, even to free

another from it."[31] "This would in fact be allowed," comments Willem Van Est, filling in the argument, "if a person were equally obliged to love himself and his neighbor."[32] The fairly obvious answer is that in no hypothesis would sin be permissible—not to save another from sin, nor to save the whole world. For the phrase *may sin* is a contradiction and *should not sin* is a tautology. From such a tautology no inference can be drawn in favor of self-preference. Once the tautology is laid bare, it is evident that a better explanation than Thomas's or Van Est's is available for the veto on this (or any) sin. "One should not do what one should not do" requires no extrinsic validation.

8. Duns Scotus's exposition of the argument from unity leads in a different direction. Since, he wrote, unity is the most perfect identity, "each person is naturally inclined to love of self, after the infinite good; but natural inclination is right."[33] This appeal to natural tendency became a favorite argument.[34] In the present century a Scholastic author still declared: "People are naturally more inclined to love of self than to love of neighbor. Since this natural inclination is implanted by nature's author, it cannot be inordinate."[35] Even Gabriel Biel, favorable though he was to self-preference, spotted the flaw in such reasoning. Sometimes, he noted, grace agrees with nature; sometimes it does not. It agrees in our greater love for ourselves than for our neighbor, but disagrees in our greater love for ourselves than for God. "It follows that natural inclination is not always right."[36] Given the variety and strength of human propensities to vice as well as to virtue, the existence of a strong and widespread inclination does not suffice to validate the inclination.

9. As a reason for placing self-love first, Scotus also suggested that "every man is for himself the immediate appointed instrument for directing a pure love towards God."[37] Commenting on the command to love one's neighbor as oneself, Bishop Butler developed an analogous argument: "Though there were an equality of affection to both, yet regards to ourselves would be more prevalent than attention to the concerns of others. And from moral considerations it ought to be so, supposing still the equality of affection commanded: because we are in a peculiar manner, as I may speak, intrusted with ourselves; and therefore care of our own interests, as well as of our conduct, particularly belongs to us."[38] Reflection on the "peculiar manner" Butler mentions reveals several possible senses. First, there is the logical impossibility of our directing anybody else's "pure love towards God," or of their doing the like for us. Second, there is the logical impossibility of our doing each other's jobs, eating each other's meals, having each other's children, or the like. Third, there is the difficulty of accurately surmising one another's preferences, and, fourth, the frequent impracticality of effectively serving them even when we do succeed in spotting them. For example, "Christianity does not advise that men brush one another's teeth. In this and many another instance, what is good for a person may be more certainly knowable and

attainable by an individual's action on his own behalf than by deeds done externally for another or by their both acting upon one another."[39] However, what concerns the norm of Christian neighbor love is not who puts on whose coat or who ties whose shoe laces, but, for instance, who gets the single coat or wears the single pair of shoes if that's the only coat or pair of shoes there is to go around. On questions like these, Scotus's and Butler's observations permit no decision.

10. Against Other-Preference and in favor of Self-Preference, the objection is sometimes made that to prefer one's neighbor to oneself would be to love him more than oneself and therefore to go against the commandment "Love your neighbor as yourself."[40] However, if taken quantitatively, the same text would tell against Self-Preference and in favor of Parity. So Scholastic authors have more frequently—and correctly— rejected a quantitative reading.

11. As evidence for Self-preference Van Est notes that "no one is bound to give another alms except from what he does not need or does not need as badly."[41] The key word here is *bound*. This alleged fact would tell against Other-Preference and in favor of Self-Preference (or Parity) only if these norms, and the "order of charity" generally, focused solely on what one is "bound" to do. The same distinction between duty and ideal applies to Fernando de Castro Palao's assertion: "The precept of saving another's life cannot oblige with serious detriment to one's own life; for that would be too harsh and hard a precept."[42] It might be too harsh a precept but not too harsh an ideal.

The further arguments I might cite are still less consequential, both quantitatively and qualitatively, than these eleven.[43] Hence, overall, Völkl's summary comments on Aquinas's position seem justified, and apply to the whole tradition he so strongly influenced: "Thomas's interest in self-love is not grounded in genuinely biblical thought but in natural-philosophical thought, especially Aristotelian. . . . But where thinking proceeds naturally, self-love, eudaemonism, and humanism necessarily gain in significance. There is at least the danger of 'harmonizing' the sayings of Scripture with those of natural ethics, that is, of reading into the sayings what they do not contain, at Scripture's expense. That would be neither scientifically proper nor advantageous for ethics."[44] Its undesirability is confirmed by the weakness of the natural-philosophical arguments.

Middle Ground

As chapter 1 documented, Parity and Other-Preference have always been spoken for; but neither has been represented by a strong, continuous tradition. The middle ground between Self-Preference on the one hand and Self-Forgetfulness and Self-Denial on the other is a theoretical void; no body of writing has grown up in defense of Parity, Other-

Preference, or Self-Subordination (the New Testament favorite), as it has in defense of those other, more extreme positions.

In support of Parity, only a single argument has been advanced in Christian literature with any frequency, and that is the argument from sameness of nature. More frequently, sameness of nature is cited simply as a reason for neighbor-love, or for the Golden Rule, not for equality of love. Thus: "As to our neighbors, we then love them as ourselves when we love them not for any advantage to ourselves, not for benefits expected or received, not for affinity or blood relationship, but for this reason alone that they share our nature."[45] Sometimes, however, in Christian as in secular writings,[46] equality of love is deduced from equality of nature: "Loving another with one's whole soul does not mean disowning or sacrificing oneself; it means loving another as oneself, on a basis of perfect equality. The one I love is my equal and I am the equal of the one I love."[47] "One is to have equal regard for self and for others, since the reasons for valuing the self are identical with those for valuing others, namely, that everyone is a human being, God's image, redeemed by Christ, called to be God's child and to participate in the eschatological kingdom."[48] Consequently, "the sacrificial aspect of love has to be looked at more closely. . . . The impartiality of love requires us to have equal respect for the irreducible dignity of each person and thus to put on a par self-regard and other-regard."[49]

The gospel challenges this idea that service should be proportioned to dignity or worth. "It shall not be so among you; but whoever would be great among you must be your servant, and whoever would be first among you must be slave of all. For the Son of man also came not to be served but to serve, and to give his life as a ransom for many" (Mk 10:43-45). "Have this mind among yourselves, which is yours in Christ Jesus, who, though he was in the form of God, did not count equality with God a thing to be grasped, but emptied himself, taking the form of a servant" (Phil 2:5-7). Christendom has never reasoned that Jesus, being divine, should have served himself above others; rather it has seen his divinity revealed in his willingness to sacrifice himself for all, even the worst. "One will hardly die for a righteous man—though perhaps for a good man one will dare even to die. But God shows his love for us in that while we were yet sinners Christ died for us" (Rom 5:7-8).

Even were it granted that equals should benefit equally, it would not follow that the benefit should be achieved in the manner Parity prescribes. If, at Christmas time, Sue gives Jim a sweater and Jim gives Sue a book, the benefit to each is no greater than if Jim bought himself the sweater and Sue bought herself the book. However, the way in which the result is reached does differ; and one way may be preferable to the other, quite apart from the quantity of benefit accruing to each party. The dominical saying, "It is more blessed to give than to receive," implies as much, prescinding as it does from the nature, dignity, and worth, whether greater, less, or equal, of the person giving and the person receiving. In the form of life which the saying suggests, each person might benefit as much, and be respected as much, as in Parity, but mutual care and respect would be given fuller expression.

In chapter 6 I shall consider whether the consequences of generalized Self-Subordination would be as beneficial to all concerned as those of generalized Parity. Here I wish merely to question the kind of inference that seems to underlie a common response to the last chapter. "I tend to agree with you," one commentator writes, "that the position of the scriptures, especially the New Testament, probably most closely approximates Self-Subordination, though I think pure reason would probably favor parity." Another reader remarks that Parity appears more "reasonable." How, though, might reason legitimately pass from likeness of nature to Parity? Not directly, without any mediating premise; for modes of relationship may have their own intrinsic value apart from the respective worth or dignity of the persons related. Nor indirectly, via equal benefit; for even if all concerned did not benefit equally, overall, in other norms than Parity, benefits would not be the only thing to consider if relationships, too, have intrinsic worth.

In confirmation, consider the kindred case of friendship. It is fine and admirable, critics may grant, for friends to be mutually other-preferring and concede each other the better part. However, let us not extend the same relationship to humankind at large; that would not be reasonable. Why not? Because of our common nature? But friends share the same nature. So if equality or inequality of nature suffices by itself to dictate equality or inequality of treatment, friends should treat each other equally. Parity should hold for them as for everybody else. If, however, there is any independent value in an other-preferring relationship between friends, there may be similar value in a similar relationship between people generally. The Christian teaching of universal brotherhood suggests as much.

Let us pass, then, to the next norm in the series. Typically, Other-Preference, in the sense defined by chapter 1, is neither clearly stated nor argued for. In extensive reading, I have encountered no author who clearly located agape's norm between Parity on the one hand and Self-Subordination on the other, or who offered any support for the position thus defined. That is, none has articulated or defended a position according less weight to the agent's equal good than to another's, yet permitting the agent's good to compete with others'. Such a perspective is often suggested, for instance by the early variation on the second commandment, "You shall love your neighbor more than your own life,"[50] or by the words of St. Francis's prayer: "O Divine Master, grant that I may not so much seek to be consoled, as to console; to be understood, as to understand; to be loved, as to love." However, sayings like these more clearly go beyond Self-Preference or Parity than they stop short of Self-Subordination, Self-

Forgetfulness, or Self-Denial. "It is in dying," Francis's prayer concludes, "that we are born to eternal life."

Parity and Other-Preference approximate more closely to Self-Subordination, favored by the New Testament, than does Self-Preference; hence, from the Christian perspective of this study they would require less powerful arguments to warrant their acceptance in preference to the New Testament norm. However, as noted, practically no grounds have been offered by Christians in these two norms' support, and the many reasons Christians have cited for Self-Preference are all weak. So if valid grounds are to be found in Christian literature for abandoning the norm of Self-Subordination, they will have to come from the other, less self-regarding end of the spectrum.

Self-Forgetfulness

A mystical, ascetical tradition, stressing self-forgetfulness and self-denial, began early in Christendom (Benedict, Basil, Chrysostom, Leo, . . .), continued strong through the Middle Ages (Bernard, Eckhart, Ruysbroeck, Suso, Tauler, . . .), carried into post-Reformation Catholic spirituality (John of the Cross, Ignatius Loyola, Francis de Sales, Fénelon, Guardini, . . .), won still more general acceptance among Protestants (Luther, Calvin, Bucer, Nygren, Bultmann, . . .), and left traces in secular Western culture (Fichte, Schopenhauer, . . .).[51] In the resulting literature, little distinction has often been made between forgetting self and denying self; an expression like *selfless love* may signify either or both. It is therefore often difficult to tell whether Self-Forgetfulness or Self-Denial is being commended. When, for instance, it is said that "we must empty ourselves of self,"[52] this may have a weaker or a stronger sense: it may mean forgetting ourselves or denying ourselves. Often, however, the drift of assertions or arguments is fairly evident. Some, for instance, point clearly to Self-Forgetfulness.

"Eros is covetous by nature," writes Werner Elert. "Agape, in its concern for others, forgets itself, is unaware of its own existence."[53] It does not take thought of its own concerns so as to act against them; it simply ignores them. All its thoughts are for its neighbor. More typically, in arguments for Self-Forgetfulness emphasis falls not on the neighbor but on taking thought for God alone, and being indifferent to all save his divine will. "When once a person has established pure love," writes Fénelon, "which no longer fears nor hopes for oneself either eternal goods or eternal ills, which perfects itself so as to obey God and not for the sake of one's own perfection, the root of all desires has been severed. This is the holy indifference of Saint Francis of Sales."[54]

Now, why is this indifference to one's own concerns considered a good thing? "In no other way," comes the reply, "but by drinking deep of this saving draught will my mind reel and my soul thereafter slumber in delightful repose. And so my love for God, with all my heart, soul, and strength, would have no place for my own interests, but only for those of Christ. And before the warmth of my love for my fellow men all self-centredness would melt away, so that my every thought and aim would be focused on them."⁵⁵ What bliss, to be emptied of self.

Concretely, though, what does this mean? That I love my friends with special warmth but do not wish their company? That I value music or poetry, but have no desire to hear any? That I appreciate nature's wonders but have no inclination to make their closer or continued acquaintance? Or does it mean that I no longer have any feeling for my friends, any appreciation of music or poetry, any liking for woodland trails, mountain views, or fresh spring air? The first alternative does not seem psychologically possible; the second does not seem humanly desirable. Or religiously preferable. How can I praise and love God for that which has no worth in my eyes? How can I resemble him if I look on what he has made and do not find it good? And if I find it good, how can I feel indifferent toward it?

In much writing on this topic, a crucial oversight appears, akin to that which gives rise to the doctrine of psychological egoism. "We must understand," writes Fénelon,

> that people who have a sincere piety, but who are not entirely dead to the comforts of life, or to reputation or friendship, allow themselves a little self-seeking in everything. We do not go straight toward it with bent head, but we let ourselves be drawn into it as though by accident. We still cling to self in all these things, and a sure sign that we cling to it, is that if anyone disturbs these natural supports, we are desolate. If some accident upsets the tranquillity of our life, threatens our reputation, or takes away from us those people whose friendship we value, we feel within ourselves a sharp pang, which shows how much self is still alive and sensitive.⁵⁶

Fénelon might have written with equal or greater truth: "Which shows how desirable and attractive are the things whose absence we regret." Missing from his analysis is any acknowledgment that the things we value are in fact valuable, that they attract us because they are valuable, and that in desiring them we focus on them more than on ourselves.⁵⁷ We may allow ourselves "a little self-seeking in everything," but we permit ourselves a good deal more other-seeking. If, for example, we feel a sharp pang when separated from "those people whose friendship we value," it is precisely because we do value them and their friendship. If we did not care for them, we would experience no pang.

I suspect that on close examination the truth in the doctrine of indifference turns out to be compatible with Self-Subordination and not in conflict with it. Consider, for example, St. Ignatius's advice that "we must make ourselves indifferent to all created things, as far as we are allowed free choice and are not under any prohibition," and that, "as far as we are concerned, we should not prefer health to sickness, riches to poverty, honor to dishonor, a long life to a short life. The same holds for all other things."[58] So are created things all worthless? Is our—or others'—enjoyment or deprivation of them a matter of indifference? No, but "man is to make use of them in as far as they help him in the attainment of his end, and he must rid himself of them in as far as they prove a hindrance to him." Such is the reason Ignatius gives for his advice, and such, accordingly, is the way it should be read. What he here opposes is any inclination to reverse the right order of means and end, "first choosing the means and then finding a way of using it toward the end,"[59] rather than the other way around. So understood, his advice does not conflict with the rule of Self-Subordination, but closely resembles or coincides with it. Benefit to self is made subordinate to service of God and neighbor.

Since the reasons alleged for Self-Forgetfulness do not survive scrutiny, let us pass on and examine those proposed for Self-Denial.

Self-Denial

There is simplicity and sureness in the image of the heart, pumping only as much blood to itself as enables it to pump much more to other parts of the body. There is appeal in the characterization of Jesus as a "man for others"—an appeal that seems to be weakened or undone by careful qualifications, as in Self-Subordination. There is beauty in the Eucharistic words and in a life that mirrors them: "This is my body, which will be given up for you . . . This is my blood, which will be shed for you and for many." With all concessions to self excluded, there can be a sense of full fidelity to the letter of the first and greatest commandment: "You shall love the Lord you God with your *whole* mind, your *whole* heart, your *whole* strength." And yet, is not the appeal of the image, the phrase, the selfless Eucharistic symbol at least partly aesthetic, and not purely ethical? Is it not fostered through abstraction from the details of concrete living and from the genuine values set aside? Must the better always be an enemy of the good? Is not beauty, in Aquinas's phrase, a splendid order, with the splendor increased by the variety and multiplicity of what is ordered? Can purity and integrity be achieved only by excluding what is disordered rather than by ordering it? Must there be narrowing and impoverishment?

1. One answer has been that no impoverishment results. "Give me your love and your grace," says Ignatius's prayer; "that is enough for me."[60] The theme is a favorite with Luther. "I will do nothing in this life except what I see is necessary, profitable, and salutary to my neighbor, since through faith I have an abundance of all good things in Christ."[61] "Christ's disciples can do nothing for themselves, for their own sins, or for their own salvation, but Christ's blood has already done everything and accom-

plished everything, and because he has loved them they no longer need to love themselves or seek or wish anything good for themselves, but what they might do and seek for themselves they must now turn to their neighbor's good and do for others the good works which they do not require for themselves."[62]

There is no need to open the shades and let in the morning sunlight, for God shines in the soul. Such, concretely, seems to be Luther's message. And yet I rather suspect that Luther opened the shades. He may even have found that God shone brighter in the soul when he did so. In general, though, if the argument "I have no need" means "I can do without," the natural answer is: "Why should you?" What is wrong with the sunlight, and what is wrong with enjoying it? What is wrong with all the varied benefits to self which make no appreciable difference to service of God or neighbor, one way or the other?[63]

2. Some would say that it simply is not fitting, in itself, that we ever serve ourselves without serving others.

> How often there come to us occasions when, with no wrong-doing, without any actual meanness for which the judgment of others could reproach us, we might win some possession we should so much like to have, reach some success which would thrill us with the glow of delight. Yet the possession and the success, did we seize them, would in some indefinable way—we could not reason it out, perhaps, but the deepest voices in us declare it—rub a little of the gold of life away for others: they would not recognise it as a loss, did we exert our power and take the prize: they will not recognise it as a gain, if we obey the better impulse and hold our hand: sacrifice there will not be in the sense of giving up something which another receives; but by our grip upon ourselves we shall have kept our relationship sweet with our fellow-men.[64]

The "voices" that dictate this reponse remain too deep for effective response and dialog. How can it come to appear that housewives who listen to music while they work or people who plant trees and flowers on their property are doing a slightly ignoble thing? Perhaps because the thesis is left abstract and not tested by its concrete implications. Perhaps because a hidden, defective logic is at work: To keep a higher good *pure* is to keep it *higher,* for the good with which it would be mixed is lower. Honey would not be as sweet if mixed with sugar. However, honey would lose none of its sweetness if put on the same table with sugar. And in well-ordered love there is no mixing, no watering down; there is just greater richness and variety.

The anti-additive thinking in a passage like the following rises more clearly to the surface: "God alone and no physical thing is worthy of our love, for physical things are not as noble as we are and they cannot return our love. As a result, if we love them, our love would be corrupted."[65] Only love of God, it would appear, is free of such "corruption." For only he escapes this degradation (revealing word!) by comparison. The answer, of course, is that there is no corruption in loving the lower as well as the higher, provided we love them in proportion; indeed, it would be unfitting to withhold from lesser things the love that is their due. A person's love of God is not tainted by his love for his wife or his admiration for Shakespeare. Nor is his neighbor-love tainted by his watching *Macbeth* or skating in the park. The service of neighbor may take precedence over service to self, as Self-Subordination suggests; but that does not signify that service to self is "worse" than service to others. It may just be less good.

In a twist on the same reductive type of reasoning, service to self may appear to be excluded by definition: "It is generally taken for granted that Fénelon was right in his claim that love itself means something incompatible with self-seeking, and that his only mistake was to treat 'pure love' as a state of perfection reserved for a few."[66] "Love is free, selfless devotion to others."[67] "Love is self-giving."[68] "To love is to give but, above all, to give oneself; and to give oneself it is necessary to abandon oneself, forget oneself."[69] Hence, "the truer love is the more it makes a person go out of himself and give himself to the beloved, so that the degree of its self-surrender indicates as well the degree of its purity and perfection."[70] This may be true, so long as the surrender is related to the giving. And it may be, as some have claimed, that service or care for oneself does not merit the label *love*.[71] However, the point is not worth debating; for substantive issues are not decided by names or definitions. Though perhaps not the highest love nor worthy of the title *love,* concern for self that does not conflict with concern for others may, nonetheless, be legitimate.

3. Other Christian writers cite extrinsic reasons for turning from creatures to the Creator. "In words which can still bring tears to the eyes," writes C. S. Lewis, "St. Augustine describes the desolation in which the death of his friend Nebridius plunged him (*Confessions* IV, 10). Then he draws a moral. This is what comes, he says, of giving one's heart to anything but God. All human beings pass away. Do not let your happiness depend on something you may lose. If love is to be a blessing, not a misery, it must be for the only Beloved who will never pass away."[72] "Turn to the Lord with your whole heart," urges the *Imitation of Christ,* "and leave behind this wretched world. Then your soul shall find rest."[73]

Lewis acknowledges the appeal of such an argument. And yet,

When I respond to that appeal I seem to myself to be a thousand miles away from Christ. If I am sure of anything I am sure that His teaching was never meant to confirm my congenital preference for safe investments and limited liabilities. I doubt whether there is anything in me that pleases Him less. And who could conceivably begin to love God on such a prudential ground— because the security (so to speak) is better? . . . There is no escape along the lines St. Augustine suggests. Nor along any other lines. There is no safe investment. To love at all is to be vulnerable.[74]

4. Lewis develops this response fully and convincingly. However, Augustine's love monism had other, deeper roots. "As metaphysician, Augustine was impelled to the conclusion that only one object of love was permissible: 'It is a simple love by which the multiplicity of loves is overcome! One love is needful to overcome the many! One good love ranged against all the evil ones!' Any love was perverse unless it was totally directed to God, for 'he loves thee less who loves ought beside thee'."[75] The same rivalry has echoed through the centuries.[76] For Aquinas, too, "man is situated between the things of this world and spiritual goods which constitute eternal beatitude, in such a way that the more he clings to either of them the more he abandons the other, and vice versa."[77] "There are two things which increase one's charity. First the heart's separation from earthly things. For the heart cannot tend perfectly towards different objects. Hence no one can love both God and the world. And therefore the farther our heart is removed from love of earthly things, the more it is strengthened in love of the divine."[78] "Keep this in mind," writes Eckhart: "to be full of things is to be empty of God, while to be empty of things is to be full of God."[79] "When," for instance, "the senses are deprived of all agreeable objects, the soul fasts from all sensible pleasure, and is, in consequence, free from all attachment to it."[80] St. Ignatius drew a natural, traditional conclusion: "The better to arrive at this degree of perfection which is so precious in the spiritual life, [a candidate's] chief and most earnest endeavor should be to seek in our Lord his greater abnegation and continual mortification in all things possible."[81]

Self-concern is seen as competing with neighbor-concern as well as with concern for God and higher things. "Love, as sheer existence for one's neighbor, is possible only to him who is free from himself."[82] "It may not cherish any collateral aims such as honour, advantage, or reward, but must, fully unrestrained in this particular, be a completely self-denying love."[83] "Radically shifting our center, by dislodging us from our concern about ourselves . . . , it works a spiritual conversion so radical and so profound that it opens our horizon to the whole of humanity."[84] Combining both reasons for Self-Denial, Nygren concludes: "Christian love moves in two directions, towards God and towards its neighbour; and in self-love it finds its chief adversary, which must be fought and conquered. . . . Agape recognises no kind of self-love as legitimate."[85]

L'amour-propre étant tout contraire
Au saint feu de l'amour divin
Il faut tout suffrir et tout faire
Pour chasser ce subtil venin.[86]

With such wide and varied backing, this challenge appears the most serious Self-Subordination must face, at least within Christendom. At first glance, it appears to deny the assumption on which the norm rests, that there can be benefits to self which make no difference to the welfare of others. Any good, it is held, that is sought or accepted for self and not for God or neighbor is a good that works against both God and neighbor. For it nourishes the enemy within. The concupiscence to which we all are heir resembles a hidden tapeworm which has to be fed lest its host die or be enfeebled but which is not to be allowed a scrap of nourishment beyond the absolute minimum. For the sake of greater service Christians may eat, drink, sleep, rest, recreate, and otherwise indulge themselves—but only for that reason and only so far as it dictates. Any further concessions are unwise.

My first response is to note that even were this dire assessment true, it would not negate the norm of Self-Subordination or its underlying supposition. The norm rests, it is true, on the assumption that benefits to self may on occasion make no difference to the welfare of others. But this may be so for two quite different reasons: either because others are unaffected or because, though affected, they are affected equally, for good or for ill, in either of two options. In urging that others are always affected, and affected adversely (at least indirectly) by concessions to self, the objection challenges the first of these two possibilities, but not the second. The indirect harm may be balanced by direct or indirect benefits.

Furthermore, to stress only the adverse effects of self-directed benefits is one-sided. It is plausible that an appetite satisfied is an appetite strengthened, which may therefore offer more resistance when the call comes to deny it for the sake of others. However, it is also plausible that an appetite constantly denied may be an appetite not deadened but aroused, from which one may fear unpleasant surprises. (Consider the desire for food and the desire for drink, which are strengthened, not weakened, by deprivation.) It is also plausible that preoccupation with self-deprivation may have the unwelcome side-effect of focusing attention on self.[87] Again, it is plausible that the benefits to self conceded by Self-Subordination provide an inner buoyancy and contentment permitting greater service. It is plausible, furthermore, to argue as Dewey and Tufts did, that "it is impossible for a man who conceives his own good to be in 'going without,' in just restricting himself, to have any large or adequate idea of the good of others. Unconsciously and inevitably a hardening and narrowing of the conditions of the lives of others accompanies the reign of the Puritanic ideal."[88] A person without appreciation of created good will not beget like appreciation in others or be sensible of it as something to further in them. It is plausible, finally, to suggest that the extra benefits permitted by Self-Subordination may evoke praise, thanksgiving, and greater love of God, which may compensate for any increase in desire and may foster greater willingness to serve. "Why be selfish," Luther asked, "when God has been so kind?"

In dealing with their children, parents recognize that excessive kindness is unkindness; the children may be spoiled. From this realization, parents might infer that kindnesses are dangerous; and in a sense they would be right. Give nice things to children, and they may come to want them inordinately. However, this is not the whole story. So parents sometimes give and sometimes do not give, as the occasion suggests. The argument for Self-Denial makes no such wise discriminations. Like many toe-in-the-door, camel's-nose-under-the-tent arguments, it suffers from excessive rigidity and universality.[89]

This results partly from considering only the dangers of benefitting self, and partly, I suspect, from maximizing those dangers, unrealistically. It is natural that inordinate self-seeking should appear especially pervasive and inveterate when a norm as severe as Self-Denial is the standard by which people's conduct is assessed. And we have already noted the tendency to view love of creatures as self-directed, not other-directed. A child or a scientist who seeks the why of things, a person lost in admiration of a sunset, a flower, an invention, or a work of art, a hearer engrossed by a symphony or held spellbound by a theatrical performance, is not centered on self. The focus is on value, and the value is real.

Exception may therefore be taken to the argument's basic strategy for dealing with disordered loves. To this problem two rival solutions are conceivable: either eliminate all loves but the highest, or love each thing as it ought to be loved, starting with the highest. (Loving all else solely "for the sake of the highest" amounts to loving only the highest.) In our present condition, neither conversion is completely realizable. But the latter alternative, according love where love is due and to the degree that it is due, is, I believe, the better,[90] more Christian solution,[91] and also the more divine. It is not possible that the intensity of a person's love of God should make him unloving or indifferent toward creation; for "God is infinite love and therefore devotion to God can never make us less loving toward a creature."[92] He looked on all that he had made, says Genesis, and found it very good.

In various ways the tactic of eliminating rival loves rather than ordering them leads to incoherence and impoverishment.[93] Luthardt, writing of St. Anselm, aptly comments on "the ascetic mood of mind which, in denying the life in the world, takes away thereby from the Christian life its God-given substantiality, in order to make the immediate relationship to God the exclusive content of life instead of that which ought to be its power."[94] The alternative approach, of ordering rival lives rather than reducing them, requires that God be loved, not solely, but above all. However, to be loved above all he must be perceived as supremely lovable; and the only way his lovableness can be perceived is through his works. The argument for Self-Denial says, in effect: "Forget his creation, since it is so attractive. Look only to his saving acts; his Son on the cross suffices to teach you love." Such a prescription seems unduly narrow and impoverishing. Why must the better always be the enemy of the good? "We do not forget the debt of gratitude we owe to God our Lord and Creator," wrote Tertullian; "we reject no creature of his hands, though certainly we exercise restraint upon ourselves, lest of any gift of his we make an immoderate or sinful use."[95]

Rejection of the "ascetic ideal" does not signify rejection of asceticism, nor does the rejection of Self-Denial mean rejection of self-denial. St. Paul spoke of the athlete who denies himself whatever conflicts with achieving his goal; in this spirit Christians have resorted to fasting and other penances. However, to fast on Fridays or during Lent is one thing; to fast every day all through the year is quite another. Periodic penances are one thing; continual penance in all things is quite another. Those who enjoin Self-Denial to counteract selfish inclinations may not recognize what great and continual denial of one's desires even Parity entails, not to mention Other-Preference or Self-Subordination. Anyone who habitually practiced Self-Subordination would hardly need further training of the will. All selfishness would already be extinct; all inclinations and desires would be well ordered. So true is this that two chief objections against Self-Subordination considered in the next chapter are its human impossibility and its excessive rigor.

Traditional understanding has supposed that in heaven our loves will be many and strong but will be perfectly ordered. We will love all creatures fittingly, for what they are, and God as the source whose transcendent goodness they reveal. At present, our loves are disordered. Yet even now we approximate that future ideal more faithfully by seeking to order our loves than by seeking to weaken or eliminate them. In the words of St. Francis de Sales, "We should indeed love something besides God, but with a love that does not equal our love of him, with the consequence that we are always ready to abandon and reject it in so far as the love of God requires."[96] We should not love creatures less than we do; we should love their Maker more than we do. "It is love alone," suggests Norman Pittenger, "which can correct the failures of our human loving."[97]

Other arguments and considerations might be added to these.[98] But I need not clinch the case for Self-Subordination or decisively refute the case for Self-Denial. In order for the New Testament's apparent preference to stand, it suffices that the arguments against it not be strongly persuasive. I have now explained why I find no Christian counterarguments sufficiently weighty. The grounds for Self-Denial look stronger than those proposed for Self-Preference, Parity, or Other-Preference; but even they fail to convince.

A Neglected Possibility

The number and quality of the advocates of Self-Denial impress me more than their arguments; I cannot help but feel misgivings when, on a matter of such difficulty and depth, I find Eckhart, Ignatius, Luther, Calvin, and many others in apparent opposition to my position. Several considerations, however, mitigate these misgivings. Whatever version of agape one espouses, one will find saints and scholars in opposition. And proponents of Self-Denial have seldom been very carefully analytic in their thinking or in the expression of their thoughts; seldom, if ever, have they envisaged or dealt with Self-Subordination as an alternative to the less altruistic stances they opposed.

The literature of self-denial has been characterized by strong antitheses more than by careful distinctions or the listing and weighing of alternatives. When, for instance, Ivo of Chartres writes, "Then no one seeks his own, in the manner of venal physicians,"[99] he conveys the impression that there are just two possibilities: either one selfishly seeks one's own or one does not seek one's own at all. Similarly, a present-day writer recounts Bonaventure's opinion that Self-Preference will not continue in heaven, then adds: "Hence in the state of glory love is entirely selfless, unselfish."[100] No alternative is recognized between selfishness or Self-Preference on the one hand (the two are not distinguished) and selflessness on the other. Thus the tendency has been to oppose "all-consuming self-love which makes a man think only of himself," at the one extreme, to the state of love in which "the soul will no longer seek its own interests, only God's and his neighbor's," at the other.[101] The middle ground between these two poles has received scant attention from advocates of Self-Denial.

A major obstacle to clear understanding and sound evaluation has been the failure to distinguish between the self-denial required by any altruistic norm, and the specific altruistic norm I have labeled Self-Denial. An illustration will make my meaning clear. Christian charity, writes Thomas Barrosse, "is disinterested since it not only does not seek its own advantage but rather disregards it or even renounces it for the good of the person loved. Thus God loves men and does not spare his only Son (Romans 8:32); Christ loves them and gives his life for them (for example, Romans 8:34; Ephesians 5:2; John 10:10-11; 15:13); and Christians must also be ready to give their lives for their neighbors (for example, John 15:12; 1 John 3:16)."[102] As chapter 1 noted, these scriptural data conform to all six altruistic norms, since all six may call for the sacrifice of life itself. Hence none of the texts Barrosse cites backs his apparent position. It is necessary to distinguish between disregard for one's good on occasion (in the sense of sacrificing it) and disregard for one's good on all occasions, as a general norm. To be sure, a person who surrenders life itself is not seeking his own advantage; but the norm he follows even then may be one that endorses benefit to self, to a greater or lesser degree. The absence of such distinctions in the literature of Self-Denial entitles one to doubt the validity of its preference.

Frequently, it also warrants doubt whether the position expressed is indeed Self-Denial. Absence of analysis means absence of clarity; so there is often reason to wonder whether apparent proponents of Self-Denial really intend a position as extreme as the one their words suggest. Charity, we may be told, is "entirely selfless giving. Hence the Middle Ages, in agreement with Aristotle, constantly repeat: 'To love is to wish someone good'."[103] Since these words of Aristotle are compatible with any version of altruism, indeed with pure egoism, one hesitates to assume that the author meant precisely what the phrase suggests when he declared charity to be "entirely selfless." One may doubt whether he, or many like him, clearly envisaged Self-Subordination and ruled it out. Sometimes one page of a work suggests one position and another page a different one; or the fluctuation may occur within a single passage. Note, for instance, the alternating indications—weak, strong, weak—in a passage of Boularand: "This surrender of our material interests into the hands of our heavenly Father . . . places our security in him alone and attaches us to the source of all good *more than* to our personal utility. Far from rendering us indifferent to the kingdom, it centers *all* our desires on him and makes us seek him *first of all,* as 'the hidden treasure' and 'the pearl of great price' which is worth more than all (*Mt.* 13, 44-47)."[104]

And yet some writers seem clearly to exclude Self-Subordination in favor of Self-Denial, while others clearly exclude Self-Denial as too rigorous. What is extremely rare in either opponents or proponents of Self-Denial is any clear statement of the position I have defined as Self-Subordination. Bourdaloue comes close.[105] So does Fénelon.[106] So does Kenneth Kirk. After strongly stressing self-denial and disregard for self, he states his position more carefully:

> Within the sphere of the actions which we desire to do, or which "interest" us, there are some whose performance would beyond question constitute a definite menace to our neighbor's legitimate well-being; such actions we do not hesitate to call selfish, or "interested." In other actions our neighbour's interests, if not actually promoted, are at least respected; here (even though the action may in some cases be self-regarding) we can fairly claim that it is "disinterested." The essence of Christian morality lies in the conviction that Jesus only desired to do, and only did, actions of this disinterested character; and that the true follower of Jesus will aspire, at however great a distance, to imitate Him in this respect.[107]

When authors thus draw back from Self-Forgetfulness or Self-Denial, we may surmise that they do not mean to retreat as far as Other-Preference and that, if questioned, they would indicate Self-Subordination as the analytic norm which best represents their thinking.

With the position left implicit, no arguments have had it as their explicit conclusion. What can be said for it, basically, from the viewpoint of Christian tradition, is that the New Testament suggests it and that the grounds proposed for alternative positions prove unconvincing. Other grounds, however, and other objections have been advanced from without the Christian fold, and evaluation will not be complete until these too have been considered.

6

A Wider Forum

Like most Christians, I view Scripture as normative for the life of the church, but not self-sufficient; I regard its authority as primary, but not absolute.[1] "The Bible is a necessary source, but it must also be in constant dialog with the many other sources of knowledge and insight through which God might be disclosing himself."[2] Accordingly, although the New Testament norm of Self-Subordination looks no less valid at the end of twenty centuries of Christian discussion than at the start, other challenges remain to be assessed. In the present chapter I turn from theological literature and Christian debate to philosophical and psychological writings and the objections they raise to the principle of Self-Subordination.

In these writings, too, the norm has seldom been stated explicitly.[3] Hence the objections raised against it are implicit, appearing in arguments for or against other positions. To introduce some order into the discussion, I have arranged these implicit critiques, roughly, according to the positions from which they arise or for which they speak. For completeness, I conclude with an objection of my own creation, as plausible as those I have culled from others' writings.

Egoism

1. Psychological Egoism

Though discredited in philosophy,[4] the doctrine of psychological egoism, according to which all human actions are basically self-seeking, still surfaces elsewhere. When it does, it challenges the idea that one's own welfare might be subordinated to others'. Thus Giles Milhaven, for example, ventures "to lay down a thesis," which he attributes to Freud: "Essentially, the thesis says: The only way to really love—the only way!—is in moving to meet my own needs. That is the only kind of love there is. This love may be, at the same time, directed at other persons and their needs. But, through and through, it is a love for me and my needs."[5] Hence it is not possible, it would seem, to place others' welfare ahead of one's own or to reduce one's own benefit to a mere by-product, as Self-Subordination would frequently prescribe. However, philosophers have long recognized that the love which brings me satisfaction is a love, not of myself or of my satisfaction, but of that which brings me satisfaction (for example, other people, their companionship, knowledge, riches, power, prestige, literature, artistic achievement, relief of suffering). It is basically object-centered, not subject-centered. A person who does not find satisfaction outside himself will not find satisfaction. Hence Self-Subordination is not excluded, psychologically; it may indeed be a possibility.

2. Egoistic "Intuition"

Of Henry Sidgwick and his ethical masterpiece, *The Methods of Ethics,* C. D. Broad observed:

> Each of the two following principles seemed to him to be thoroughly self-evident when he considered it in isolation. (i) Each man's primary and unconditional duty is to try to maximize the *general* happiness; he ought to seek his own happiness so far and only so far as it is a part or a condition of the general happiness. (ii) Each man's primary and unconditional duty is to try to maximize *his own* happiness; he ought to seek the happiness of others so far and only so far as it will contribute in the long run to his own. Now it was perfectly plain to Sidgwick that these two equally self-evident principles would in many cases dictate different courses of action, even when we make the utmost allowance for the pleasures and pains of sympathy, of an approving or a guilty conscience, of public opinion, and of legal rewards and punishments. He could discover no more ultimate principle from which to deduce these two and by which to adjudicate between them in cases of conflict.[6]

To say that two principles concerning what is "primary" can be considered "in isolation" seems incoherent. To say that two contradictory principles are equally "self-evident" seems equally untenable. At least one of the two must be wrong. And there can be little doubt which of these two principles is mistaken. A purely egoistic principle, according not only preferential treatment but exclusive claims to each of six billion competing human agents, is hardly the fruit of intuition.[7] "Let the whole race perish if only I may be saved" is not a self-evident truth of morality.

3. The "Rationality" of Egoism

Max Hocutt writes: "In response to a claim that you ought to do such and so, it is always appropriate to ask, Why? (When you may not ask this question, the answer is all too obvious.) This fact indicates, I think, that you ought to do something only if you have a good reason to do it. So far as I can see, however, the only good reason for doing something is that it is in one's interests."[8] Others' interests do not count—except when others are the agents; then my interests do not count. Why this should be so is not explained. Yet its reasonableness is far from self-evident.[9] Indeed it seems counterintuitive to assert that the only reason for preserving or promoting any value—pleasure, love, health, knowledge, beauty, creativity, and so forth—is the fact that it is mine.

4. Each Person His or Her Own End

Ayn Rand writes: "The basic *social* principle of the Objectivist ethics is that just as life is an end in itself, so every living human being is an end in himself, not the means to the ends or the welfare of others—and, therefore, that man must live for his own sake, neither sacrificing himself to others nor sacrificing others to himself. To live for his own sake means that *the achievement of his own happiness is man's highest moral purpose.*"[10] This reasoning passes from an acceptable premise to an egoistic conclusion by means of a double or triple non sequitur. A man can be an end in himself and *also* a means to others' welfare. He can be an end in himself without being the end to which he devotes himself (he may develop as a person through regard for others). His happiness can be the end to which he devotes himself without its being either the sole or the "highest," preeminent purpose of his life. There is no incompatibility, therefore, between the norm of Self-Subordination and the principle, "Every living human being is an end in himself."

5. Effects on the Recipients

Self-Subordination falls within the likely target area of warnings against the "special dangers and evils attendant upon an exaggeration of the altruistic idea":

(i) *It tends to render others dependent,* and thus contradicts its own professed aim: the helping of others. Almost every one knows some child who is

so continuously "helped" by others, that he loses his initiative and re-
sourcefulness. Many an invalid is confirmed in a state of helplessness by the
devoted attention of others. . . .

(ii) *The erection of the "benevolent" impulse into a virtue in and of itself
tends to build up egoism in others.* The child who finds himself unremit-
tingly the object of attention from others is likely to develop an exaggerated
sense of the relative importance of his own *ego*. The chronic invalid, con-
spicuously the recipient of the conscious altruism of others, is happy in nature who avoids the slow growth of an insidious egoism. Men who are the
constant subjects of abnegation on the part of their wives and female
relatives rarely fail to develop a self-absorbed complacency and uncon-
scious conceit.[11]

A benign reading of these complaints would take them as directed
against a "benevolent" impulse which employs inappropriate means to its
purported goal, and not against a norm such as Self-Subordination, which
enjoins effective service. An altruist is not required to spoil children, confirm invalids in their dependence, or otherwise disregard the moral
welfare of others. If anything stronger is intended, then Ewing's remarks
become pertinent: "It can hardly be good for a person to be the constant
recipient of unreasonable sacrifices, and is likely to make him selfish and
exigent. Yet there is nothing that calls forth greater admiration than
devoted and cheerful sacrifice of great goods or incurring of great
hardships where it is really called for if another person is to be saved from
unhappiness."[12] One beneficiary may be moved to dependence, another
to gratitude and admiring imitation. The possible bad effects may be
balanced or overridden by the possible or certain good effects. In general
it can therefore be said that although an abstract norm like Self-Subordination is no substitute for realistic reckoning of true benefits, unrealistic
reckoning or failure to reckon is not a valid reason for rejecting the
norm.[13]

6. *Self-Seeking Maximizes Happiness*

"The conclusion forced on us," wrote Herbert Spencer, "is that the
pursuit of individual happiness within those limits prescribed by social
conditions is the first requisite to the attainment of the greatest general
happiness. To see this it needs but to contrast one whose self-regard has
maintained bodily well-being with one whose regardlessness of self has
brought its natural results; and then to ask what must be the contrast between two societies formed of two such kinds of individuals."[14] Spencer's
description of these contrasting individuals leaves little doubt where the
preference should go.

Bounding out of bed after an unbroken sleep, singing or whistling as he
dresses, coming down with beaming face ready to laugh on the smallest

provocation, the healthy man of high powers, conscious of past successes, and by his energy, quickness, resource, made confident of the future, enters on the day's business, not with repugnance, but with gladness; and from hour to hour experiencing satisfactions from work effectually done, comes home with an abundant surplus of energy remaining for hours of relaxation. Far otherwise is it with one who is enfeebled by great neglect of self. Already deficient, his energies are made more deficient by constant endeavors to execute tasks that prove beyond his strength, and by the resulting discouragement. Besides the depressing consciousness of the immediate future, there is the depressing consciousness of the remoter future, with its probability of accumulated difficulties and diminished ability to meet them. Hours of leisure which, rightly passed, bring pleasures that raise the tide of life and renew the powers of work, cannot be utilized: there is not vigor enough for enjoyments involving action, and lack of spirits prevents passive enjoyments from being entered upon with zest. In brief, life becomes a burden.[15]

Obviously, a community composed of individuals like the first will be vibrant and joyous, whereas one composed of individuals like the second will be miserable. Hence, "it must be admitted that conduct causing the one result is good, and conduct causing the other is bad."[16]

Spencer's account is highly selective. It is as though he related the light-hearted laughter at Versailles and the varied entertainments but said nothing about the Sun King's wars or the conditions in the countryside. True, an enlightened egoist might avoid idleness, wars, and oppression. But so might an enlightened altruist take care of himself—physically, emotionally, intellectually, aesthetically, morally, and religiously. We must therefore distinguish, as above, between genuine altruism and spurious, mindless altruism. As bona fide altruism is concerned for the genuine good of others, so too it is concerned for the genuine good of oneself, required for the service of others. (The heart pumps ample blood to itself—enough to stay healthy and efficiently nourish other parts of the body.)

7. Survival of the "Superior"

Earlier in the same work, Spencer adopts an evolutionary perspective:

Any arrangements which in a considerable degree prevent superiority from profiting by the rewards of superiority, or shield inferiority from the evils it entails—any arrangements which tend to make it as well to be inferior as to be superior, are arrangements diametrically opposed to the progress of organization and the reaching of a higher life.

But to say that each individual shall reap the benefits brought to him by his own powers, inherited and acquired, is to enunciate egoism as an ultimate principle of conduct. It is to say that egoistic claims must take precedence of altruistic claims.[17]

Let dog eat dog, and only the scrappiest, strongest, most intelligent dogs will survive. But such dogs are obviously happier. To illustrate: "The mentally inferior individual of any race suffers negative and positive miseries; while the mentally superior individual receives negative and positive gratifications. Inevitably then, this law in conformity with which each member of a species takes the consequences of its own nature; and in virtue of which the progeny of each member, participating in its nature, also takes such consequences; is one that tends ever to raise the aggregate happiness of the species, by furthering the multiplication of the happier, and hindering that of the less happy."[18]

Were brains and brawn the chief sources of human happiness, there might be something to this argument, at least pragmatically. But they are not, and the pragmatic perspective is not the sole or chief one to consider. Kant emphasized respect for persons; Rawls stressed fairness;[19] Christians set great store by an altruistic form of life, in itself. Consequences are not the only determinant of morality, nor is happiness the only goal, especially if it signifies simply "enjoyment." I need not belabor these familiar points, to which I shall return in objection 24.

Reflection also suggests that Spencer's formula, if acted on, would more likely perpetuate unhappiness than diminish it. No matter how healthy, strong, or intelligent people became through survival of the fittest, there would always be some that were superior and others that were inferior; and so long as the Spencerian norm held sway, the inferior would suffer the consequences. Besides, since "survival of the fittest" here has a less radical sense than when applied to animal evolution, Spencer's means would not achieve the goal he envisages. Short of a systematic program of eugenics, little or no improvement in the race would result from making life unpleasant for the "inferior" and pleasant for the "superior." More promising as a formula for heightened human happiness would be altruistic efforts by the better endowed to eliminate birth defects, remedy handicaps, improve public health, further education, assure adequate housing and nutrition, provide incentives, broaden opportunity, and the like.

8. Economic Effectiveness

The economic version of Spencer's survival-of-the-fittest is familiar. Charles Patterson writes:

> Some of the advantages of the selfish motive as the basis for conduct are well illustrated in the better features of the capitalist system. Take, for example, the small businessman who knows that the amount of profits he will make depends on successful competition with others who are engaged in the same line of work. Any laziness or inefficiency on his part will give an advantage to his competitors, and this will lessen his own chances of making prof-

its for himself. On the other hand, the harder he works and the more effective use he makes of the abilities he possesses the greater income he will receive. And it is not only the businessman who gains by working at his full capacity. The competitive system tends to eliminate the businessmen who give the poorest type of service to the public. The business goes to the one who is able to give the public the most for its money.[20]

The same competitive system would eliminate an ineffectual altruist, who produced too little or too poorly, as surely as it would an ineffectual egoist. And the altruist would be less likely to overcharge, to pass off shoddy or dangerous products, to pollute the environment, to skimp on safety, and so forth. Thus the claim of "advantages" is misleading. Insofar as it is true, it means merely that selfish motives, in a system based on selfishness, may bring incidental benefits to the public, along with the contrary; it does not mean that such motives are more beneficial, in that system or generally, than altruistic motives. And of course economic advantages are not the only ones to be considered; as Marx and others have emphasized, there are values more important to a society and its members than increased productivity.

Self-Preference

9. Social Effectiveness

"Every ego," Friedrich Paulsen suggests, "arranges all other egoes around it in concentric circles; the farther away the interests from this centre, the less weight and motive force they possess. That is a law of psychical mechanics. Its teleological necessity is obvious: if the different interests were to influence us according to their objective value, it would lead to the most curious confusion in our natures. A corresponding confusion in our actions would render the latter utterly fruitless; the efficacy of all aid generally decreases in direct proportion to the distance between the giver and the recipient."[21] But the nearest of the near is the giver himself—the ego at the center of the concentric circles. Thus, Dewey and Tufts extend this line of reasoning and apply it to the agent: "It is profitable for society, not merely for an individual, that each of us should instinctively have his powers most actively and intensely called out by the things that distinctively affect him and his own welfare. Any other arrangement would mean waste of social energy, inefficiency in securing social results."[22]

These contentions contain an obvious kernel of truth, of a kind already noted in the last chapter's response to Butler. If a woman desires her hair to be combed with minimal fuss, in the manner she prefers, let her comb it herself. If a man wants his tie tied properly, let him do it himself. As for endeavors like getting an education or becoming a concert pianist, there is no substitute for personal effort; no one else can do the learning for you. However, there is no good reason to suppose that, for example, a person who studies medicine with future earnings in mind applies himself more "actively and intensely" than a person whose goal is a lifetime of service; or that a doctor whose aim is profit will heal more people more expertly than one whose aim is the alleviation of suffering.

Citing different examples, Paulsen suggests at least a partial response:

> On the contrary, the value of works composed "for others" is perhaps much more doubtful than the value of those whose authors were interested solely in the subject itself, and perhaps occasionally thought of their fame. . . . The true poet writes poetry for himself, and the true artist creates for himself and gives expression to what his soul conceives. Of course, if there were no "others" nothing would be created. No orator would speak without an audience to hear him, no poet make poetry without a people to read or sing his songs, no author write unless there were, at least in his imagination, persons who would read what he wrote. Nevertheless, if a man is not so full of his subject that he cannot help speaking of it, if he must first be impelled to do so by his consideration of others and their good, he may save his efforts without endangering the welfare of others.[23]

As it stands, Paulsen's argument is easily answered. Largely by means of the ambiguous phrase *for himself* it poses a false dichotomy between working for others and taking an interest in the work itself. If a person had no interest in poetry or art, altruism (for example, Self-Subordination) would dissuade him from either occupation; if he had a keen appreciation of words or a passion for visual representation, altruism would see that as one good reason for choosing a life of service through poetry or art. The supposed conflict is illusory. However, there is more to Paulsen's objection than appears in his formulation. I am reminded, for instance, of Maisie Ward's portrayal of G. K. Chesterton's parents:

> They belonged to a generation which cheerfully created a home and brought fresh life into being. In doing it, they did a thousand other things, so that the home they made was full of vital energies for the children who were to grow up in it. Gilbert recollects his father as a man of a dozen hobbies, his study as a place where these hobbies formed strata of exciting products, awakening youthful covetousness in the matter of a new paint-box, satisfying youthful imagination by the production of a toy theatre.[24]

Some of these things the elder Chesterton did with and for his children, while enjoying them himself (enjoying them the more because of their enjoyment). Yet one senses that too careful a calculation of what was for their good, damping his personal interests and enthusiasms, might have benefited them less in the long run. And in that case society would have been the loser.

This objection acquires its apparent strength from the fusion of a plausible impression with a plausible surmise, and can be answered by distinguishing between them. First there is the impression that such a manner of life is beneficial to others as well as to the person himself. This impression, whether accurate or inaccurate, does not conflict with an altruistic norm such as Self-Subordination. What is genuinely good for others, Self-Subordination would favor. Second there is the surmise that Chesterton's father did not calculate benefits very carefully—did not, for instance, apply the norm of Self-Subordination and see that it was satisfied by his manner of life. The accuracy of this surmise is irrelevant to the question of the norm's validity. Were we to imagine his father choosing mindlessly, without regard for other's good, or choosing more reflectively, but with no one else's benefit in view, his way of life might look admirable but his manner of adopting it would not. Confusion of these two aspects—the objective and the subjective—accounts for the objection's prima facie plausibility.

10. *"Common Sense"*

An altruistic norm like Self-Subordination is often thought to make unrealistic demands and therefore to conflict with common sense.[25] "To take some present examples from my own life," writes James Fishkin,

> is it a *moral* question what my wife and I serve at a dinner party? Or what courses I decide to teach next fall? Is it a moral question what law school my brother decides to attend? Or even, to take a question of greater importance, is it a *moral* problem that my wife and I should consider when we discuss whether or not—or when—to have a second child?
>
> Under some possible conditions any of these questions might pose a moral problem. But under normal conditions most of us would not think about them in that way. The way of life we assume would permit us, as a matter of course, to classify these actions, and a host of others, within the zone of moral indifference—the realm of permissibly free personal choice.[26]

An agapistic norm like Self-Subordination would draw no such "zone of moral indifference"; any action that affects human welfare is of moral interest to it. So a critique is implicit in Fishkin's further comments: "If I am incorrect in this assumption, then two results would immediately follow. The most obvious result would be that most of us must be immoral in the entire way of life we take for granted. For we would then be ignoring a host of obligations as a matter of course. Unless by blind luck we always do the right thing anyway—without even being aware of the moral questions involved—we must be subject to a host of failed obligations of both omission and commission."

This consequence would follow only if we paid no attention to the effects of our choices on ourselves and others; to act in accordance with a norm does not require that we formulate and explicitly apply it (though doubtless that would help). Thus our doing the right thing need not be "blind luck." Furthermore, our shortcomings need not be "failed obligations." Fishkin's critique does not discriminate between trivial matters or slight differences, on the one hand, and weighty discrepancies between alternative choices, on the other. Thus, although serving one dish rather than the other—say the guests' favorite dessert rather than the host's—may accord better with the norm of Self-Subordination, it does not follow that the host is "morally obliged" to serve the dish his guests prefer.[27] Finally, with regard to more serious matters, there is nothing unrealistic about supposing that people very often treat moral matters prudentially, not morally, or misjudge their genuine obligations, or fail to live up to the obligations they recognize. Earlier, our society countenanced slavery, child labor, religious coercion, and imprisonment for debt; presently, it countenances vacations in the Bahamas while millions starve to death in Africa and Asia.

11. *"Heroism" is Supererogatory*

Fishkin's anti-altruism is aroused by the implications Peter Singer draws from a norm less stringently altruistic than Self-Subordination. "Strictly," Singer concludes, "we would need to cut down to the minimum level compatible with earning the income which, after providing for our needs, left us most to give away."[28] "We ought to give until we reach the level of marginal utility—that is, the level at which, by giving more, I would cause as much suffering to myself or my dependents as I would relieve by my gift. This would mean, of course, that one would reduce oneself to very near the material circumstances of a Bengali refugee."[29] Although these two statements of Singer's do not perfectly agree, and the norm stated in the first might not call for the verdict stated in the second, still, the norm of Self-Subordination would warrant basically similar inferences, and Fishkin's comments are therefore germane to it as well:

> I believe that one reason we find Singer's extremely demanding conclusions troubling is that we commonly approach this kind of problem with another assumption, whose application to this problem Singer rejects. This is the assumption that some levels of sacrifice or risk must be *heroic* or "beyond the call of duty." Let us call this assumption the *cutoff for heroism.* . . . Because we commonly assume such a cutoff for heroism, Singer's conclusion is theoretically perplexing as well as morally disturbing. For by defini-

tion, we cannot be *obligated* or required to perform acts that are also *supererogatory*. We cannot be morally required to be heroes.[30]

I question both Fishkin's equation of the heroic with the supererogatory and his conclusion that no action can be morally mandatory if it calls for notable sacrifice. When Tom O'Brien chose to risk his life rather than devastate the neighborhood (see chapter 1), his action was surely heroic; but shall we say that he was under no obligation to avoid the slaughter? True, we would be slow to accuse him—to say "You sinned"— if he chose the easy way out; yet he, in retrospect, might truly say, "I should have tried to save all those people." "It makes a difference," I have elsewhere remarked, "whether one is judging oneself or another. In the latter case one is slower to condemn or to impose an obligation. Reactions also vary according to the magnitude of the divergence among competing alternatives and the clarity with which the disparity is seen. If we fix on cases where the value-gap is great and clearly perceived, we are inclined to assert obligation, especially if we are judging ourselves."[31]

I have cited Tom O'Brien because his sacrifice would be required by any form of altruism, even Self-Preference. If Fishkin's objection were a valid complaint against Self-Subordination, it would implicate all six altruistic preference-rules, not just Self-Subordination; for all six sometimes call for extreme self-sacrifice. However, reflection reveals that even were Fishkin correct in linking heroism with the absence of obligation and claiming a "cutoff for heroism," Self-Subordination might still be a valid norm. It might indicate the better thing to do and explain many an obligation. The obligations it imposed would just be fewer, by reason of this further stipulation. To the cutoff of gravity would be added the cutoff of sacrifice. Before employing the heavy artillery of moral terminology (*ought, obliged, duty, sin*) we would need to consider not only the seriousness of the matter and the discrepancy between one course of action and another but also the degree of difficulty for the agent.

12. *"Moral Fanaticism"*

One aspect of the objection from common sense deserves closer scrutiny, since it does not merely reduce the area of obligation imposed by Self-Subordination but eliminates as well the whole area of what is better though not "obligatory." "If we were to give up the robust sphere of indifference," Fishkin writes, "then we would accept the pervasive intrusion of morality into virtually every minor aspect of our daily lives. A recognizable form of life would result, but one that is distinctly foreign to modern secular Western culture. The result would be what Marcus Singer has called in a provocative choice of terms, 'moral fanaticism'—'the idea that no action is indifferent or trivial.' Allowing for some hyperbole, he has

identified the consternation most of us would feel at such a way of life."
Here, Fishkin notes—indeed stresses—the difference between grave and
trifling matters. However, phrases like "the robust sphere of indifference,"
"the realm of permissibly free personal choice," and "indifferent or
trivial," unaccompanied by any compensating reference to what is "better," "preferable," or "indicated by the norm," suggest a minimalizing tendency at odds with Christian agape of any stripe. The abstract stipulations
of a norm like Self-Subordination, leaving room for differences of degree,
are more adequate guides than all-or-nothing dichotomies like Fishkin's.

13. The Impossible Does not Oblige

"Any moral judgment," notes Neil Cooper, "which prescribes or
commends or commits one to the prescription or commendation of what
it is impossible to perform is irrational or pointless."[32] "Should" supposes
"can"; "cannot" entails "no obligation." Yet as Kierkegaard remarks, "a
man would not be able to live every moment exclusively in the highest
Christian ideals any more than he could live only on the food from the
Lord's table."[33] And doubtless Self-Subordination qualifies as such an ideal.
However, fine distinctions aside, it might with equal truth be said that no
one can invariably live up to all his obligations, whatever they may be, or
always do the better thing. Yet the individual obligations would still be
obligations, and the better thing would still be the better thing. As for the
individual injunctions of a norm like Self-Subordination, Cooper himself
observes: "It is a mistake to argue that it is irrational to recommend what
is 'practically impossible'; this is a highly contestable claim, for practical
impossibility is only very great difficulty, and it follows from the very
meaning of the word 'difficult' that it is possible to perform the action if
one tries hard enough."[34] Besides, even if people fall short of the ideal,
they may come closer by trying to reach it than they would if they did not
hold it as an ideal or strive to achieve it.

14. Counterproductive

According to one common objection, "The moral teaching of Jesus is
so far above our ordinary conduct that we tend not to take it quite
seriously, to regard it as a rather remote ideal which should have some effect on our conduct but not very much, just because we think that what it
actually prescribes is impossible."[35] "Excessive demands are likely to provoke a reaction: by encouraging a sense of unworthiness they may produce greater laxness than we would otherwise encounter."[36] "Might it
not be counter-productive to demand so much? Might not people say: 'As
I can't do what is morally required anyway, I won't bother to give at all'? If,

however, we were to set a more realistic standard, people might make a genuine effort to reach it."[37]

To place this recurring objection in proper perspective, consider a simple comparison. A coach, say, knows that an athlete can jump seven feet; he's done it before. He also knows that the man can't jump that high all the time or even most of the time. Insisting that he jump seven feet every time might discourage him; settling for less might prevent him from doing his best. A good coach will avoid both these extremes; he will encourage the man to jump seven feet but will not demand it, and will not treat an effort of six feet ten inches as a disgrace. Much will depend on the coach's tone and the relationship between him and his charge. However, the question of teaching technique should not be confused with the question of the ideal. The ideal is still to jump the maximum.

Thus Peter Singer writes: "It is important to get the status of this objection clear. Its accuracy as a prediction of human behaviour is quite compatible with the argument that we are obliged to give to the point at which by giving more we sacrifice something of comparable moral significance. What would follow from the objection is that public advocacy of this standard of giving is undesirable. It would mean [for example] that in order to do the maximum to reduce absolute poverty, we should advocate a standard lower than the amount we think people really ought to give."[38] A general exhortation to compassion may often be more effective than spelling out the requirements of Self-Subordination. Yet no single tactic is universally preferable. Much depends on the manner, the recipient, and the circumstances of the advice. What can be more generally asserted is that "ideals that are easily attained are useless as ideals. It is only as we strive to reach the so-called impossible ideals that we can make a steady moral advance."[39]

15. Excessive Burden

"In our research into, and therapy of, a neurosis," remarks Freud, "we are led to make two reproaches against the super-ego of the individual. In the severity of its commands and prohibitions it troubles itself too little about the happiness of the ego, in that it takes insufficient account of the resistances against obeying them—of the instinctual strength of the id, and of the difficulties presented by the real external environment."[40] The Christian love command is an oft-cited illustration.

Developing this objection, Thomas Green writes:

When we compare the life of service to mankind, involving so much sacrifice of pure pleasure, which is lived by the men whom in our consciences we think best, and which they reproach themselves for not making one of more complete self-denial, with the life of free activity in bodily and intellectual exercises, in friendly converse, in civil debate, in the enjoyment of beautiful sights and sounds, which we commonly ascribe to the Greeks, and which their philosophers certainly set before them as an ideal, we might be apt, on the first view, to think that, even though measured not merely by the quantity of pleasure incidental to it but by the fulness of the realisation of human capabilities implied in it, the latter kind of life was the higher of the two. Man for man, the Greek who at all came up to the ideal of the philosophers might seem to be intrinsically a nobler being—one of more fully developed powers—than the self-mortifying Christian, upon whom the sense of duty to a suffering world weighs too heavily to allow of his giving free play to enjoyable activities, of which he would otherwise be capable.[41]

In response to this objection, Green himself remarks that "such a comparison of man with man, in abstraction from the rest of mankind, is not the way to ascertain the real value of the virtue of either in its relation to the possibilities of the human soul." What of the slaves who made the Greek ideal possible? What of the needy and underprivileged of every time whose plight does not trouble the healthy hedonist? A variety of other considerations further blunt the edge of the objection:

1) Service to others requires due regard for one's own physical, emotional, intellectual, moral, and spiritual well-being.[42] (As Nolan and Kirkpatrick remark, "The idealization of selfless love in religious literature and among some saints fails to give an accurate picture of the extent of their actual wholesomeness, true state of mental health, and actual interpersonal relationships."[43])

2) The dictates of enlightened self-interest and of enlightened altruism largely coincide. (A healthy heart requires a healthy body; a healthy body requires a healthy heart.)

3) Self-Subordination makes more provision for one's own interests than do more purely altruistic norms. The fringe benefits it approves once the service of others is assured are of daily, even hourly, occurrence.

4) Concern for others brings something more than inevitable crosses. It also elicits appreciation, admiration, and liking; it cements friendships, fosters community.

5) A mere altruistic formula, minus the love it expresses, may seem burdensome. For then attention centers on one's own losses rather than on others' gains. Love of others takes pleasure in their pleasure, is made happy by their happiness, rejoices in their welfare. ("I was a sinner," St. Francis recalls at the start of his *Testament,* "and found it hard to look at lepers, and the Lord God led me among them, and I was merciful to them. As I left them, what had previously seemed bitter turned into sweetness of body and soul."[44])

What theory suggests, experience confirms. The most altruistic people I have known have been cheerful, happy, peaceful people. Others report the same experience. Henry Fehren's description of his long-time housekeeper, Meriam Lux, illustrates what Self-Subordination might look like if lived out. On the one hand,

> Her generosity was legendary; she simply gave away everything. "Money just causes trouble," she said. She did not know that she was echoing St. Paul when he told Timothy that money is the root of all evil (1 Tim 6:10). She never heard of voluntary poverty but she practiced it. There were never more than a few dollars in her old purse. A housekeeper's salary is below the poverty level but the Internal Revenue Service investigated her in 1968. They said she listed too much for charity in comparison to her salary. I sent them her canceled checks and showed that she had not even listed all her charities in her income tax report.[45]

Yet despite what others might term her deprivations, despite the fact that she was not beautiful, her feet were bad, her clothes haphazard, her slip always showing, "she just laughed about these things. Indeed, she was always cheerful, even during some times of great stress and difficulty. . . . Even when she was cheated she did not complain. She always sensed that she was in the hands of the Lord and He would take care of her."[46] This further source of comfort—trusting faith—does not appear in secular, Freudian calculations.

True, not all can live as an unmarried housekeeper is able to; but suppose we change our paradigm:

> If a girl chooses the career of teaching French in school, she should not hope to commit the prescribed texts and grammars to memory and then turn her mind to other things. She should dedicate part of her life to the French language, to the superb literature of France, to French art and history and civilization. To become a good teacher of French, she will build up a growing library of her own French books, spending one year (for instance) reading Balzac, the next year reading Proust, the next with Molière, and the next with Giraudoux, Cocteau, Romains, and the other modern playwrights. She will visit France, if and when she can save up enough money to do so—which will be fearfully difficult with salaries at their present low level. She may take summer courses in French at a university. Certainly she will see every available French film, and learn to enjoy Raimu's rich Marseillais accent, to guffaw with Fernandel. For it will not all be serious work and planned self-improvement. It will be living, and therefore it will contain enjoyments, and even frivolities, like the latest records by Lucienne Boyer and Charles Trenet. But it will be learning at the same time, and it will make better teaching.[47]

Better teaching is what Self-Subordination would typically ask of a teacher. So what better teaching requires, the norm would sanction. From this illustration it appears that the burden of self-subordinating service may be less crushing than unrealistic assessments or isolated instances of heroic self-sacrifice suggest.

However, a further misgiving arises and had better be addressed, since the impression of excessive burden is the most frequent, powerful objection the norm of Self-Subordination is likely to evoke. Urging love's demands, Thomas Green writes:

> It is no time to enjoy the pleasures of eye and ear, of search for knowledge, of friendly intercourse, of applauded speech or writing, while the mass of men whom we call our brethren, and whom we declare to be meant with us for eternal destinies, are left without the chance, which only the help of others can gain for them, of making themselves in act what in possibility we believe them to be. Interest in the problem of social deliverance, in one or other of the innumerable forms in which it presents itself to us . . . forbids a surrender to enjoyments which are not incidental to that work of deliverance, whatever the value which they, or the activities to which they belong, might otherwise have.[48]

Perhaps the French teacher should abandon her agreeable profession and join Mother Teresa in the slums of Calcutta. Isn't that where the greater good beckons?

I need not decide this particular case, but in answer to the general objection which it illustrates I can make three points. First, given the dire needs of humanity, any altruistic norm may deliver a like verdict; even Self-Preference may direct a person to a less enjoyable occupation, in response to a greater need. Second, the same suppositions that create the difficulty—the greater need elsewhere, the ability to remedy it—provide a ready answer to the complaint of excessive burden. If the need really is so great and can in fact be met, then the cost required to achieve it, even if considerable, may not be disproportionate. Third, a person who senses the need and responds to it may learn the truth of the gospel saying that he who loses his life will save it. Viktor Frankl speaks of humans' basic need for meaning in their lives,[49] and the examples he cites suggest that meaning typically comes from service to others.[50] The Mother Teresas of the world find fulfillment.

16. Suicidal

They also provide living refutation of the objection that "a man who loved all men in universal brotherhood would be destroyed for that love, and succeed in assisting few people"; that "he would then sacrifice himself to them all and help none of them."[51] The fate of Jesus and of many a martyr testifies how risky authentic charity may be. But the majority of saints renowned for their generosity died in their beds. And those who did not generally succeeded in assisting many more than a handful. The responses to the preceding objection suggest why this is so. A person intent on service does not seek self-diminishment or self-annihilation.

17. Unfair

A possible critique of Self-Subordination is implicit in the comparison Derek Parfit draws between two forms of "Consequentialism," one individualistic, the other collective:

> Consider the question of how much the rich should give to the poor. For most Consequentialists, this question ignores national boundaries. Since I know that most other rich people will give very little, it would be hard for me to deny that it would be better if I gave away almost all my income. Even if I gave nine-tenths, some of my remaining tenth would do more good if spent by the very poor. Consequentialism thus tells me that I ought to give away almost all my income.
>
> Collective Consequentialism is much less demanding. It does not tell me to give the amount that would in fact make the outcome best. It tells me to give the amount which is such that if we all gave this amount, the outcome would be best. More exactly, it tells me to give what would be demanded by the particular International Income Tax that would make the outcome best. This tax would be progressive, requiring larger proportions from those who are richer. But the demands made on each person would be much smaller than the demands made by C[onsequentialism], on any plausible prediction about the amounts that others will in fact give.[52]

This collective norm's demands are right and fair, it has been said; the other norm's are not.[53] Why should some be punished for the stinginess of others? The same complaint might be leveled at Self-Subordination, for it too ignores what the world would be like and what would be required if all did their share, and instead considers the world as it is, with its suffering and unmet needs.

Three comments suffice to deal with this objection. First, it applies to any of the six forms of altruism listed in chapter 1, so does not tell in favor of any Christian alternative to Self-Subordination. Second, it is true that it is unfair for the whole burden to fall on a few; others should do their share. Third, this does not signify, however, that the norm and its demands are unfair; the objection shows too much concern for the giver, too little for those in distress. It is not their fault that their needs are ignored by the majority.

18. Guilt Feelings

A further Freudian objection, besides the one already cited (*Excessive Burden*), warns that insistence on high ideals "is an occasion for the intensification of guilt feelings, even when the departure is merely a thought or wish (Freud, 1930:71). The love commandment is often interpreted in a way that makes it impossible or exceedingly difficult to fulfill, yet its enforcement is uncompromisingly strict. . . . The psychic cost to the individual is 'extraordinary severity of conscience'."[54]

Christians sometimes appear to corroborate this critique. Consider C. H. Dodd's comments on the Sermon on the Mount:

> The one thing that all such sayings clearly enforce is the unlimited scope of God's commands. They leave no room for complacency. It is impossible to be satisfied with ourselves, when we try our conduct by these standards; and yet, since God is here in His kingdom, these standards are obligatory. It is put briefly in the maxim: "When you have done every thing say, 'We are un-profitable servants: we have only done our duty'" (Luke 17:10). Such sayings as these invite us to recognize how far away from God's demands our best has been. They provide an objective standard for self-criticism. In other words, they bring home God's judgment upon us. To accept this judgment is the first step in what the New Testament calls "repentance."[55]

"In genuine prophetic Christianity," writes Reinhold Niebuhr, "the moral qualities of the Christ are not only our hope, but our despair."[56]

However, to this first, negative phase of repentance there suc-ceeds a second:

> These seemingly harsh and uncompromising demands . . . are set within a picture of the Kingdom of God which holds out the prospect of fulfillment and satisfaction beyond all measure, because God is what He is. "Fear not, little flock; it is your Father's good pleasure to give you the Kingdom." Thus, repentance passes from the negative action which is the acceptance of God's judgment upon our evil to the positive realization of new possibilities. The transition from the negative to the positive is what is called in the gos-pels the forgiveness of sins. I need hardly remind you how large a place forgiveness holds in the gospels, not only in the teaching of Jesus, but even more in the record of His actual dealing with the moral failures of society (the "publicans and sinners" of the gospel narration).[57]

Why, in fact, do so few Christians verify Freud's misgivings? Why do so few appear oppressed by guilt at having fallen short of what Christian charity requires? Many, no doubt, seldom advert to its requirements. Many have little awareness of what its requirements are. Those who are more reflective recognize how frequently service and self-interest coincide; dis-tinguish between major and minor offenses; and trust that even their major lapses, if repented, are forgiven. If, nonetheless, some regrets and self-accusation remain, no doubt that is as it should be. Where there is guilt, guilt-feelings are appropriate.[58]

Parity

19. Agents Made Means

In an argument somewhat similar to Ayn Rand's but offered in support of Parity, Ahad Ha'am declares:

> The altruism of the Gospels is neither more nor less than inverted egoism. Altruism and egoism alike deny the individual as such all objective moral value, and make him merely a means to a subjective end; but whereas egoism makes the "other" a means to the advantage of the "self," altruism does just the reverse. Judaism, however, gets rid of this subjective attitude entirely. Its morality is based on something abstract and objective, on *absolute justice,* which attaches moral value to the individual as such, without any distinction between the "self" and the "other."[59]

The premise of individual worth permits neither the conclusion of egoism, as in Rand, nor of Parity, as here. No norm, if ethical, reduces either party to a mere means or denies him "all objective moral value." Any preference-rule, whether egoistic, altruistic, or egalitarian, is impartial. It applies equally to all, and attends equally to the welfare of all. Only the manner of realization differs. And the egoistic or altruistic manner is as "abstract and objective" as the egalitarian.

Ha'am's objection might have had more semblance of validity had he argued that altruism denies the individual *as agent* (not "as such") all objective moral value. Even then, the intended target would have to be a form of altruism more extreme than Self-Subordination, which permits independent consideration of the agent's own welfare. Only Self-Forgetfulness or Self-Denial might be said to reduce the agent, as agent, to a mere means to others' welfare. However, the qualifier "as agent" is important. First, because agents are also recipients and therefore beneficiaries of the same norm. Second, because they are seen, by proponents of such a norm, as achieving their highest perfection through their generous giving of self. The refining process may be rigorous in the extreme, but the persons thus formed are also precious in the extreme—immortal diamonds, finite images of God. Thus, even against these least self-regarding versions of agape, Ha'am's objection is ineffectual. No Christian preference-rule demotes those who follow it to mere means.

20. Momentary Selves

"From the Buddhistic-Whiteheadian standpoint," writes Charles Hartshorne, "when one says 'I' he not only refers to the consciousness associated with his body rather than someone else's, but he normally intends only some limited part of the sequence of conscious states which he calls his. If I now plan for my future welfare, 'I' here means one or more momentary subjects in the Hartshorne personal sequence and 'my' qualifies some future stretch of that sequence."[60] The future stretch is as distinct from the present, momentary self as is the consciousness associated with other people's bodies. Hence, "the present self enjoys itself; but beyond that, so far as it is rational or ethical, it concerns itself with whatever future selves, in no matter what body, can profit or suffer by inheriting from this present self."[61] In the realm of action, which looks beyond the present moment, egoistic and altruistic norms are transcended, and only Parity applies; for future selves are no more mine than thine. The lives Tom O'Brien, Maximilian Kolbe, and Arland Williams saved by their supposedly generous deeds were as much their own as anybody else's, and no self-sacrifice was in fact involved.

Such paradoxical results are to be expected when thinkers abandon or misrepresent the familiar meanings of words. And that is what has happened in this instance. Suppose I tell someone that I am listening to Brahms's Fourth Symphony or that I saw my friend Bill drive by in his Chevrolet. Would it be accurate to say that by "Brahms's Fourth Symphony" I mean only the notes I am hearing at that moment or that by "Bill" I mean only the parts of his body I observed as he drove by (the surface of his left arm, say, and the left side of his head)? Surely not. But Hartshorne's semantic reductions are of this variety. There is no better backing for his double restriction, temporal and mental: "he normally intends only some *limited part* of the sequence of *conscious states* which he calls his." In everyday speech and thought, selves are not momentary conscious states but subjects identified by spatio-temporal continuity, bodily appearance, memories, abilities, personality, and so forth. And regardless of how some philosopher redefines terms (or empties them of coherent content),[62] these differences remain to differentiate one future self from another. The man named Tom O'Brien, who stayed in his cab and steered his crane's load safely into the pit, was the same man who was seriously injured as a result, spent months in the hospital, and never fully recovered.[63]

21. Contradiction

As Neil Cooper observes, the quasi-logical difficulties cited against ethical egoism "are symmetrical and apply to both egoism and altruism; they cannot therefore be exploited in order to eliminate one to the advantage of the other."[64] However, they can, if valid, be exploited to eliminate both egoism and other-preferring altruism in favor of Parity. Hence Self-Subordination may be implicated in the charge of self-contradiction Kurt Baier directs against ethical egoism. Any ethical theory, he plausibly contends, is subject to the principle: "One ought never to aim at preventing another from doing what he ought."[65] From this principle plus the egoistic principle it would follow that in cases of irreconcilable conflicts of interest, each party should and should not oppose the other: should, because egoism requires self-seeking of him; should not, because egoism requires the same thing of the other. But this requirement is contradictory.[66] The like might be urged not only against egoism or self-preference but against any form of other-preference, including Self-Subordination. When interests conflict, each altruist should and should not oppose the other's efforts to assist him: should, because altruism requires sacrifice from him; should not, because altruism requires sacrifice from the other. For example, those to whom Arland Williams passed the lifeline should and should not have opposed him.

In first answer, it might be proposed that in accepting the lifeline, one allows Arland Williams to be altruistic, and that his altruism rates higher in value than even his physical life. This reply is suggested by Paul's words to the Philippians: "It was kind of you to share my trouble. And you Philippians yourselves know that in the beginning of the gospel, when I left Macedonia, no church entered into partnership with me in giving and receiving except you only; for even in Thessalonica you sent me help once and again. Not that I seek the gift; but I seek the fruit that increases to your credit" (Phil 4:14-17).

It might be objected that the Philippians' gifts were equally generous whether Paul accepted them or returned them, and that Arland's offer, similarly, was equally altruistic whether the others accepted the lifeline or refused it. So Baier's difficulty might appear still to hold: were an altruistic norm like Self-Subordination valid, the Philippians and Arland would be obliged to make their offers and the others would be obliged to refuse them. The solution I prefer is that the intended recipients would not be obliged to refuse, but that even if they were, no contradiction would result.

The first part of this answer is suggested, once again, by Paul's words to the Philippians. What they graciously offered he graciously accepted. He freely shared the gospel with them; they freely shared their sustenance with him. To have returned their gifts would have created an inequality, an imbalance, with him alone the giver and they only receivers, in place of the "partnership in giving and receiving" he favored. For Christians, mutual service, not just willingness to serve, is a good and holy thing. The inner must become outer; the spirit must become incarnate. And it cannot do so if every time service is offered it is rejected. View persons atomistically, and Baier's objection may seem to hold; view them non-atomistically, and the objection is answered. The value of lived community requires and justifies "partnership in giving and receiving."

In view of the distinctions I have made between striving and succeeding, offering and actually giving, a back-up solution also looks available. If Self-Subordination requires Arland to offer the lifeline and the others to refuse it, there is no contradiction. He is not obliged both to make the offer and not to make it; they are not obliged both to refuse the offer and not to refuse it. Their refusal is perfectly compatible with his doing all he is obliged to do, namely, make the offer. He cannot be obliged to do anything contingent on their acceptance, namely, to succeed in actually passing them the lifeline. He is bound, not to save their lives, but to try to save them.

Searching for more troublesome examples, I recall the movie *Shane*. In this classic western a monumental battle between Shane and his friend, waged to determine who will risk his life against their common enemy, ends with Shane knocking out his opponent. It might be said that Shane thereby prevents the other from even trying to do what he thinks he should do; however, even here the answer is evident: his friend put up a terrific fight, and this was all that could be required of him. He was not duty-bound to win the fight. Shane, for his part, could not prevent him from trying, but he could and did prevent him from succeeding, as his love for his friend and for his friend's family urged.

Thus it is possible to accept Baier's principles without drawing inferences that conflict with altruism. It may be that "one ought never to aim at preventing another from doing what he ought,"[67] but that all the other is obliged to do is to try. It may be that "one's right to do A implies other people's obligation to let one try,"[68] but not their obligation to let one succeed.

22. Incoherence

The charge of incoherent motivation, like that of self-contradiction, has been leveled both at egoism[69] and, with parallel reasoning, at altruism.[70] Generally, the version accused is Self-Forgetfulness or Self-Denial ("pure egoism"), not Self-Subordination.[71] Thus Herbert Spencer objects: "To make pure altruism possible for all, each must be at once extremely unegoistic and extremely egoistic. As a giver, he must have no thought for self; as a receiver, no thought for others. Evidently this implies an inconceivable mental constitution."[72] With minor modification ("slight thought" in place of "no thought"), this critique can be made to implicate Self-Subordination as well as Self-Forgetfulness and Self-Denial.

Clearly, the criticism does not hold for many cases. When, for instance, Tom O'Brien saved the lives of those in the buildings and streets roundabout, there was no selfishness in their receiving. They had no idea what was happening and no way of stopping him or refusing his self-sacrifice. As for those to whom Arland Williams passed the lifeline, one possible solution has already been suggested: he could have generously offered the lifeline, they could have generously refused it. Perhaps that is what Self-Subordination would dictate. However, the prospect of Arland

and others passing the lifeline back and forth till they all drowned elicits another common objection to any such altruistic norm—an objection to which I shall now turn before concluding my response to the charge of incoherence.

23. Inadequacy

"We usually expect an ethical theory to be able to settle conflicts of interest," it is said;[73] but in a world where self-subordinating altruism reigned, "life would be a kind of series of curtsies and retreats. 'You take the food'; 'No, you take it' and so on. Who would end up taking the food?"[74] How would Alphonse and Gaston ever manage to get through the door? ("After you, my dear Gaston," "No, you first, my dear Alphonse." ...)[75]

In response it may be noted, first, that this problem does not arise in many cases, perhaps not in the majority. Chapter 1's examples look representative. An Alphonse-Gaston alternation was possible between Arland Williams and those he sought to save, but could not very readily develop between Maximilian Kolbe and the man whose place he took, and was out of the question when Tom O'Brien, alone in the cab of his giant crane, chose to risk his life for the people passing in the street and working in the buildings nearby. It should also be observed, with regard to those cases where conflict can occur, that they do not count against Self-Subordination and in favor of any rival norm, since no preference-rule—whether egoistic, altruistic, or in between—can conceivably settle all cases. Parity would not even indicate what Alphonse and Gaston should *try* to do, but would leave them entirely on their own. Both might legitimately attempt to go first; both might legitimately insist on the other going first. Pure ethical egoism and Self-Preference might put them at egoistic loggerheads; Other-Preference, Self-Subordination, Self-Forgetfulness, and Self-Denial might set them at altruistic loggerheads. However, such need not be the case; a common-sense egoist might let the other go first ("It's not worth a fight"); a common-sense altruist might accept the other's invitation and go first ("We can't dither here all day"). Neither an egoistic nor an altruistic norm requires us to suppose that both parties are idiots. If both Alphonse and Gaston want to get through the door, and if the only way to get the other through the door is to precede him, then Self-Subordination endorses this apparent lack of deference.

24. Maximizing Value

In my *Christian Moral Reasoning,* an historical, analytic survey led to the verdict: "If Christian moral reasoning is to be both consistent and true to its past, it must be based on the balance of values; value-maximization must be its logic and its law."[76] But, "if Well-being or Good in general be the supreme end," Rashdall and others object, "my good is a part of that end: and my happiness is a part of my good, though not the whole of it. It ought not, therefore, to be sacrificed to promote a less amount of it in others."[77] Yet that is what Self-Subordination dictates; it enjoins that benefit to others take precedence over benefit to self, regardless of the proportion between them. The norm of Self-Subordination might therefore seem to clash with the supreme norm of value-maximization.

This impression comes from equating the value of an action with the value of its consequences, without regard for the value of the action in itself. So in answer I would stress, as others have, the importance of reasons "which assign objective value to a certain kind of behaviour, rather than to any goal of that behaviour."[78] "There are forgiving, mild, humble, friendly, devout *ways of doing the things* we do and of leading our lives in pursuit of varied values. And these aspects of behavior are themselves important values: 'Love is patient; love is kind and envies no one. Love is never boastful, nor conceited, nor rude' (1 Cor. 13:4)."[79] And love "seeks not its own." This, too, Christians have seen as intrinsically admirable. Jesus' washing of his disciples' feet is not made attractive by the special cleanliness imparted to their feet.

The same consequentialism that gives rise to the present objection accounts as well for the impression of incoherence considered two objections back. Viewed consequentially, preference for others' good over one's own does not make sense; only Parity does. However, consequentialism is notoriously deficient as an overall guide to conduct. As the mere quantity of benefits conferred by a law does not guarantee that the law is just, so the mere quantity of value achieved by an act does not guarantee that the act is admirable. As one distribution of benefits may be preferable, so one manner of achieving value for self and others may be preferable, and doubtless is. All preference-rules, including Parity, go beyond mere value-maximization. All see value in one mode of action rather than another. If Self-Subordination has its own preferred manner of achieving good, and therefore enjoins that I seek another's good while he or she seeks mine, there is no inconsistency in that.

25. Disproportion

According to C. D. Broad, "When Altruism is clearly formulated as a general principle, it plainly does not commend itself to the common-sense of enlightened and virtuous persons"[80]—not if it enjoins, as Self-Subordination does, that "you ought to sacrifice *any* amount of happiness in yourself if you will thereby increase the total happiness of others *to the slightest degree* more than you could by any other course of action open to you."[81] Paulsen agrees. "Can we grant that the sacrifice of personal interests, even when it really promotes the welfare of others, is invariably meritorious and praiseworthy, or even a duty? I do not believe it. Ought I, in order to give others a little pleasure, to ignore my own important and essential interests?"[82] Granted, altruistic action may be preferable as such, and may tip the scales to some extent; but does it really weigh as heavily as this? Is the blessedness of giving always decisive, no matter how great the prospective benefit to self and how slight the benefit to others?

Perhaps the norm of Self-Subordination would not hold without exception in all conceivable worlds, but in our actual world—the world for which the norm is intended—it may be generally valid. The reason appears when Paulsen continues: "Ought I to sacrifice my possessions, health, and life in order to fulfil a sick man's harmless whims, and to lighten his lot? Is that my duty, or, if not my duty, always meritorious or praiseworthy?" Surely not, and Self-Subordination would not say it was. To sacrifice possessions, health, and life—indeed to sacrifice one's possessions, health, *or* life—would prevent services more important than fulfilling a sick man's harmless whims. And such is generally the case. It is difficult to conceive any real-life situation in which a slight benefit to others achieved at great cost to oneself would clearly redound to others' overall, long-term welfare. And the norm of Self-Subordination is intended for human beings as they are, not as they conceivably might be, in some ill-defined alternative mode of existence.

26. "The Saint's Dilemma"

In order to demonstrate "the perils of naive benevolence," Nicholas Rescher reformulates the familiar "Prisoner's Dilemma" as "The Saint's Dilemma." In the original version,

> Two prisoners, held incommunicado, are charged with being accomplices in the commission of a crime. For conviction, the testimony of each is needed to incriminate the other. If each confesses, the result is mutual incrimination, and both will divide the penalty of twenty years' imprisonment. If only one turns state's evidence and confesses, thereby incriminating the other (who maintains silence), the whole penalty will fall on this hapless unfortunate. But if both maintain silence and neither confesses, both will suffer a much-diminished penalty (say two years' imprisonment). The prisoners face the problem of whether to take a chance on confession or to opt for the possible benefit of silence, accompanied by an even greater risk.[83]

Here, it will be very much to their mutual benefit for both to be altruistic rather than selfish. A norm of ethical egoism, if followed naively, would be counterproductive. However, there is no difficulty, says Rescher, "in showing that social-interaction situations can unquestionably arise in which the parties are led to a mutually suboptimal result by being *too mindful* of the welfare of others."[84] Simply rewrite the values in the payoff matrix, he suggests, and a situation results in which "prudential selfless-ness produces the result that is, among all possibilities, the one most damaging to the general interest."[85]

Other-Preference is not implicated by Rescher's substitute matrix; Self-Subordination is. Yet such hypothetical configurations pose no real threat to Self-Subordination. For one thing, the mere assigning of values in a payoff matrix does not demonstrate that situations can *in fact* arise in which Self-Subordination would have adverse effects for others as well as for oneself. The dilemma as originally stated is already unreal; Rescher's revision looks still more fantastic. Furthermore, arbitrary reassignment of values might create a similarly adverse result for any preference-rule, and not just Self-Subordination. Finally and fundamentally, no such configura-tion, even if realized, would invalidate any preference-rule, whether Self-Subordination or any other. The key assumption in each form of the dilemma is ignorance of what the other person intends, or is likely, to do. And there is no need of game theory to teach us that ignorance of various kinds, or miscalculation, may and frequently does cause egoists to harm themselves and altruists to harm others. When this occurs, we rightly blame the ignorance or miscalculation, not the norm.

Self-Forgetfulness or Self-Denial

27. Overkill

A high school football coach I heard about taught his players to tackle head-on, figuring that the law of self-preservation would operate at the last moment. The result would then be a solid shoulder tackle, whereas if they attempted a shoulder tackle and flinched, the result would be an inef-fectual arm tackle. Analogous reasoning might appear to favor Self-Forgetfulness or Self-Denial over Self-Subordination. Thus Bourdaloue writes:

> Isn't it a paradox of our religion to say that we are obliged to respect others' interests, at the same time as God commands us to sacrifice our own, and to say that the law of charity requires us to be attentive to whatever concerns our neighbor, after the same law requires us to renounce in mind and heart whatever concerns ourselves? . . . It was right, says Saint Ambrose, and his reflection is sound—it was right for God to establish this order among human beings, that is, for him to order us to be zealous for our neighbor's in-terests, while he obliges us to a sincere detachment from all self-interest.

Why? Because he knew, the holy doctor adds, that no matter how detached we were from our own interests, we would still be only too attentive and ardent in their behalf, and that on the contrary no matter how much zeal we had for others' interests, we would with difficulty ever have as much as the exact law of complete justice demands.[86]

This objection concedes the essential in advance, namely that the ideal to be aimed at falls short of complete self-denial or self-forgetfulness. All the rest is psychology or pedagogy.[87] And psychologically or pedagogically, too much should not be expected of a mere formula. Without love, no altruistic norm will take effect; with love, there will be no flinching. Besides, an excessive, inaccurate norm may provoke as much resistance as it obviates. Those who have found Self-Forgetfulness or Self-Denial quixotic, fantastic, or irrational[88] have not fallen back just to Self-Subordination. Overkill may bring backlash, all the way to Parity or Self-Preference.

Conclusion

The last chapter reviewed various arguments in favor of alternatives to Self-Subordination and found the arguments wanting. The present chapter has run through numerous arguments against Self-Subordination and found them, too, unconvincing. From this double negation it does not follow, however, that Self-Subordination wins through elimination. What can be said positively in its favor?

The intrinsic attractiveness of such a form of life, obscured by verbal formulae and complex debates, appears in those who practice it. In particular, the figure of Jesus, the man for others, has virtually universal appeal. Yet I have never seen or heard it suggested that he followed any less altruistic norm than Self-Subordination. On the other hand, details like his presence at Cana, his producing large quantities of first-rate wine, or his prayer in the garden (see chapter 4) are rarely held against him. Thus the widespread acceptance of Jesus as the gospels portray him amounts to implicit acceptance of the norm of Self-Subordination.

Approved in Jesus' practice, the norm is also approved by his teaching. The mind of Christ, Christians believe, reflects the mind of God; and the New Testament reveals the mind of Christ. Hence, after ascertaining, in chapter 4, the New Testament's apparent verdict favoring Self-Subordination, in the last two chapters I have followed a procedure similar to J. Philip Wogaman's "methodological presumption." This he characterizes as

the method of arriving at a judgment despite uncertainties by making an initial presumption of the superiority of one set of conclusions and then testing that presumption by examining contradictory evidence. If, after examining the contradictory evidence, substantial doubt or uncertainty remains we decide the matter on the basis of the initial presumption. Methodological presumption seems peculiarly useful in approaching moral judgments in the face of continuing uncertainty. If we can establish in advance what is *probably* the best line of decision in the light of our most basic moral traditions, then we have a clear basis for proceeding—even though this method will by no means banish uncertainty altogether.[89]

The succinctness of my answers to successive critiques may have created an illusory impression of clarity and certainty. However, although non-scriptural considerations may not clearly favor Self-Subordination, they speak no more clearly, or still less evidently, in favor of rival norms. Hence Wogaman's principle applies, and a reply can now be given to this study's original query. "If Christians wish to be both consistent and true to their heritage," I asked, "what preference-rule for mine and thine should they adopt?" The answer I now propose, on the strength of New Testament evidence, is Self-Subordination. That is: "One may and should give independent consideration to one's own benefit, but only on condition that maximum benefit to others is first assured (whether directly or indirectly, through benefit to oneself)."

7

The Inquiry's Significance

"We have to find the proper compromise," writes Stace, "between absolute altruism and absolute egoism. . . . Morality, if it is to be a reality, must in some way specify the *right* point on the line for a man to occupy. A moral code which told a man only to occupy a point somewhere between the two extremes, but specified nothing further, would be like a Government department which ordered a light-ship to be anchored somewhere between New York and Southampton, but gave no further directions. In other words it would be entirely useless."[1] Numerous Christian ethicians, some well known, have had so little to say with regard to love's preference-rule that their names have not appeared in this study. Many others have responded, in the varied ways we have seen, to the need Stace points out. Yet the charge of neglect made in chapter 1 still stands and has now been fully confirmed. The various Christian responses have not previously been analyzed, catalogued, and compared, as in chapter 1. The New Testament's preference among them has not been sought, as in chapter 4. Its preference has not been put to the test of subsequent Christian and non-Christian thinking, as in chapters 5 and 6. Hence previous proposals have lacked the backing which would entitle their advocates to assert: "This is the Christian norm of neighbor-love."

Such a claim can now be made for the principle of Self-Subordination. Still, what has been achieved? Is the outcome really worth all the effort? By way of initial motivation, chapter 2 argued the value of a study like the one pursued in subsequent chapters. However, only now that a result has been reached can the inquiry's significance be fully assessed. What is the value not only of *an* answer to Stace's query, but of *this* answer—Self-Subordination?

Theory and Practice

From one point of view the clarification of agape's norm looks supremely important; from another it appears worthless. The truth, I believe, lies somewhere between these extremes.

Supreme Importance

In brief summation of the favorable point of view, it may plausibly be claimed: 1) that agape is central to Christianity, 2) that the objective norm relating self and others is central to agape, and, accordingly, 3) that no question is more crucial to Christendom than the one here examined.

The first part of this *plaidoyer* should occasion little debate, for the centrality of agape to both faith and morals has been proclaimed by countless Christian writers. As Nygren notes:

> To the religious question, now stated in theocentric terms, What is God? Christianity replies with the Johannine formula: God is ἀγάπη. And to the ethical question, What is the Good, the 'Good-in-itself'? the answer is similar: The Good is ἀγάπη, and the ethical demand finds summary expression in the Commandment of Love, the commandment to love God and my neighbour.
>
> We have therefore every right to say that ἀγάπη is the centre of Christianity, the Christian fundamental motif *par excellence,* the answer to both the religious and the ethical question.[2]

The centrality of agape's objective norm is less frequently proclaimed. In Christians, in Jesus whom they imitate, and in the Father whose love he reveals, agape is attitude as well as action—loving disposition as well as loving service. And emphasis has often fallen on the attitude rather than the service.

> Since, according to Christian teaching, belief, faith and commitment precede their results in the form of behaviour, it is impossible without distortion to consider behaviour as though it were independent of these other factors, or as though it came first in importance. The aim of the Christian life is not in the first place to achieve Christian behaviour according to some discoverable pattern; its aim is union with God, from which true Christian behaviour can alone derive.[3]

Simply put, the tree is more important than its fruit, since without the tree there can be no fruit. However, without the fruit the tree cannot be known for what it is (Mt 7:16). "To be sure, the tree is also known by its *leaves*, but the fruit is still its essential mark. If, therefore, one knew by the leaves that a tree was of a certain kind but in the fruit season found that it bore no fruit—then one would know that it really was not the tree which according to the leaves it appeared to be. The recognisability of love is just like this."[4]

It is not merely that acts of love are the surest signs of love; in final analysis, love is defined in relation to behavior. "No act," it is often said, "can rightly be called good in the moral sense of the term unless it proceeds from a good motive."[5] Yet what is a good motive? A motive of self-preferring charity? Of Parity? Of Other-Preference? Of Self-Subordination? Of Self-Forgetfulness? Of Self-Denial? Such norms not only describe and guide action; they also define the attitudes and intentions of agents. A charitable person is one who is inclined to act in such-and-such a manner; a charitable intention is the intention to behave in such-and-such a way. And both times "such-and-such" describes a behavioral norm or pattern, or conduct corresponding to it. Thus, whether objectively or subjectively, "By their fruits you shall know them."

It is important to distinguish such cognitive primacy from causal, existential primacy; for often, as here, they do not coincide. In this instance, what comes first in the order of being does not come first in the order of knowledge. Hence in ethics, which aims at understanding, agape as conduct, not agape as virtue, is of prime concern. More specifically still, the relation of self and other (not, for instance, of self and God or of nearest and neediest) is of primary interest. For as was noted earlier, among the questions treated in the "order of charity" the two which are at the same time most practically significant and most theoretically obscure are the question concerning self and others and the question concerning nearest and neediest; and the first of these two has still more constant application than the second.

In vindication, then, it might be said that from the viewpoint of knowledge and the desire to understand, this inquiry has focused on the most important single question concerning the most important single aspect of Christianity. Agape-love is rightly described, in Nygren's words, as "the centre of Christianity, the Christian fundamental motif *par excellence.*" And the aspect of agape-love most in need of clarification is the relation it stipulates between self and others.

Minimal Importance

From a practical perspective, however, such an inquiry may appear to have little or no importance. "All the while we speculate about these things, people out there in our society are hurting. The important question is whether we are doing justice, whether and how we are involved in helping suffering and oppressed people. We don't have to postpone the mission to needy people until we have all our theories straight."[6] Even if we got them straight, what would that accomplish in an individualistic society in which, it has been reported, "the scale of value against which both sexes now tend to measure everything is solitary gratification."[7] Their scale of values may be wrong, and another may desperately be needed; but what are the chances that a mere formula will effect the substitution? As Massillon observed, even when higher values are acknowledged, "it is with the duty of charity as with all the other duties of the law: in general the obligation is not, even in idea, denied; but does the circumstance of its fulfilment take place? A pretext is never wanting, either to dispense with it entirely, or at least to be quit for a moiety of the duty."[8] What is needed is conversion, and mere preference-rules do not convert. "Vain is the discourse of philosophy by which no human heart is healed."[9]

It would seem that Jesus' way was more attuned to human needs. As Dodd remarks, the ethical teaching of the Gospels is "not so much detailed guidance for conduct in this or that situation, as a disclosure of the absolute standards which alone are relevant when the Kingdom of God is upon us. These standards, however, are not defined in general and abstract propositions, but in dramatic pictures of action in concrete situations; and they are intended to appeal to the conscience by way of the imagination."[10] The master forgives the staggering debt, the Samaritan cares for the man by the wayside, the father receives the prodigal with open arms, the rich man dines luxuriously and spares not a crumb for the beggar at his door. There can be little doubt about the superiority of this teaching strategy.

Besides, the great divide, practically speaking, is not that which separates one version of altruism from another but that which separates altruism from egoism. Even the weakest version of altruism calls for continual sacrifice of self. Even the norm of Self-Preference can lead to deeds as heroic as that of Tom O'Brien, cited in chapter 1, or of Jesus himself, who died "that the whole nation should not perish" (Jn 11:50). Time and again, all six preference-rules concur in their verdict.

So too, for that matter, do egoism and altruism repeatedly agree when both are enlightened. Indeed it may be as Paulsen claims, that "the opposition between individual and general welfare, selfish and altruistic motives, is not the rule, but the exception. As a rule, there is harmony in the effects as well as in the motives."[11] And though the occasions on which the application of one preference-rule rather than another would make a difference may be more numerous than Paulsen's words suggest (see chapter 1), it may be felt, nonetheless, that "such exact calculations are . . . to be found only in the works of moral theorists."[12] A Vincent de

Paul or a Mother Teresa does not carefully balance pros and cons or estimate benefits to self versus benefits to others. A need is seen, the heart is moved, the loving deed is done. By comparison, a calculating attitude may seem positively pernicious. And a study that inculcates it, through careful discriminations like those in chapter 1, may appear a worse than futile enterprise.

"To speak plainly," declares Gérard Gilleman, "our treatises have systematized into a science the pulsing vitality of concrete Christian life."[13] Now it may seem that I have done the like for Christian charity. And yet, in Gilleman's words, "what Christian love finally encounters is a Person (Jn. 14:21). That is why it fosters a spirit of deep interior life rather than a mere observance of the letter of the law. . . . Our manuals of moral theology, at first glance, do not seem to be written in the same perspective. Law rather than love is their dominant theme. Where there should be a spiritual impulse, we find a fixed body of doctrine. Even inspiration and liberty are precisely codified."[14] Even Christian sympathy is now stated as a "preference-rule"!

Counterconsiderations

Such an indictment sounds impressive; yet reflection reveals its one-sidedness. Worth notice, for example, is the fact that the New Testament contains precepts as well as parables, and that most or all of the strictures just urged against Self-Subordination would apply equally to these scriptural prescriptions. A norm like the Golden Rule, or the injunction to love one's neighbor as oneself, does not effect conversion but presupposes it. Neither rule is equivalent to action. Neither precludes rationalization. Neither stops short at the elimination of pure egoism. Neither makes any difference on the many occasions when altruism's verdict agrees with that of egoism. Neither functions in the vivid, concrete way Dodd describes. Hence both are implicated in T. E. Jessop's critique: "Christian casuistry is not logical but imaginative. When we want to know what is the right thing to do in a given situation, we are not to make a rigorous deduction from a general rule, but are to frame a vivid picture of what in that situation neighborly love would do. A picture of love in action is, if right, likely to be self-evidently right, and if wrong to be self-evidently wrong; and when right, it moves as rules do not."[15]

What, then, may be said in reply, to rescue not only agapistic preference-rules but also well-known scriptural precepts from the charge of futility? First, that sharp dichotomies like Jessop's tend to be misleading, and that his is no exception. Such an account is sometimes apt, sometimes not, depending on the case in question. And other possibilities exist besides "rigorous deduction," on the one hand, and imaginative intuition, on the other. Jessop appears to have nourished his thinking with too limited a diet of examples. And even the cases that provoke remarks like his call for fuller comment.

"There can be little doubt," I remarked on one such episode, "that an uninstructed person who is yet profoundly Christian will both do and judge the good far more readily and effectively than a person who, though fully informed on the matters here discussed, is less concerned, generous, disinterested and receptive to grace."[16] However, who is "profoundly Christian"? What preference-rule has he or she interiorized? Self-Preference? Parity? Other-Preference? Self-Subordination? Self-Forgetfulness? Self-Denial? And how did it come to be assimilated? Was no such rule ever mentioned, either implicitly or explicitly? Jessop's account not only minimizes the role of rules in judging prospective behavior, but also slights—indeed ignores—their role in forming the people who, he alleges, judge with such unerring ease.

In most areas of human activity the distinction between rules known and learned and rules explicitly cited and applied is an important one. A motorist who stops on red and starts on green does not call to mind the traffic laws he knows and draw the proper conclusions; yet doubtless at an early date he or she heard the relevant rules of the road. A speaker who says "She moves" rather than "She move" may not have heard the rule of grammar that covers this case, but he or she has observed it consistently adhered to. In ethics there is no such constancy. In particular, people are not uniformly egoistic or altruistic. So the pertinent rule of neighbor-love had better be clearly stated and imparted, even if, once learned, it operates implicitly and "a picture of love in action" then appears "self-evidently right."

Let me be specific. Why does the vow of poverty, as lived by many religious, offer such weak, uncertain witness in a consumeristic society? For various reasons, no doubt. Because Self-Preference was till recently the dominant position in Catholic moral theology. Because poverty was viewed principally in an ascetical, other-worldly perspective, rather than in relation to others' needs. Because as ascetical, world-denying motivation has declined, altruistic motivation has not adequately replaced it. Because even today too few novices are told, in simple explanation of the first vow: "Charity seeks not its own." Hence, once vowed, they do not readily grasp why one might deny oneself the good things of life—the movies, the shows, the ice cream parlors, the restaurants. Indeed, the thought of such curtailment often does not occur to them. If, ideally, the poor should not be poor, why "live as poor people do"? Given the basic generosity of most religious, I believe they would live their vow more convincingly if they perceived it as a direct expression of neighbor-love. And how are they to know what neighbor-love calls for in specific detail if they do not know what it calls for in general?

I do not deny the possibility of direct intuition,[17] but intuitions are helped by good rules and hindered by bad. A person trained in a rule that commends a wrong action is less likely to see it as wrong; a person trained in a rule that condemns a good action is less likely to see it as admirable. Chapter 1 provides ready illustrations. If a proponent of Self-Preference envisaged Kolbe's self-sacrificing action, he would not see it as patently preferable. If an advocate of Parity imagined passing the life-belt as Arland Williams did, he would not recognize it straight off as the more Christian thing to do. If formed by the rule of Other-Preference, the girl would not consider it most admirable to distribute all her chocolates to her friends and keep none for herself. If taught to accept Self-Subordination but not Self-Denial as a norm, Reinhold Niebuhr would see nothing admirable in denying himself the more attractive alternative of marriage.

Furthermore, once acquired, a rule does not thereafter vanish from view; it inevitably surfaces from time to time as people deliberate or discuss moral issues. For first intuitions do not always suffice. And Christians differ with fellow Christians regarding the norms they accept, act on, and articulate, and differ still more notably with people of other traditions.

Surely, on a theme as central as neighbor-love, Christians should be ready to give an account of the faith that is theirs, whether to fellow believers or to nonbelievers. This is a further advantage of a study like the present one. No clear or convincing answer can be given to the numerous, varied criticisms of the Christian position unless and until that position is more clearly determined. Objections that hold against one formulation do not hold against another. Arguments that favor one formulation do not favor another. So long as six variants remain in contention, Christians cannot effectively defend or urge the norm of fraternal charity, which they recognize as central to their faith and to their lives.

A still more evident reason for fuller investigation is that Christians themselves may err on this crucial issue. Indeed, so long as all six preference-rules have Christian advocates, five factions out of six are in error. What is more, given the wide spectrum of opinion covered by the rules, the error of some positions must be notable. In such a situation, mere "intuition" does not suffice; the evidence and arguments cited by various parties must be surveyed and assessed. This has now been done.

Social Significance

"In the New Testament," as Jessop remarks, "the primary interest is in personal relations, in individuals; Christian love is for one's 'neighbour,' a term which in the parable of the Good Samaritan is widened to mean anybody who is within our direct reach and whom we can therefore directly serve."[18] This emphasis has continued. "More often perhaps, Christianity has exalted the sphere of morality that is concerned with personal relationships; for the Christian emphasis on love is more at home in this sphere than in the more public, impersonal realm of civic duty."[19] Within the realm of personal relationships, the specification of agape's norm has great theoretical and considerable practical significance; within "the more public, impersonal realm," the norm's relevance is less apparent. Still, it seems evident that agape has more than purely personal significance. "If every time the Good Samaritan went down that road from Jerusalem to Jericho," Stephen Mott observes, "he found people wounded and did nothing about the bandits, would his love be perfect? Spontaneous, simple love, following the dictates of its own concern for persons in need, grows into a concern for the formal structure of society. It expands from attention to single individuals to the interaction of groups with which the individuals are caught up."[20] Thus, "the fact that the love taught by Jesus is not politically and socially motivated does not mean that important political and social results cannot be and have not been derived from it."[21] Illustrations of love's larger relevance—economic, social, and political, in the present and in the past—abound. To cite a striking instance from the last century,

> The slave-holding oligarchy which ruled the South before the War numbered only about ten thousand men. But to protect their private interest in an immoral source of profit, they forced an outgrown and inefficient form of labor on their communities, kept the poor whites in poverty, retarded the industrial development of the South by one generation or more, muzzled and perverted the social conscience of their people, and were willing permanently to disrupt the Union.[22]

Reflection suggests that any serious problem of society—crime, crowding, corruption, poverty, drugs, illiteracy, racism, war, oppression, inadequate health care—has roots in the selfishness of individuals. Consider, for instance, the effect of self-seeking on public finance. "The town, the city, the state, the nation are the most inclusive organizations for the common good, offering every citizen a thousand forms of protection and service. The problem for our selfishness then is, how to contribute as little in the way of taxes and service to the community, and how to get as many benefits from it as possible—especially somewhat more than our neighbor is getting."[23] Each person looks out for himself. In concrete illustration:

> Different residents of New York City had different attitudes toward whether to build a bridge connecting Brooklyn with Staten Island. The homeowners who would have had to find new places to live were vehemently against building the bridge. The people who lived on Staten Island, as well as those who wanted to live there but could not because ferry service was too slow, were strongly in favor of the bridge. Motorists in general were in favor of it, as were those who commuted back and forth. Taxpayers who were not

likely to want to go to Staten Island but who would have had to pay increased taxes for the bridge were against it.[24]

The same narrow self-interest explains why teachers are underpaid, roads
and bridges are not repaired, toxic dumps are not cleared, pollution is not
curbed, struggling nations are not assisted.

And yet the relevance of personal ethics for the social sphere has
often been contested.[25] "Together with the subjectively enthusiastic nature of ethics," Albert Schweitzer observes, "goes the fact that it is impossible to succeed in developing the ethic of ethical personality into a serv-
iceable ethic of society. It seems so obvious, that from right individual
ethics right social ethics should result, the one system continuing itself
into the other like a town into its suburbs. In reality, however, they cannot
be so built that the streets of the one continue into those of the other. The
plans of each are drawn on principles which take no account of that."[26]

Schweitzer supports his claim as follows: "When the individual is
faced with the alternative of having to sacrifice in some way or other the
happiness or the existence of another, or else to bear the loss himself, he
is in a position to obey the demands of ethics and to choose the latter. But
society, thinking impersonally and pursuing its aims impersonally, does
not allow the same weight to consideration for the happiness or existence
of an individual. In principle humaneness is not an item in its ethics."[27]
This is puzzling. Does not society consist of individuals? Are not social
decisions the decisions of individuals? And should not their decisions be
humane? Schweitzer's meaning may appear if we consider the prominence of impersonal justice, rather than personal charity, in social
morality.

Justice versus Self-Subordination

"Justice," writes John Rawls, "is the first virtue of social institutions,
as truth is of systems of thought."[28] And justice differs from charity or Self-
Subordination.[29] Person may yield to person in private situations; that is an
individual decision. But laws and institutions do not work that way. In social dispositions—zoning, voting, licensing, loans, taxes, tariffs, subsidies,
minimum wages, old-age benefits, and the like—which decide simultaneously for many, a multitude of Alphonses and Gastons cluster at the
common legislative door. The only way to clear it and keep traffic moving,
it would seem, is to treat all equally.

This argument from sheer practicality works no better for societies
than it does for individuals (see chapter 6). Traffic does in fact move; it just
flows in a predominantly egoistic rather than an altruistic direction. Individuals and individual interest groups contend for preference (home-
owners against motorists, motorists against taxpayers, taxpayers against

residents, and so forth), and one wins while another loses. Self-Subordination might simply reverse the process. Each would strive, successfully or unsuccessfully, to have others' interests preferred. The norm itself would not unclog the legislative door, but its practitioners would keep the traffic moving, as the practitioners of egoism or self-preference currently do.

That such self-subordination seems far removed from present actualities does not invalidate it. Consider Rawls's own norm: "All social primary goods—liberty and opportunity, income and wealth, and the bases of self-respect—are to be distributed equally unless an unequal distribution of any or all of these goods is to the advantage of the least favored."[30] This prescription, too, is honored more often in the breach than in the observance, for the least favored are typically least powerful, and so cannot coerce conformity. Yet concessions are sometimes made in their behalf by the better-favored, more powerful elements in society.

Neither is the imbalance resulting from successful Self-Subordination a valid objection against it, as it would be were the imbalance involuntary. "Each person," observes Rawls, "possesses an inviolability founded on justice that even the welfare of society as a whole cannot override. For this reason justice denies that the loss of freedom for some is made right by a greater good shared by others. It does not allow that the sacrifices imposed on a few are outweighed by the larger sum of advantages enjoyed by many."[31] The key word here is *imposed.* There is no injustice when the sacrifices are not only accepted but are preferred, pursued, and achieved by those adversely affected.

A more serious objection against the extension of Self-Subordination to social determinations is the message the norm would convey to society's least favored members. "Make no effort to better your lot," it would exhort them; "give the preference to others."[32] However, it would convey the same message to all—to the rich as well as to the poor, to the powerful as well as to the weak. And the traditional Christian preference for the needy may take precedence over Self-Subordination, and suggest that the least favored give priority to the needs of their own class. Furthermore, Self-Subordination itself would often dictate that those at the bottom seek to better their lot, if only for the benefit of society as a whole.

An important ambiguity lurks in this last reply. Individual members of a least-favored class might seek, as individuals, to better the lot of their class and thereby of themselves, for the benefit of society as a whole; or a least-favored class as a whole might seek to better its lot, for the benefit of other segments of society. This second possibility, extending Self-Subordination from individual selves to social selves, has received surprisingly little attention in ethical literature, but requires consideration here, to permit full assessment of the present study's implications.

Social versus Individual Selves

"Strictly speaking," declares Lindsay Dewar, "it is meaningless to tell groups that they must 'love' one another. Love is a relationship between persons, and groups of men and women are not persons. Trade unions are not persons; nations are not persons, and, therefore, it is no good telling them that they must settle their differences by loving one another."[33] And yet, whether strict or loose or somewhere in between, talk of societies as moral selves is common. So is talk of charity between such selves, for instance between nations or states. Thus, according to Thomas Higgins, "the Natural Law commands States to exercise charity towards other States."[34] For Edgar Brightman, "there can be no doubt from the standpoint of ethical science that the relations of states to each other ought to be governed by the same moral laws as guide the conduct of the good individual."[35] Reinhold Niebuhr speaks of "national animosities" which "might be appeased if nations could hear the accusing word, 'Let him who is without sin cast the first stone.' Only a forgiving love, grounded in repentance, is adequate to heal the animosities between nations. . . . It is a very rare achievement among individuals; and the mind and heart of collective man is notoriously less imaginative than that of the individual."[36] Johannes Messner writes in like vein about varied social groupings: "Among the chief individual obligations of social charity in the society of today is that of mutual respect on the part of races, classes, and nations as members, equal in value, of the state or of the community of nations. Such respect implies readiness to promote a proportionate distribution of material and cultural welfare within the political and international community, even at some sacrifice."[37]

Given the readiness with which Christian ethicians have spoken of love and respect between various social entities, and the manner in which many have urged Other-Preference, Self-Subordination, Self-Forgetfulness, or Self-Denial as a norm for individual conduct, it is surprising that no one, to my knowledge, has proposed that any such norm be extended to societies. Indeed, the possibility is seldom considered, and when it is, is generally rejected out of hand. The reasons for this neglect and this rejection merit scrutiny.

The chief reason cited against collective other-preference, by Christians and non-Christians alike, is its alleged impossibility. According to Ahad Ha'am, a nation can never believe that its moral duty lies in self-abasement or in the renunciation of its rights for the benefit of other nations. "Hence Christian nations have not been able to regulate their relations with one another on the moral basis of their religion; national egoism has inevitably remained the sole determining force in international affairs, and patriotism, in the Bismarckian sense, has been elevated to the position of the supreme moral criterion."[38] Reinhold Niebuhr's assessment sounds similarly pessimistic. "This new life in

Christ," he writes, "represents the perfection of complete and heedless self-giving which obscures the contrary impulse of self-regard. It is a moral ideal scarcely possible for the individual and certainly not relevant to the morality of self-regarding nations."[39] "Not only a ruling class but a ruling nation, and a ruling oligarchy within a class, and the rebellious leadership of a subject class, and a functional group within a class, and a racial minority or majority within a functional group; all these and many more are bound to judge a total human problem from their own particular perspective."[40]

Despite their similar sound, Niebuhr's and Ha'am's claims differ. It is one thing to assert, with Niebuhr, that no nation has ever engaged in "complete and heedless self-giving"; it is quite another to maintain, with Ha'am, that "national egoism has inevitably remained the sole determining force in international affairs." The first claim may be accurate; the second is clearly excessive. Granted, it might be argued with some plausibility that famine aid, earthquake aid, and all forms of foreign assistance inevitably redound to the benefit of the giving nation and profit it as much as, or more than, stinginess would. But it is not plausible to maintain that egoistic calculations invariably explain such assistance. To cite a single counterinstance, John Bennett notes that in 1945 and again in 1946 the Gallup Poll showed that seventy percent of the American people were willing to go back to food rationing in order to send food to people in other countries.[41] Thus egoism is not the only alternative to complete self-denial. A range of possibilities between pure egoism and pure altruism lies open to group action as well as to individual choice. And even if it did not, altruistic group-members would still need to know what ideal they should pursue in their attempts to shape group policy. They could not simply acquiesce in collective selfishness.

This response to Ha'am's claim is reinforced by the reflection that, were collective egoism really inevitable, the "justice" or Parity he argues for would likewise be impossible. Parity's dictates, like Self-Subordination's, might sometimes coincide with those of pure self-interest as perceived by the population, and the nation might then conform to the principle's demands. But when Parity called for sacrifice, as it sometimes does, obedience would be impossible, as it allegedly is for more altruistic rules of preference. Ha'am seems unaware that really even-handed charity, treating the good of another on a par with equal good for oneself, may call for self-sacrifice as great as any required by Self-Subordination or Self-Denial (see chapter 1). Once this fact is recognized, the practical difference between Parity and Self-Subordination is seen as a matter of degree. "It is true that the higher the recognised ideal, the greater the demands it makes on those who acknowledge it, the more difficult it is to live up to its requirements, and, therefore, the less likely it is that people as a whole will do so consistently."[42] However, no individual, and a fortiori no collectivity, is likely to comply consistently with the dictates of either

Parity or Self-Subordination. Some compliance is possible, and greater can be striven for.

A second reason, implicit yet powerful, blocking the application of agape's norm to societies as well as to individuals may be the apparent conflict—or at least the unclear relation—between the two applications. Applied to a collectivity, Self-Subordination would counsel preference for other collectivities' interests; applied to the individual members of a collectivity, who make its choices, it would advise preference for the interests of others generally, including the interests of other members of the collectivity. Do these verdicts conflict? Or does the double application just result in a gradated preference: fellow-members over oneself, foreign members over fellow-members?[43]

Comparison with individual charity suggests the latter answer. Single persons have bodily members; and one member is preferred to another (foot to toe, head to foot, etc.). But member by member, Self-Subordination enjoins other-preference (better to lose one's own foot than deprive another of his, better to lose one's own head than make another lose his, etc.). However, the analogy between individual selves and social selves is stronger in some instances, weaker in others; and this complication further impedes the extension of agape's norm to societies.

For nations, the analogies with individual persons are multiple and strong.[44] Nations, too, have points of view on the world, perspectives fixed by their unique stream of experience; they, too, have hopes and fears and aspirations; they, too, may be said to take pride in their achievements, make choices, and attempt to better their lot.[45] Like individuals, they "conclude contracts, take precautions, apologize for actions, and make promises."[46] As much cannot be said, however, of all types of groups or classes—for instance of "the young, the old, the active population, unwed mothers, cadres, the middle class, and the proletariat"—though these too are termed "social units."[47] Nations themselves have only recently achieved their present functional unity, moral cohesion, and psychic dominance; a few centuries ago they offered fewer grounds for treating them as moral persons.[48]

Given this diversity, the extension of Self-Subordination to social entities may appear not only theoretically shaky but practically ominous. It may be feared that application of the norm to all sizes, stages, and varieties of social entity would result in moral chaos; altruistic preferences of varying strength and sureness would criss-cross every which way. A first response to this objection would be to point out that the situation is not simplified by switching from charity to justice: one type of relation would just replace the other. The entities related would be as numerous and varied as ever. A second, simplifying response might be that agape's norm applies to groups as well as individuals only to the extent that the groups closely resemble individuals; the resemblances must be numerous and strong.

There are those, however, who would argue that even the analogies cited for entities like nations are illusory. According to Jeremy Bentham, "the community is a fictitious *body,* composed of the individual persons who are considered as constituting as it were its *members.* The interest of the community then is, what?—the sum of the interests of the several members who compose it."[49] For Howard Harrod, "there is no such thing as a 'social mind.' The correlates of memory and projection in the social world are analogous in function but not identical in form to those that pertain to individual agents. When we speak of social past and social future, the realities to which we refer are dependent upon the continual intersubjective intending of a social world by individual agents."[50] According to Andre Donner, nations and states are mere "concepts of the mind, simple technical institutions, made for the maintenance of law and order and the defense of earthly interests."[51] They are not genuine persons, subject to moral norms.

The inadequacy of such reductive analyses has often been remarked. "There are facts about the functioning of social institutions that cannot be reduced to facts about individuals taken as isolates."[52] These irreducible facts include those most relevant for our present question. With regard to individuals, preference-rules are required because people have interests and these interests conflict. But societies, too, have interests, interests which conflict; and the interests and their conflicts cannot be reduced without remainder to those of individuals. Furthermore, as Joseph Allen notes, not only is the common good common "in the sense that it is something in which all the members share, and not merely a collection of the goods of its individual members"; it "is—or can be—common in the sense that it is the shared objective of the community's members."[53]

Ernest Gellner concedes that "individuals do have holistic concepts and often act in terms of them";[54] but he also remarks, reductively: "Take as an example a generalization such as 'The committee decided to appoint Jones.' This means, amongst other things, that each of the members of the committee came in the end to accept a certain conclusion."[55] On the contrary, this is not even one of the things such a statement signifies. Agreement, a vote, or acceptance of the vote generally need not be unanimous. Nor is a committee decision a mere summation of individual acts. Who belongs to the committee, who has active voice, what constitutes a quorum, what majority is required, for what types of questions—these and other stipulations define the committee as a social entity and determine, for example, whether a given action is a vote, a valid vote, a consultative vote, a decision. These are further facts—further relevant facts—"about the functioning of social institutions that cannot be reduced to facts about individuals taken as isolates." And they have their analogues in cities, states, churches, councils, clubs, and corporations.

Considerable grounds can therefore be found for viewing at least some social entities as moral agents, with conflicting interests to which preference-rules apply. It may still be questioned, however, whether the same rule that applies to individuals applies to societies. For a further obstacle remains to be considered. According to a traditional rule, in equal need one should give priority to one's nearest and dearest. In a conflict between the interests of members of one's own family, club, community, corporation, or nation and the interests of members of other such groups, one should favor the former. However, extend the rule of Self-Subordination to such entities as wholes, and it seems that this verdict would be reversed. Preference would go to other families, clubs, communities, corporations, or nations, and their members. The two rules would conflict.

This difficulty arises from a confusion of perspectives. Preference for one's nearest and dearest governs one's individual actions, not the actions of one's group as a group; whereas Self-Subordination, if extended to societal agents, would govern the actions of such agents, that is, the collective actions of such collective persons. It would not dictate the conduct of a mother in relation to her children or the conduct of a president in relation to the citizens of his or her country, but would suggest, for example, the preferable conduct of the whole family or country in relation to other families or countries. If a father showed preference for other children over his own or a president showed preference for the citizens of another country over those of his own, that would appear problematic, to say the least. But if a whole family or a whole country willingly placed the interests of another family or country ahead of its own, "what would that be but a new creation and resurrection from the dead?"[56] From a Christian point of view, it would be as admirable as the other-preferring conduct of individual persons, but a still greater marvel.

Competitive Individuals in a Competitive Society?

The social implications of Self-Subordination come to specially sharp focus with reflection on the competitiveness of Western society. "We compete in the marketplace for sales, jobs, and promotions. We compete in schools for admission and grades. We compete in politics for political office. We may even compete with others for a marital partner."[57] "Besides sports, the need of competition—that is, the need to take part in a struggle where each contends with others for the first place—likewise gives rise to numerous activities expressly designed to satisfy this need: card games, checkers, singing contests, beauty contests, etc. Furthermore, in a society of strongly competitive structure, the need for competition is continually solicited, indeed provoked, in a hidden manner, by all kinds of participation in social life (professional, political, etc.)."[58] There are, for example, first violins in orchestras and first chairs in school bands, inviting youngsters to concentrate harder on "being the best" than on making music for others to enjoy.[59]

Such competition may be characterized in Samuel Johnson's words as "the action of endeavouring to gain what another endeavours to gain at the same time."[60] A recent, narrower definition of competition describes it as "an attempt (according to agreed-upon rules) to get or keep any valuable thing either to the exclusion of others or in greater measure than others."[61] The attraction of competition, rule-governed or other, is explained thus by Aquinas: "The reason that human nature takes pleasure in defeating another is that it makes one appreciate one's own superiority. This is why games in which there is competition, and the possibility of winning, give the greatest pleasure; indeed, this is true of all competitive activities, in so far as they offer a hope of being victorious."[62]

Such an attitude does not clearly conflict with Parity, which indicates no preference between self and others; still less does it clash with Self-Preference. But the conflict with Self-Subordination is unmistakable. Hence the general relevance of the norm for a society pervaded by the attitude is evident. Just how relevant the norm is can be seen by examining paradigm forms of competition, for instance in sports.

Athletic competition seems the very antithesis of yielding to others the better part.[63] Altruistic participants are caught in a dilemma: if they wish to win, they wish to have for themselves what others wish for themselves; if they don't wish to win, the activity loses its point and becomes a mere charade. "Consider a boxing match. Each of the two fighters has reason to try to knock the other out and prevent the other from knocking him out, to employ his own strength and skill to best advantage and to prevent his opponent from doing so. At the same time he will agree that his opponent has similar reasons. It is evidently absurd to suggest that, in agreeing to this, he is acknowledging a justification for wanting or helping his opponent to succeed."[64]

The situation is similar in games like baseball, basketball, or football. Although some players may think more of their team than of their personal fame and success, still,

> Each team tries not only to maximize its own score, but also to hold to a minimum the score of the opposing team. Each team attempts to reduce the achievement of the other by directly interfering with it. There is only a relative standard of achievement and no objective, independent one, such as time in a race, or total crop harvested. The extent of the defeat of one team is the measure of the achievement, the victory, of the other team. This is true also of boxing or chess matches. Achievement consists mainly in defeating the opponent, more than in attaining a goal in itself worthwhile.[65]

It may be said that "in any competition in sports man is really *competing with himself.* He is *his own rival.* At least he should be."[66] Or, looking to the future, it may hopefully be surmised that "eventually, the world of sport is going to take the emphasis off winning-at-any-cost. The new direction will be toward helping athletes make personally chosen modifications in behavior; toward the joyous pursuit of esthetic experience; toward wide variety of personality types and values."[67] However, given the nature of the activities athletes engage in, such hopes and exhortations seem illusory. Michel Bouet comments in persuasive detail:

> Contrary to the view so frequently and complacently expressed, according to which "the essential is not to win but to take part," it seems that everything in sports competition contributes to arouse, develop, and excite in each competitor the desire to win. Even if, at the start, certain individuals may feel themselves only distantly concerned, the attraction is such that little by little the emulation and rivalry take hold on them and they "enter into the game." A winner must emerge. And each must wish to be the winner. The counting of points or goals as the competition progresses, the announcing of results, then the distribution of rewards, as likewise, before the contest, the preparation, the exhortations, the predictions, the bets—all combine to make of the winner and his victory the very meaning of the competitive structure. But above all it is the perpetual interaction of the protagonists during the contest that stimulates their efforts and gives rise to an unceasing psychological chain reaction. . . . Thus the competitive structure, of itself, constitutes a motivating situation for those who take part in it and necessarily reinforces and nourishes in them the desire to win. Just as a task once undertaken is a factor that inclines a person to continue and complete it, so a contest holds the competitor or player in the specific tension which it defines as a system of adversarial interactions, and inclines him to try to resolve the tension to his own advantage.[68]

This is not just theory. "Drugs and violence remain problems, but the pressure to win, even for nonprofessional teams, remains the greatest problem, in spite of numerous books and articles stressing other goals and values."[69] From the viewpoint of Self-Subordination there is a problem not only for the individual competitor but also, and especially, for the activity he takes part in. In such an endeavor, "one wins before others, over others, and at the expense of others. To win is essentially to take; it is to monopolize the place desired as well by one's opponents, and to take it from them in the very moment of their desire, since it is nothing but the realization of that desire and of the will to be the victor."[70]

The problem is similar in education, where competition, in the form of debate tournaments, spelling bees, oratorical contests, academic state fairs, and the like, is widespread. "Theoretically, at least, modern educators regard emulation as highly unethical," wrote William McGucken in 1932,

> but in practice there has hardly been a school where it has not been employed to some extent. The Jesuits frankly accepted it; they believed that

competition in school was a good preparation for competition in later life. Classes were divided into camps; the "Romans" were pitted against the "Carthaginians"; each boy had his competitor or *aemulus;* he was ever on the alert to catch his opponent. Classwork became an absorbing game; the Jesuits saw no reason why competition, altogether correct on the playing field, should be immoral in the classroom.[71]

Immoral is perhaps too strong a word. But McGucken's *plaidoyer* may be inverted. If competition is not "altogether correct" on the playing field, it is not altogether correct in the classroom.

Robert Schwickerath appeals to different comparisons:

The Greeks rewarded the conqueror in their national games with a wreath; the Romans had various crowns for citizens who in different ways had de- served well of their country. And now-a-days no one objects if a victorious general or admiral is offered a token of public recognition, in the form of a precious sword, or even a more useful object. The soldiers of our genera- tion are justly proud if their bravery is rewarded by a badge, and even the scholars of modern Europe, perhaps such as strongly denounce the cor- rupting influence of premiums in Jesuit schools, do not hesitate to accept a decoration, or the title of nobility in recognition of their labors for the ad- vance of science. Why, then, should this principle of rewarding success be so rigorously excluded from the schools?[72]

This question, and these comparisons, suggest the need for agape's norm. Schwickerath does not distinguish between competitive and noncompeti- tive rewards; Self-Subordination would. As there could be but a single vic- tor in the Greek national games, his victory meaning others' defeat, so there could be but a single victorious side in scholastic combats between "Romans" and "Carthaginians." Crowns, medals, titles, and the like, on the contrary, can go to as many citizens as deserve well of their country and to as many soldiers as distinguish themselves by their bravery. Such honors and achievements are not inherently competitive. Neither are various analogues in academe, most notably grades. If a whole class is outstanding, let the whole class get A's.

The same distinction, between competitive and noncompetitive rewards, is still more clearly called for when Schwickerath turns to Scrip- ture for support:

Does not the Divine teacher of mankind act similarly? He demands great sac- rifices and arduous exertions of man: purity, humility, meekness, patience, self-denial, but he always points also to the reward, "theirs is the kingdom of heaven," "your reward in heaven is exceedingly great." God promises also earthly blessings to those that observe his commandments: "Honor thy father and thy mother, that thou mayest be long lived upon the land which the Lord thy God will give thee." Why, then, should it be unlawful and immoral to employ rewards in the education of the young, who are not yet able to grasp the highest motives of well-doing?[73]

Such a defense suggests what a subtly pervasive influence the doctrine of Self-Preference has had. Self-Subordination would note immediately the difference between rewards and competition. People do not compete for places in heaven; longer life for one does not mean shorter life for another; the blessedness of some does not preclude the blessedness of others. Numerous forms of academic activity, on the contrary, are not only comparative, as are grades, but are intrinsically competitive, in the manner of the "Romans" and the "Carthaginians."

Garrett Hardin's critique of Peter and Brigitte Berger calls for similar comment. "What would the educational system produce," he asks,

> if we saw to it that competitive excellence was not rewarded? Suppose we should decide to eliminate individualistic competition among our medical students, permitting them to practice the virtue of "solidarity" whenever they take examinations? Suppose we create two classes of medical schools, one of which is the individualistically competitive sort we have now, and the other a noncompetitive, solidarity-serving sort in which failure is impossible. Let the graduates of the two types of schools be clearly labeled in the telephone directory and on the brass plates at their doors. ("Competitive M.D." and "Solidarity M.D." would do.) Then let sociologists choose their *personal* physicians—while the rest of us watch with keen interest![74]

By lumping together success, comparison, and competition, Hardin obscures the fact that a pass-fail system might assure competence and a comparative system of grades might certify excellence without either system's involving competition. It is only right that medical students should strive for excellence; lives will depend on their competence. It is only right that their competence should be certified to those who will seek their services. What alone is questionable, Hardin might have noted, is any system that replaces absolute achievement with relative—that incites students, for example, to hide library books which other students need, in an effort to beat them out for the top grade.

McGucken's description of scholastic rivalry as "a good preparation for competition in later life" elicits misgivings about later life, as experienced in our society, as well as about the preparation. "In various societies, such as Fiji and Kwakiutl," Albert Lauterbach observes, "people compete in giving things away rather than in acquiring them."[75] In other societies, such as one Ruth Benedict described, no one works with another and no one shares with another. ("They look upon a good garden crop as a confession of theft, for everyone is engaged in making magic to induce into his garden the productiveness of his neighbor's.")[76] Our capitalist, semi-Christian society lies somewhere between these two extremes—the egoistic and the altruistic. And it may be doubted whether the point it occupies is an entirely happy mean.

Christian criticism has focused on the profit motive as the chief failing of capitalism. "In all the operations of capitalistic industry and commerce the aim that controls and directs is not the purpose to supply human needs, but to make a profit for those who direct industry. This in itself is an irrational and unchristian adjustment of the social order, for it sets money up as the prime aim, and human life as something secondary, or as a means to secure money."[77] "Compromise is as impossible between the Church of Christ and the idolatry of wealth, which is the practical religion of capitalist societies, as it was between the Church and the State idolatry of the Roman Empire."[78]

Even humanists might concur with this critique. But from the perspective of Self-Subordination what is most problematic is not so much the fact of personal gain[79] as the fact that the gain is, and is known to be, at others' expense. The system is intrinsically competitive. Workers, managers, owners, middlemen, consumers—all compete for a larger piece of the economic pie. Companies vie with companies for markets; executives vie with executives for top positions; nations vie with nations for economic advantage. In such a system, "the simple truth is that whatever I gain, I gain at someone else's cost."[80]

To a considerable extent, this mutual exclusiveness is inevitable, given the nature of material wealth. In sports and education, benefits need not be exclusive. How high one person jumps or climbs puts no limit on how high another jumps or climbs. One person's appreciation of Mozart or Shakespeare does not diminish another's. The excellence of one person's writing, drawing, singing, or dancing is no hindrance to others' performance. In these areas, achievement may replace winning, and one's achievement is compatible with others'. But material wealth is different. If one's share is larger somebody else's is smaller. Even the elimination of profit or private property would not alter this fact of life, so long as human needs and desires continue to exceed available resources.

It might therefore appear that solutions of the kind available in other areas are not feasible in economic life. The challenge of reading Virgil in the original may replace the challenge of beating the "Romans"; the challenge of climbing Everest may replace the challenge of winning a gold medal at the Olympics; and so forth. Excitement, entertainment, and personal development may be had, without their coming at anyone else's expense. But it may appear that such substitutions cannot be contrived in economics. Hence the relevance of agape's norm may appear limited. Individuals may mend their ways and not seek to maximize profit at others' expense; but they cannot escape the fact that their profit will be at others' expense. Participants may be converted, but the system itself cannot be brought into conformity with the dictates of Self-Subordination.

Such defeatism overlooks a pertinent parallel. In other areas of endeavor, the inescapable fact is human inequality. One person can jump higher, run faster, swim farther, sing more beautifully, write more creatively, type more flawlessly than another. And each person *may* view his abilities and achievements relative to others'; his interest *may* center on surpassing others rather than on doing his best. But it need not. The social question is whether attention should be focused, institutionally, on achievement or on the better-worse relationship. In economics, the ineluctable fact is that a greater share for one person means a lesser share for someone else, somewhere else in the system. But that does not mean that a relationship of dog-eat-dog, or a corresponding attitude, is unavoidable. Institutions may emphasize competition or mimimize it; they may stimulate rivalry or mitigate it. Consumer cooperatives eliminate producer-consumer rivalry. Credit cooperatives bypass lender-borrower rivalry. Producer cooperatives, profit sharing, joint ownership, social ownership, joint management, and the like reduce worker-owner or employee-manager conflict. Communes, monasteries, and various other types of religious community have minimized all four types of competition.[81] Other experiments—the United States of America, the Common Market, the World Council of Churches—have been tried; and doubtless many others will be attempted in the future.

I am not championing any particular solution, in business, sports, education, or elsewhere; my presentation has been too one-sided for that. I am simply arguing the relevance of Self-Subordination in most areas of life, not only for individuals but also for institutions. In the balancing and trade-offs most social choices demand, Self-Subordination would suggest that the competitive aspect be taken more seriously than it generally is, even by Christians. It is often thought sufficient to cite some benefit resulting from competition, or some loss resulting from its absence; the legitimacy of competition is thereby established. If competitions are "useful promoters of efficiency,"[82] if they "provide joy and excitement and help us probe our limits and our capacities,"[83] no further justification is required. Yet similar benefits can be cited for numerous noncompetitive activities—for surfing, diving, skiing, gliding, spelunking, mountain climbing, shooting rapids. Even if they could not, it would still be necessary to ask whether the hoped-for results justify the competitive means. Of warfare, too, it could be said that, for many, it provides "joy and excitement and helps us probe our limits and our capacities."

What values are most important? Where does primacy lie? Russell Shaw, reviewing Howard Bray's *The Pillars of the Post,* draws a suggestive contrast:

> The Washington Post is a great newpaper. But what makes a newspaper great? To judge from Howard Bray's investigative account, in the case of The Post it is The New York Times. Competition. . . . Bray paints a picture of a driven institution operated by driven people. It is not in all respects a pretty

picture, and the account of the ugly 1975 strike by Post pressmen is especially painful. Putting aside the merits of the respective positions of labor and management, it appears that somewhere in the newspaper's rush for excellence a crucial element, the human element, was lost sight of. It is a fault of many contemporary institutions.[84]

Even were competition the only route to excellence, its desirability might be questioned if charity and humanity were the price exacted. I do not think that competition is in fact an indispensable means to success or that excellence must come at such a cost.[85] However, the conflict of which Shaw writes, between the "rush for excellence" and the "human element," typifies our society. Thus Frank Knight plausibly surmises:

> The competitive economic order must be partly responsible for making emulation and rivalry the outstanding quality in the character of the Western peoples who have adopted and developed it. The modern idea of enjoyment as well as of achievement has come to consist chiefly in keeping up with or getting ahead of other people in a rivalry for things about whose significance, beyond furnishing objectives for the competition itself, little question is asked. It is surely one function of ethical discussion to keep the world reminded that this is not the only possible conception of value and to point out its contrast with the religious ideals to which the Western world has continued to render lip-service—a contrast resulting in fundamental dualism in our thought and culture.[86]

Even were it true that rivalry does nine-tenths of the world's work,[87] that "competition has been, ever since the origin of Man, the spur to most serious activities,"[88] that "the most effective way of utilizing human energy is through an organized rivalry,"[89] we might still hesitate, for both intrinsic and extrinsic reasons, to have recourse to such means.[90] Some competition cannot be avoided. Not everyone can preside over the court or conduct the orchestra; not everyone can win the election or be admitted to civil service.[91] But if Self-Subordination accurately defines agape's norm, approval cannot be given to "competition as a basis for an ideal type of human relations, or as a motive to action. It fails to harmonize either with the pagan ideal of society as a community of friends or the Christian ideal of spiritual fellowship."[92]

Conclusion

Considering individual members of society, then societies as persons, then society as a whole, I have suggested that agape's authentic formulation, Self-Subordination, has social as well as personal significance. It is clear that genuine concern for others entails concern for the structures that affect them. It is clear that, other things being equal, noncompetitive structures should be preferred to competitive ones. It is somewhat less clear whether and to what extent individuals and groups should go beyond mere justice in their social dispositions and endeavors; for social groupings differ sufficiently from individual persons and are so varied that it is not immediately evident which of them, if any, should count as moral persons subject to agape's norm. Fuller light on the social implications of Self-Subordination and of agape in general can be expected from a further study investigating the relationship, not between self and neighbor, but between various categories of neighbor (children, parents, friends, etc.) and others.[93]

Yet so much is already clear, and was before I wrote, that Kierkegaard's blunt words bring a blush of recognition:

> We artful dodgers act as if we do not understand the New Testament, because we realize full well that we should have to change our way of life drastically. That is why we invented "religious education" and "christian doctrine." Another concordance, another lexicon, a few more commentaries, three other translations, because it is so difficult to understand. Yes, of course, dear God, all of us—capitalists, officials, ministers, house-owners, beggars, the whole society—we would be lost if it were not for the "scholarly doctrine"![94]

The plea in my defense might be that I have restored the New Testament message, not obscured it, and that the restoration has ecumenical significance. Catholic moralists favored Self-Preference. Protestant moralists favored Self-Denial. Self-Subordination strikes a balance between them, and accommodates the truth in both positions. Paul, it appears, would have approved such an advance—or rather, such a recovery. "This is my prayer," he wrote the Philippians (1:9), "that your love may grow ever richer and richer in knowledge and insight of every kind, and may thus bring you the gift of true discrimination."

Notes

Abbreviations:

CCSL Corpus christianorum, series latina
     (Turnhout-Paris: Brepols, 1953—)
CSEL Corpus scriptorum ecclesiasticorum latinorum
     (Vienna: Apud C. Geroldi filium, 1866—)
PG Patrologiae cursus completus, series graeca
     (Paris: Migne, 1857-1866)
PL Patrologiae cursus completus, series latina
     (Paris: Migne, 1844-1890)

Preface

1. Anders Nygren, *Agape and Eros,* trans. P. Watson (London: SPCK, 1953), 27.

Chapter 1

1. Paul H. Furfey, *The Morality Gap* (New York: Macmillan, 1969), 34.
2. Ibid., 56.
3. Rudolf Bultmann, *Theology of the New Testament,* trans. K. Grobel, vol. 1 (New York: Scribner's, 1951), 19. See idem, *Essays Philosophical and Theological* (London: SCM, 1955), 79-80.
4. St. Thomas Aquinas, *Commentum in evangelium s. Mattaei,* chap. 22, n. 4.

5. Dominic M. Prümmer, *Handbook of Moral Theology,* trans. G. Shelton (New York: P. J. Kenedy, 1957), 98.

6. Bruce C. Birch and Larry L. Rasmussen, *Bible and Ethics in the Christian Life* (Minneapolis: Augsburg, 1976), 187.

7. Jean-François Collange, *De Jésus à Paul: l'éthique du Nouveau Testament* (Geneva: Labor et Fides, 1980), 142.

8. Martin Luther, *Lectures on Romans,* trans. and ed. W. Pauck (Philadelphia: Westminster Press, 1961), 407-8.

9. Sören Kierkegaard, quoted (with approval) in Rudolf Bultmann, *Jesus and the Word,* trans. L. Smith and E. Lantero (New York: Scribner's, 1958), 115.

10. Paul Ramsey, *Basic Christian Ethics* (New York: Scribner's, 1950), 99. See Alexander of Hales, *Glossa in quatuor libros sententiarum Petri Lombardi,* book 3, dist. 29, n. 9; Petrus Pictaviensis, *Sententiarum libri quinque,* book 3, chap. 23 (PL 211, 1098).

11. John Burnaby, *Amor Dei: A Study of the Religion of St. Augustine* (London: Hodder and Stoughton, 1938), 116.

12. Aquinas, *Opusculum* 54, chap. 3.

13. Durandus a Sancto Porciano, *In Petri Lombardi sententias theologicas commentariorum libri IIII,* book 4, dist. 17, q. 6.

14. Francis Suarez, *Tractatus de charitate,* disp. 9, section 3, n. 7.

15. John Stuart Mill, *Utilitarianism,* in *Collected Works of John Stuart Mill,* vol. 10, *Essays on Ethics, Religion and Society,* ed. J. Robson (Toronto: University of Toronto Press, 1969), 218.

16. St. Justin, *Dialogue with Trypho,* chap. 93 (PG 6, 697-98).

17. Origen, *Commentary on the Song of Songs,* trans. R. Lawson (Westminster, Md.: Newman, 1957), 188.

18. St. Basil, *Homilia 7 in divites,* PG 31, 282 ("Whoever loves his neighbor as himself owns no more than his neighbor").

19. See chapter 5, or Etienne Gilson, *The Christian Philosophy of Saint Augustine,* trans. L. Lynch (New York: Random House, 1960), 137-38.

20. St. Maximus, *The Four Centuries on Charity,* trans. P. Sherwood (Westminster, Md.: Newman, 1955), 146-47, 158.

21. William of St. Thierry, *Expositio altera super cantica canticorum,* chap. 2 (PL 180, 518).

22. St. Robert Bellarmine, *Opera oratoria postuma,* ed. S. Tromp, vol. 7 (Rome: Gregorian University Press, 1946), 280.

23. Jacques Bénigne Bossuet, *Oeuvres complètes,* ed. F. Lachat, vol. 6 (Paris: Vivès, 1862), 80, 181.

24. Reinhold Niebuhr, *An Interpretation of Christian Ethics,* 4th ed. (London: SCM, 1948), 120.

25. Joachim Wiebering, *Handeln aus Glauben: Grundriss der theologischen Ethik* (Berlin: Evangelische Verlagsanstalt, 1981), 148-49.

26. Raoul Cappanéra, "Amour de soi, vertu de l'apôtre," *Nouvelle Revue Théologique* 97 (1975):609.

27. Johann Arndt, *True Christianity,* trans. P. Erb (New York: Paulist Press, 1979), 129; see also 238.

28. Boniface Wöhrmüller, *The Royal Law: Little Chapters on Charity,* trans. E. Graf (New York: Benziger, 1931), 11.

29. Peter Schineller, "The Same Love," *America* 139 (1978): 480.

30. Joseph Mausbach, *Katholische Moraltheologie,* vol. 2, *Die spezielle Moral,* part 1 (Münster: Aschendorff, 1960), 135.

31. St. Nilus, "The Tradition to the Disciples," in *A Treasury of Russian Spirituality,* ed. G. Fedotov (New York: Sheed and Ward, 1948), 92.

32. St. Leo the Great, Sermon 42, n. 2, in *A Select Library of Nicene and Post-Nicene Fathers of the Christian Church,* 2d ser., vol. 12, ed. and trans. L. Feltoe (New York: The Christian Literature Company, 1895), 156.

33. *Disputationum Roberti Bellarmini,* vol. 4, *De controversiis christianae fidei adversus hujus temporis haereticos* (Naples: J. Paravicini, 1871), 722.

34. St. Ambrose, *Duties of the Clergy,* book 3, chap. 2, n. 13, in *Nicene and Post-Nicene Fathers,* 2d ser., vol. 10, trans. H. De Romestin, 69.

35. Werner Elert, *The Christian Ethos,* trans. C. Schindler (Philadelphia: Muhlenberg, 1957), 272.

36. John P. Reeder, Jr., "Assenting to Agape," *Journal of Religion* 60 (1980): 19.

37. Karl Barth, *Ethics,* ed. D. Braun, trans. G. Bromiley (New York: Seabury, 1981), 329.

38. St. Aelred of Rivaulx, *The Mirror of Charity,* trans. G. and A. Walker (London: Mowbray, 1962), p. 15 (part 1, chap. 10).

39. Jürgen Moltmann, *The Crucified God,* trans. R. Wilson and J. Bowden (London: SCM, 1974), 230.

40. Jeanne-Lydie Goré, *La notion d'indifférence chez Fénelon et ses sources* (Paris: Presses Universitaires de France, 1956), 17.

41. Norbert J. Rigali, "Christian Ethics and Perfection," *Chicago Studies* 14 (1975): 239.

42. Gerhard Uhlhorn, *Christian Charity in the Ancient Church* (New York: Scribner's, 1883), 59.

43. St. Ambrose, *Seven Exegetical Works,* trans. M. McHugh (Washington: Catholic University Press, 1972), 138-39, 387; *Funeral Orations,* trans. L. McCauley and others (New York: Fathers of the Church, 1953), 186.

44. St. Augustine, *De civitate Dei,* book 14, chap. 28 (PL 41, 436; CSEL 40/2, 57; CCSL 48, 451).

45. St. Basil, *Concerning Baptism,* in *Ascetical Works,* trans. M. Wagner (New York: Fathers of the Church, 1950), 428.

46. The Rule of St. Benedict, chap. 72 (CSEL 75, 163).

47. St. John Chrysostom, Homily 25 on 1 Corinthians, n. 4, in *The Homilies on the First Epistle of St. Paul the Apostle to the Corinthians* (Oxford: J. Parker, 1839), 343.

48. St. Leo the Great, Letter 14, n. 12; Letter 105, n. 2; and Sermon 88, n. 4— all in *Nicene and Post-Nicene Fathers,* 2d ser., vol. 12, ed. and trans. L. Feltoe (19, 76, and 199).

49. A Kempis, *De imitatione Christi,* book 2, chap. 11.

50. St. Albert the Great, *In decem libros Ethicorum,* book 4, chap. 3, n. 13.

51. St. Bernard of Clairvaux, *On the Love of God,* trans. T. Connolly (New York: Spiritual Book Associates, 1937), 55; *The Letters of St. Bernard of Clairvaux,* trans. B. James (Chicago: Regnery, 1953), 44 (letter 12); *On the Song of Songs,* trans. and ed. a religious of C.S.M.V. (London: Mowbray, 1952), 37.

52. St. Catherine of Siena, *Dialogue,* trans. A. Thorold (Westminster, Md.: Newman, 1944), 155.

53. *Meister Eckhart: A Modern Translation,* by R. Blakney (New York: Harper, 1941), 241.

54. Hugh of St. Victor, *The Divine Love,* trans. a religious of C.S.M.V. (London: Mowbray, 1956), 10.

55. Jan Van Ruysbroeck, *The Seven Steps of the Ladder of Spiritual Love,* trans. F. Taylor (Westminster, Md.: Dacre, 1944), 40, 47.

56. See Burnaby, *Amor Dei,* 274-76.

57. Henry Suso, *The Exemplar,* ed. N. Heller, trans. M. Edward, vol. 1 (Dubuque, Iowa: Priory Press, 1962), 50.

58. Johannes Tauler, *The Inner Way,* ed. A. Hutton (London: Methuen, 1901), 26-27, 229-30, 248-49; and *The Sermons and Conferences of John Tauler,* trans. W. Elliott (Washington: Apostolic Mission House, 1910), 11-12. See C. Ernst Luthardt, *History of Christian Ethics,* vol. 1, *History of Christian Ethics before the Reformation,* trans. W. Hastie (Edinburgh: T. and T. Clark, 1889), 357.

59. William of Auvergne, *De virtutibus,* in *Opera omnia,* vol. 1 (Paris: Pralard, 1674), 137-38 (part 1, chap. 11). See Zoltan Alszeghy, *Grundformen der Liebe: Die Theorie der Gottesliebe bei dem hl. Bonaventura* (Rome: Gregorian University Press, 1946), 269.

60. *The Book of the Poor in Spirit,* ed. and trans. C. Kelley (New York: Harper, n.d.), 58, 181.

61. Bossuet, *Oeuvres,* vol. 6, 648.

62. Martin Bucer, *Instruction in Christian Love,* trans. P. Fuhrmann (Richmond: John Knox, 1952), 16, 28-30, 47-48.

63. John Calvin, *The Institutes of the Christian Religion,* book 2, chap. 8, n. 54.

64. St. Ignatius Loyola, *Spiritual Exercises,* n. 189, and *The Constitutions of the Society of Jesus,* n. 103.

65. St. John of the Cross, *The Ascent of Mount Carmel,* book 1, chap. 13; book 2, chap. 4. See Goré, *La notion d'indifférence,* 67.

66. Martin Luther: *Lectures on Romans,* 407-8; *Letters of Spiritual Counsel,* ed. and trans. T. Tappert (Philadelphia: Westminster Press, 1955), 196; *The Christian in Society,* vol. 2, ed. W. Brandt (Philadelphia: Muhlenberg, 1962), 296; *The Freedom of a Christian,* in *Luther's Works,* vol. 31, *Career of the Reformer: I,* ed. H. Grimm (Philadelphia: Muhlenberg, 1957), 365-68.

67. See Goré, *La notion d'indifférence,* 73, quoting from *Entretiens,* ed. Coste, vol. 12, 230 ff. (no further data).

68. Arndt, *True Christianity,* 31, 78, 83, 150.

69. Sylvester Birngruber, *Morals for Lay People,* trans. W. Kane (Chicago: Scepter, 1960), 125.

70. Emil Brunner, *The Divine Imperative: A Study in Christian Ethics,* trans. O. Wyon (London: Lutterworth, 1937), 189-90.

71. *Theology of the New Testament,* vol. 1, 344.

72. Catherine de Hueck Doherty, *The Gospel without Compromise* (Notre Dame: Ave Maria, 1976), 13.

73. Olivier DuRoy, *La réciprocité: Essai de morale fondamentale* (Paris: Epi, 1970), 48-49.

74. Romano Guardini, *The Virtues: On Forms of Moral Life,* trans. S. Lange (Chicago: Regnery, 1967), 127.

75. Dag Hammarskjöld, *Markings*, trans. L. Sjöberg and W. Auden (New York: Knopf, 1964), 93. See Daniel D. Williams, *The Spirit and the Forms of Love* (New York: Harper and Row, 1968), 193.

76. Carl F. H. Henry, *Christian Personal Ethics* (Grand Rapids: Eerdmans, 1957), 394-95.

77. John Knox, *The Ethic of Jesus in the Teaching of the Church* (Nashville: Abingdon, 1961), 34.

78. William E. H. Lecky, *History of European Morals from Augustus to Charlemagne*, 3d ed. (New York: Appleton, 1884), vol. 2, 9.

79. Wilhelm Lütgert, *Ethik der Liebe* (Gütersloh: C. Bertelsmann, 1938), 92.

80. Nygren, *Agape and Eros*, 217.

81. George F. Thomas, *Christian Ethics and Moral Philosophy* (New York: Scribner's, 1955), 58.

82. A rare refinement of Self-Preference does draw a sharp line when it stipulates that preference goes to oneself when benefit is equal, but that "the neighbor's greater need, even with respect to a good of the same order, takes precedence over our lesser need." (Parity agrees with the second stipulation, not with the first.) See A. Peinador, *Cursus brevior theologiae moralis*, vol. 2 (Madrid: Coculsa, 1950), 234.

83. See the answer to objection 21 in chapter 6. Compare John Hospers, *Human Conduct: An Introduction to the Problems of Ethics* (New York: Harcourt, Brace and World, 1961), 165.

84. Richard H. Schneider, "The Man Who Wouldn't Jump," *Reader's Digest,* May 1985, 95-99.

85. See, e.g., Patricia Treece, *A Man for Others* (San Francisco: Harper and Row, 1982), chaps. 15-16.

86. Alan Donagan, *The Theory of Morality* (Chicago: University of Chicago Press, 1977), 79.

87. For similar verdicts, see, e.g., John of St. Thomas, *Cursus theologicus in IIam IIae. De Caritate,* q. 64, d. 9, a. 3, nn. 5 and 24; Francisco Toledo, *In Summam Theologiae S. Thomae Aquinatis enarratio,* vol. 2 (Rome: S. Congregatio de Propaganda Fide, 1869), 186, 201; Gregorio de Valencia, *Commentariorum theologicorum tomi quatuor* (Paris: Ex Typographia Rolini Theoderici et Petri Chevalerii, 1609), vol. 3, col. 652; Rodrigo de Arriaga, *Disputationes theologicae in secundam secundae D. Thomae* (Antwerp: B. Moretus, 1649), 540; Antonio a S. Joseph, *Compendium Salmanticense,* vol. 1 (Pamplona: B. Cosculluela, 1791), 191.

88. Claire Safran, "Hero of the Frozen River," *Reader's Digest,* September 1982, 49-53.

89. Concerning these latter illustrations, involving division, it may be objected that if each piece of chocolate would produce the same amount of satisfaction in the girl and in her playmates, and if each dollar of the couple's winnings would confer as much benefit on others as on them, then Other-Preference, like Self-Subordination, would dictate that the girl give all the chocolates away and that the retired couple distribute all their winnings. True, each chocolate is divisible, given a sharp knife; and each dollar can be split into quarters, dimes, nickels, and cents. But the same objection would hold at each level of analysis. One can therefore sense where such reasoning would lead. If, for example, a person had a pie to

divide with half a dozen people, Self-Preference would forbid her taking so much as a forkful for herself. The disposition of every crumb would pose a separate decision problem, subject to the same norm as the pie, a slice, or a slice of a slice. This way of stating the objection suggests where its fallacy lies, namely in equating a decision concerning a whole with a decision concerning each of its parts, ad infinitum. Human deliberations, hence human decisions, are not superanalytic; and at whatever level such a decision is humanly posed—regarding the whole box of chocolates or a single piece, regarding the whole winnings or a single dollar, regarding the whole pie or a single slice—Other-Preference and Self-Subordination may render different verdicts.

90. Richard W. Fox, *Reinhold Niebuhr: A Biography* (New York: Pantheon, 1985), 126-27.

91. Ernst Troeltsch, *The Social Teaching of the Christian Churches,* trans. O. Wyon (New York: Macmillan, 1931), vol. 2, 1005.

92. Charles E. Harris, Jr., "Love as the Basic Moral Principle in Paul Ramsey's Ethics," *Journal of Religious Ethics* 4 (1976):240.

93. Gerard J. Budde, "Christian Charity, Now and Always: The Fathers of the Church and Almsgiving," *American Ecclesiastical Review* 85 (1931):576 and 577; St. Caesarius of Arles, *Sermons,* trans. M. Mueller, 3 vols. (New York: Fathers of the Church, 1956-73), vol. 1, 80; St. Paschasius Radbertus, *De fide, spe et charitate,* book 3, chap. 9 (PL 120, 1475).

94. St. Caesarius of Arles, *Sermons* 74 and 75.

95. Julianus Pomerius, *The Contemplative Life,* trans. M. Suelzer (Westminster, Md.: Newman, 1947), 137.

96. Budde, "Christian Charity," 577-78.

97. "Caeterum Viva, Tamburinius, Mazzotta et Roncaglia, cum communiori, censent, satisfacere probabiliter divites, erogando in pauperes communes quinquagesimam partem suorum reditum, sive duos aureos ex centum; sed non in eadem proportione, si divitiae multum excedant" (St. Alphonsus Liguori, *Theologia moralis,* ed. L. Gaudé, vol. 1 [Rome: Vatican Press, 1905], 329). More recently, see, e.g., Heribert Jone, *Moral Theology,* trans. and adapted by U. Adelman (Westminster, Md.: Newman, 1945), 87.

98. Compare, e.g., Benedict H. Merkelbach, *Summa theologiae moralis,* vol. 1, *De principiis,* 3d ed. (Paris: Desclée, 1938), 708-10.

99. With both considerations in mind, reflect on an explanation like that of Fernando de Castro Palao, *Operis moralis* (Venice: N. Pezzana, 1702), 401: "Praemitto primo triplicem esse proximi necessitatem, aliam extremam, aliam gravem, aliam communem. Extrema est, si proximus in probabili, & moraliter certo periculo vitae versetur, nisi illi succuras. Ad haec reduci potest periculum mutilationis membri, perpetui carceris, aut alicujus infirmitatis perpetuae: quia haec morti comparantur. . . . Gravis necessitas est, in qua proximus periculum moraliter certum subiit alicujus damni, tum in corpore, tum in honore, tum in pecunia; a quo tamen nisi adjuvetur, se liberare non potest. Communis necessitas est, quam pauperes communiter patiuntur, cuique non possunt succurrere, nisi cum magna difficultate, & extraordinaria diligentia."

100. "Est advertendum," writes Castro Palao (ibid.), "necessaria ad statum non spectanda esse, praecipue ex praesenti conditione; sed ex ea, quae probabiliter futura est."

101. Ronald J. Sider, *Rich Christians in an Age of Hunger: A Biblical Study* (London: Hodder and Stoughton, 1977), 150.

102. Ibid.

103. Charles E. Harris, Jr., "Can Agape be Universalized?," *Journal of Religious Ethics* 6 (1978):23-24.

104. Reinhold Niebuhr, "Love and Law in Protestantism and Catholicism," *Journal of Religious Thought* 9 (1951-52):102.

105. St. Bonaventure, *Opera Omnia,* vol. 9 (Quaracchi: Ex Typographia Collegii S. Bonaventurae, 1901), 467.

106. Troeltsch, *Social Teaching,* vol. 1, 59.

107. L. Malevez, "Amour païen, amour chrétien," *Nouvelle Revue Théologique* 64 (1937):947.

108. Newman Smyth, *Christian Ethics* (New York: Scribner's, 1892), 249.

109. Birger Gerhardsson, *The Ethos of the Bible,* trans. S. Westerholm (Philadelphia: Fortress, 1981), 101.

110. David N. Freedman, "The Hebrew Old Testament and the Ministry Today. An Exegetical Study of Leviticus 19:18b," *Pittsburgh Perspective* 5 (1964), no. 1:13-14.

111. In *Faith and Ethics: Recent Roman Catholicism* (Washington: Georgetown University Press, 1985), Vincent MacNamara mentions the little attention paid to the related "problem of self-love" (p. 169) and cites a sampling of possible views (pp. 244-45), of which a couple can be identified with positions in my more unified listing of six. The similar but shorter listing in Garth L. Hallett, *Reason and Right* (Notre Dame: University of Notre Dame Press, 1984), 139-42, which includes pure egoism, is not proposed as a summary of Christian positions; and in my *Christian Moral Reasoning: An Analytic Guide* (Notre Dame: University of Notre Dame Press, 1983), 149-50, the four alternatives I distinguish are not all identified as having in fact been adopted by Christians.

Chapter 2

1. Pages 148-51.

2. Donagan, in *The Theory of Morality,* came closest. For a protracted comparison between his treatment and mine, backing and clarifying the present claim, see Garth L. Hallett, "Christian Norms of Morality," in *The Philosophical Assessment of Theology: Essays in Honour of Frederick C. Copleston,* ed. Gerard Hughes (London: Search Press, and Washington: Georgetown University Press, 1987), 187-209.

3. Nygren, *Agape and Eros,* 27.

4. J. Krishnamurti, *Commentaries on Living,* ed. D. Rajagopal (Wheaton, Ill.: Theosophical Publishing House, 1956), 16. Albert Schweitzer writes: "In the history of ethics there is downright fear of what cannot be subjected to rules and regulations. Again and again thinkers have undertaken to define altruism in such a way that it remains rational. This, however, is never done except at the cost of the naturalness and living quality of ethics" ("He That Loses His Life Shall Find It," in *Moral Principles of Action: Man's Ethical Imperative,* ed. R. Anshen [New York: Harper and Brothers, 1952], 678).

5. Jean Baptiste Massillon, "On Charity," in *20 Centuries of Great Preaching,* ed. C. Fant, Jr., and W. Pinson, Jr. (Waco, Tex.: Word Books, 1971), vol. 2, *Luther to Massillon,* 425. See Robert Johann, *The Meaning of Love: An Essay towards a Metaphysics of Intersubjectivity* (Westminster, Md.: Newman, 1959), 7.

6. Francis J. Sheed, *Theology and Sanity* (New York: Sheed and Ward, 1946), 9.

7. Ibid.

8. "Dilige, et quod vis fac" (*In epistolam Joannis,* tract. 7, chap. 4 [PL 35, 2033]).

9. Caesarius of Arles, *Sermons,* vol. 1, 145.

10. John A. T. Robinson, *Honest to God* (Philadelphia: Westminster Press, 1963), 115. See DuRoy, *La réciprocité,* 178.

11. See the quotations from Furfey and Bultmann at the start of chapter 1, and, e.g., William K. Frankena, "The Ethics of Love Conceived as an Ethics of Virtue," *Journal of Religious Ethics* 1 (Fall 1973):32; L. H. Marshall, *The Challenge of New Testament Ethics* (London: Macmillan, 1966), 67, 105. Donald Evans suggests reasons for the mistaken notion of agape as "a self-sufficient faculty by which a man rightly perceives what he ought to do." See "Does Religious Faith Conflict with Moral Freedom?" in *Religion and Morality: A Collection of Essays,* ed. G. Outka and J. Reeder, Jr. (Garden City, N.Y.: Doubleday, 1973), 371.

12. R. S. Downie and Elizabeth Telfer, *Respect for Persons* (London: Allen and Unwin, 1969), 63. See W. Norman Pittenger, *Love Looks Deep* (London: Mowbray, 1969), 17-18.

13. St. Bernard, source not traceable.

14. Bernard Häring, *Free and Faithful in Christ: Moral Theology for Priests and Laity,* vol. 2 (New York: Seabury, 1979), 469-70. See Mt 5:38-42 and a striking passage to the same effect in Denis the Carthusian, *Commentaria in tertium librum Sententiarum* (Tournai: Typis Cartusiae S. M. de Pratis, 1904), dist. 29, q. 1.

15. George H. Tavard, *A Way of Love* (Maryknoll, N.Y.: Orbis, 1977), 57.

16. Rufus Jones, "The Two Loves—Agape and Eros," in *20 Centuries of Great Preaching,* ed. Fant and Pinson, vol. 7, *Watson [Maclaren] to Rufus Jones,* 313.

17. Otto A. Piper, *Christian Ethics* (London: Nelson, 1970), 219.

18. Louis Colin, *Love One Another,* trans. F. Murphy (Westminster, Md.: Newman, 1960), 52 and 91.

19. Smyth, *Christian Ethics,* 227.

20. Ibid., 229.

21. George H. Palmer, *Altruism: Its Nature and Varieties* (New York: Scribner's, 1919), 100.

22. Furfey, *The Morality Gap,* 55-56.

23. Anthony Quinton, *Utilitarian Ethics* (London: Macmillan, 1973), 11.

24. Ibid.

25. St. Gregory Nazianzen, *Funeral Orations,* trans. L. McCauley and others (New York: Fathers of the Church, 1953), 58-59.

26. Augustine, *De moribus ecclesiae catholicae,* book 1, chap. 20 (PL 32, 1327).

27. Oliver O'Donovan, *The Problem of Self-Love in St. Augustine* (New Haven: Yale University Press, 1980), 112.

28. St. Anthony the Great, on Saintly Life, in *Early Fathers from the Philokalia* (London: Faber and Faber, 1954), 26.

29. Pomerius, *The Contemplative Life,* 77.

30. Peter Knauer, "La détermination du bien et du mal moral par le principe du double effet," *Nouvelle Revue Théologique* 87 (1965):367.

31. Bernard Häring, *What Does Christ Want?,* trans. A. Wimmer (New York: Alba House, 1968), 35.

32. Nygren, *Agape and Eros,* 683. See Michael Harper, *The Love Affair* (Grand Rapids: Eerdmans, 1982), 192 (citing Irenaeus).

33. The 32d General Congregation of the Society of Jesus, "Union of Minds and Hearts," n. 26, in *Documents of the 31st and 32nd General Congregations of the Society of Jesus* (St. Louis: Institute of Jesuit Sources, 1977), 476. See Heinz-Dietrich Wendland, *Ethik des Neuen Testaments: Eine Einführung* (Göttingen: Vandenhoeck & Ruprecht, 1970), 14; Sören Kierkegaard, *Works of Love,* trans. H. and E. Hong (New York: Harper, 1962), 247; L.-E. Bautain, *Philosophie morale,* vol. 1 (Paris: Dezobry, E. Magdeleine, 1842), 418-19, 424; Gaston Rotureau, *Amour de Dieu et amour des hommes* (Tournai: Desclée, 1958), 103, 112.

34. "Die evangelische caritas . . . ist von Anfang ihres Erscheinens an un-ethisch, denn nicht die Handlungen des Menschen untereinander sind hier als Wertmassstäbe gedacht, sondern Gott und göttliches Handeln sind der Ausgangspunkt dieser Liebe. Göttliches Handeln aber kann vom Menschen aus stets nur paradox verstanden werden" (Maria Fuerth, *Caritas und Humanitas: Zur Form und Wandlung des christlichen Liebesgedankens* [Stuttgart: Frommann, 1933], 119).

35. In addition to the authors cited above, see, e.g., John Burnaby, "Love," in *Dictionary of Christian Ethics,* ed. J. Macquarrie (Philadelphia: Westminster Press, 1967), 198; Louis Bourdaloue, *Oeuvres complètes,* vol. 6, 3d ed. (Paris: Berche & Tralin, 1878), 566-69; St. Francis de Sales, *Oeuvres complètes,* vol. 5, 5th ed. (Paris: L. Vivès, 1875), 293; J. D. Jones, *The Greatest of These: Addresses on the Thirteenth Chapter of First Corinthians* (New York: George H. Doran, 1925), 122; C. Spicq, *Agapè dans le Nouveau Testament,* 3 vols. (Paris: Gabalda, 1958-60), vol. 1, 282-84, 310, 314; Thomas Barrosse, "The Unity of the Two Charities in Greek Patristic Exegesis," *Theological Studies* 15 (1954):388; Henry W. Clark, *The Christian Method of Ethics* (New York: Fleming H. Revell, 1908), 175-76; Herbert Preisker, *Die urchristliche Botschaft von der Liebe Gottes* (Giessen: A. Töpelmann, 1930), 50; Edward P. Cronan, *The Dignity of the Human Person* (New York: Philosophical Library, 1955), 118-22; Thomas, *Christian Ethics and Moral Philosophy,* 50; William Lillie, *Studies in New Testament Ethics* (Philadelphia: Westminster Press, 1963), 163-64; Victor P. Furnish, *The Love Command in the New Testament* (Nashville: Abingdon, 1972), 157-58 ("As in the Fourth Gospel, the point is not just that brotherly love should be 'like' the divine love. Rather, the love expressed among men is to be the extension, the completion—the 'perfection'—of God's own love").

36. Joseph Butler, sermon on human nature, in *Christian Ethics,* ed. W. Beach and H. Niebuhr (New York: Ronald, 1955), 335-36. See Gene Outka, *Agape: An Ethical Analysis* (New Haven: Yale University Press, 1972), 73-74.

37. Butler, sermon on human nature, 338.

38. Joseph Butler, *Works,* 2 vols. (Oxford: Oxford University Press, 1849-1850), vol. 2, 31-32.

39. A. C. Ewing, *Ethics* (New York: Macmillan, 1953), 38.

40. André Godin, "'Le Primat de la Charité': Psychological and Educa-

tional Considerations on a Book by Rev. Fr. G. Gilleman, S.J.," *Lumen Vitae* 9 (1954):579.

41. Ibid., 580.

42. F. X. Hürth, "Hodierna conscientiae christianae problemata metaphysica, psycologica, theologica," *Periodica* 42 (1953):244.

43. Frankena, "The Ethics of Love," 22.

44. See Hallett, *Christian Moral Reasoning,* chap. 2 and 88-90.

45. Anthony Kosnik et al., *Human Sexuality: New Directions in American Catholic Thought* (New York: Paulist Press, 1977), 89.

46. Joel J. Kupperman, *The Foundations of Morality* (London: Allen and Unwin, 1983), 147.

47. Ibid., 147-48.

48. Book 1, chap. 1.

49. Karl Barth, *Church Dogmatics,* 4/2: *The Doctrine of Reconciliation,* trans. G. Bromiley (Edinburgh: T. and T. Clark, 1958), 831.

50. Franz Keller, *Caritaswissenschaft* (Freiburg im Breisgau: Herder, 1925), 64.

51. Quoted in Frankena, "The Ethics of Love," 22.

52. John R. Sheets, "The Scriptural Notion of Service," *Worship* 42 (1968):280.

53. Hallett, *Christian Moral Reasoning,* 128-33.

54. Spicq, *Agapè dans le Nouveau Testament,* vol. 1, 310.

Chapter 3

1. Joseph H. Deibert, "Thou Shalt Love Thy Neighbor as Thyself," *Lutheran Quarterly* 13 (1961):67. See Norman L. Geisler, *Ethics: Alternatives and Issues* (Grand Rapids: Zondervan, 1971), 155.

2. Hallett, *Christian Moral Reasoning,* 76.

3. See ibid., 75-78.

4. William Law, *A Serious Call to a Devout and Holy Life* (London: Romsey, 1816), 93.

5. Kurt Baier, *The Moral Point of View: A Rational Basis of Ethics* (Ithaca, N.Y.: Cornell University Press, 1958), 203-4.

6. If this contrast sounds confusing, consider countless parallels: A realtor needs to consider whether a property is large or small, or how much larger or smaller it is than another and by how much, but has no need of any abstract definition defining large and small; a doctor needs to know whether the patient's discomfort is great or slight but not where the border lies between "great" and "slight"; etc. The unimportance of the counsel-precept distinction has been obscured by its being confused with the question of universality: what holds universally has been seen as a matter of precept; what does not has been seen as a matter of counsel. See, e.g., Keller, *Caritaswissenschaft,* 62-63.

7. Jone, *Moral Theology,* 87. On this traditional estimate of 2%, see Liguori in note 97 of chapter 1.

8. For a *reductio ad absurdum* of such thinking, see the tables of percentages for various incomes and family sizes, in Arthur Vermeersch, *Theologiae moralis principia, responsa, consilia,* vol. 2, 3d ed. (Rome: Gregorian University

Press, 1945), 71; reproduced in Antonio M. Arregui, *Summarium theologiae moralis,* 18th ed. (Bilbao: El Mensajero del Corazón de Jesús, 1948), 87. It has been suggested to me that "Jone is really suggesting that we say something like this: 'In general I'm sure that (other things being equal) if you don't give *at least* 2% you are probably seriously sinning. How much more you are obliged to give, I'm not in a position to say'." This would be more reasonable, but it does not square with the quotation just given, nor with many another that might be cited.

9. Compare Francis J. Connell, *Outlines of Moral Theology,* 2d ed. (Milwaukee: Bruce, 1958), 91 ("As regards those in common necessity the rule is that those who have superfluous wealth must give the poor some portion of this wealth. It is difficult to lay down a definite rule as to the amount that must be given, but it would seem that ordinarily about 5 per cent or 7 per cent of a person's superfluous wealth would suffice, as far as the strict *obligation* of charity is concerned"); Eusebius Amort, *Ethica christiana* (Augsburg: Veith, 1758), 326 (a *seventh* of one's superfluity should be given to the poor); Caesarius of Arles, quoted in Johannes Walterscheid, *Das grösste Gebot des Evangeliums* (Cologne: J. P. Bachem, 1941), 53 (*all* of one's superfluity should go to the poor).

10. In *Contemporary Moral Theology,* vol. 1 (Westminster, Md.: Newman, 1958), 86, John C. Ford and Gerald Kelly spoke of "Catholic morality, which distinguishes clearly between obligations imposed under pain of mortal sin or of venial sin, and those works of supererogation which are not of precept but of counsel." "Distinguishes with assurance" might have been more accurate than "distinguishes clearly." The distinction between mortal and venial sin was at least fairly clearly defined, in relation to salvation and damnation; but no justification was given, or could be, for reading the mind of the eternal Judge and declaring that anyone who transgressed this or that border (e.g., 2% of one's superfluity) would surely be damned for all eternity. For the difference between venial sin and imperfection there was not even a demarcation such as that between salvation and damnation; the border was completely nebulous.

11. For a fuller listing, see for instance Aquinas, *Summa theologica,* II-II, introduction to q. 26.

12. See Garth Hallett, "The 'Incommensurability' of Values," *Heythrop Journal* 28 (1987):373.

13. John G. Gill, "An Abstract Definition of the Good," in *Human Values and Natural Science,* ed. E. Laszlo and J. Wilbur (New York: Gordon and Breach, 1970), 227.

14. See Hallett, *Christian Moral Reasoning,* 209.

15. W. G. Maclagan, "Respect for Persons as a Moral Principle—II," *Philosophy* 35 (1960):294.

16. Palmer, *Altruism,* 77.

17. Charles V. Heris, *Spirituality of Love,* trans. D. Martin (St. Louis: Herder, 1965), 24.

18. St. Augustine, *City of God,* ed. V. Bourke (Garden City: Doubleday, 1958), 329 (book 15, chap. 5). See Caesarius of Arles, Sermon 128, 3, in *Sermons,* vol. 2, 225.

19. See the first pages of Garth L. Hallett, "The Place of Moral Values in Christian Moral Reasoning," forthcoming in *Heythrop Journal,* and idem, *Christian Moral Reasoning,* 127-28, 163-65.

20. Aquinas, *Summa theologica,* II-II, q. 26, a. 4, ad 2, repeating what is said in the body of the article. Compare Cajetan's commentary on the *Summa theologica,* in Aquinas, *Opera omnia,* vol. 8 (Rome: S. C. de Propaganda Fide, 1892), 213 ("Pro beatitudine autem et virtute cuiusque communitatis nemo debet peccando sibi nocere"); James Moffatt, *Love in the New Testament* (London: Hodder and Stoughton, 1929), 99 ("The sister in *Measure for Measure* rightly feels that she dare not sacrifice her honour for the sake of saving her brother's life; it is a hard but a true conviction at which she arrives, since love cannot be expected to do anything for others which would impair or forfeit its own worth").

21. Robert J. Ringer, *Looking out for Number One* (New York: Funk and Wagnalls, 1977), 4.

22. Garth Hallett, "'Happiness,'" *Heythrop Journal* 12 (1971):302.

23. I. M. Crombie, "Moral Principles," in *Christian Ethics and Contemporary Philosophy,* ed. I. Ramsey (New York: Macmillan, 1966), 243.

24. St. Augustine, *Soliloquies,* trans. T. Gilligan, in *Writings of Saint Augustine,* vol. 1 (New York: Cima, 1948), 369-70.

25. See C. Dyke, "The Vices of Altruism," *Ethics* 81 (1971): 249, and Henry Hazlitt, *The Foundations of Morality* (Princeton: Van Nostrand, 1964), 89-90 (quotations from Jeremy Bentham's *Deontology*).

26. Irving Stone, *The Agony and the Ecstasy: A Novel of Michelangelo* (Garden City, N.Y.: Doubleday, 1961), 387.

27. Ibid., 389.

28. Kierkegaard, *Works of Love,* 36.

29. See Nicholas Rescher, *Unselfishness: The Role of the Vicarious Affects in Moral Philosophy and Social Theory* (Pittsburgh: University of Pittsburgh Press, 1975), 16.

30. Barth, *The Doctrine of Reconciliation,* 821.

31. Richard Völkl, *Die Selbstliebe in der heiligen Schrift und bei Thomas von Aquin* (Munich: Karl Zink, 1956), 84.

32. Albert Decourtray, "Renoncement et amour de soi selon saint Paul," *Nouvelle Revue Théologique* 74 (1952):21-22.

33. Frank C. Sharp, *Ethics* (New York: Century, 1928), 477.

34. Milton Mayeroff, *On Caring* (New York: Harper, 1971), 22.

35. See Butler, Sermon 11, in *Works,* vol. 2.

36. Henry Sidgwick, *The Methods of Ethics,* 7th ed. (New York: Macmillan, 1907), xix.

37. Quoted by Sidgwick, ibid., xx.

38. Hallett, *Christian Moral Reasoning,* 45.

39. Ibid.

Chapter 4

1. James A. Fischer, "Ethics and Wisdom," *Catholic Biblical Quarterly* 40 (1978):295.

2. See Ian Henderson, "Self-Love," in *Dictionary of Christian Ethics,* ed. Macquarrie, 315: "One wonders if [Butler's] enthusiasm for cool self-love is compatible with the kind of reckless behavior which is sometimes praised in the Bible. The three valiant men (II Sam. 23.13-17) who fetched the water of Bethlehem for

14

King David were obviously little concerned for their expectation of life. Nor was the widow (Mark 12.42-44) who put her last coin into the collection plate paying much heed to her calory intake."

3. Gérard Gilleman, *The Primacy of Charity in Moral Theology,* trans. W. Ryan and A. Vachon (Westminster: Newman, 1959), 206-7.

4. Bucer, *Instruction in Christian Love,* 30-31.

5. Mt 19:19; 22:39; Mk 12:31,33; Lk 10:27; Rom 13:19; Gal 5:14; Jas 2:8.

6. Aquinas, *Summa theologica,* II-II, q. 26, a. 4. See ibid., q. 44, a. 8, ad 2; *Commentum in evangelium s. Mattaei,* chap. 22, n. 4.

7. Luther, *Lectures on Romans,* 407-8.

8. See, e.g., Christoph Burchard, "Das doppelte Liebesgebot in der frühen christlichen Überlieferung," in *Der Ruf Jesu und die Antwort der Gemeinde,* ed. E. Lohse (Göttingen: Vandenhoeck & Ruprecht, 1970), 57; Albert C. Knudson, *The Principles of Christian Ethics* (New York: Abingdon-Cokesbury, 1943), 127.

9. Völkl, *Selbstliebe,* 105-6.

10. On this obscure text, see Lyder Brun, *Segen und Flucht im Urchristentum* (Oslo: Jacob Dybwad, 1932), 106-8. James Moffatt, *The First Epistle of Paul to the Corinthians* (New York: Harper, n.d.), suggests: "'*Expel* him, as I have in due form done already. Realize that this is a sin, and make him realize it also, for your own sake as well as for his'." "The church must be concerned for its own purity as an instrument dedicated to the service of God in the world" (*The Interpreter's Bible,* vol. 10 [Nashville, Tenn.: Abingdon, 1953], 353-54). Compare 2 Cor 2:6-8.

11. "So long as such a one is permitted to remain among them he imperils the life and witness of the church. The responsibility for his moral lapses cannot be confined to himself: they will bring the entire church into disrepute" (*The Interpreter's Bible,* vol. 10, 61). See Maurice Goguel, *The Primitive Church,* trans. H. Snape (New York: Macmillan, 1964), 233-35; C. K. Barrett, *A Commentary on the First Epistle to the Corinthians* (New York: Harper and Row, 1968), 127, 132; Gordon D. Fee, *The First Epistle to the Corinthians* (Grand Rapids: Eerdmans, 1987), 209-14.

12. Compare the critical view of *The Interpreter's Bible,* vol. 7, 473, with that of Philip A. Micklem, *St Matthew* (London: Methuen, 1917), 182 ("The passage . . . deals not with the forgiving temper, which is presupposed throughout, but with the course to be taken to win the offender to repentance").

13. Paul E. Johnson, *Christian Love* (New York: Abingdon-Cokesbury, 1951), 39.

14. "Many commentators," writes Freedman ("The Hebrew Old Testament," 13), "seem to regard it as equivalent to an adverb of degree, thus limiting the force to the verb, as, e.g.: 'You shall love your fellow-man as much as you love yourself." See Edward A. Westermarck, *Christianity and Morals* (London: Kegan Paul, 1939), 73 ("No such right to prefer one's own lesser good to the greater good of another is recognised in the precept 'Thou shalt love thy neighbour as thyself'"); Barrosse, "Unity of the Two Charities," 367 ("The Law commands love of neighbor 'as thyself'; Christ loved us 'more than Himself'").

15. Aelred of Rievaulx, *The Mirror of Charity,* 133.

16. Aquinas, *Summa theologica,* II-II, q. 44, a. 7 (translation from Blackfriars edition, vol. 35, trans. T. Heath [New York: McGraw-Hill, 1972], 157). See St. Bonaventure, *In III Sententiarum,* dist. 29, art. un., q. 3, *ad* 2; Peter Lombard, *Libri iv sententiarum,* book 3, dist. 27, chap. 5, n. 192.

17. Homily 13, 2.7, in *Nicene and Post-Nicene Fathers*, 1st ser., ed. P. Schaff, vol. 9, 428 (English modernized).

18. "Recte sanctus Hieronymus in cap. 5 *ad Gal.* et Sanctus Bernardus serm. 50 *in Cantica* dicunt, idem esse *dilige proximum sicut te ipsum*, et *Matt.* 7,12: *Quaecumque vultis vobis fieri, et vos facite*; et *Tob.* 4,16: *Quod tibi non vis fieri, alteri ne feceris*" (Bellarmine, *Opera oratoria postuma*, vol. 5, 335). See Harvey K. McArthur, "Golden Rule," in *Dictionary of Christian Ethics*, ed. Macquarrie, 137.

19. Ibid. See DuRoy, *La réciprocité*, 32.

20. Donagan, *The Theory of Morality*, 59. See Sidgwick, *The Methods of Ethics*, 379-80.

21. Karl Schelkle, *The Second Epistle to the Corinthians*, trans. K. Smyth (New York: Herder and Herder, 1969), 126.

22. Otto Kuss, *Die Briefe an die Römer, Korinther und Galater* (Regensburg: Pustet, 1940), 228 ("Die 'Gleichheit' soll massgebendes Gesetz sein"); Sider, *Rich Christians*, 150.

23. Schelkle, *Second Epistle*, 126 ("But no one can or ought to be urged or compelled to do the extraordinary"); Heinz-Dietrich Wendland, *Die Briefe an die Korinther*, rev. ed. (Göttingen: Vandenhoeck & Ruprecht, 1968), 200 ("Seine Mahnung ist kein Befehl . . . , aber er möchte doch, dass ihre Liebe nicht hinter derjenigen der Mazedonier zurückstünde"). For similar hesitancy to impose the better thing, compare 1 Cor 7.

24. Compare the more familiar distinction between the viewpoint of the individual, altruistic Christian citizen and that of the Christian legislator, who cannot and should not show partiality.

25. See C. K. Barrett, *A Commentary on the Second Epistle to the Corinthians* (New York: Harper and Row, 1973), 223; Ralph P. Martin, *2 Corinthians* (Waco, Tex.: Word Books, 1986), 263-64.

26. Paul S. Rees, *The Epistles to the Philippians, Colossians, and Philemon* (Grand Rapids: Baker, 1964), 38. In like vein, see J. Hugh Michael, *The Epistle of Paul to the Philippians* (New York: Harper, n.d.), 82 ("The Apostle does not prohibit interest in one's own affairs; it is selfish preoccupation with one's own affairs that he condemns"); Suzanne Dietrich, *Toward Fullness of Life: Studies in the Letter of Paul to the Philippians* (Philadelphia: Westminster Press, 1966), 44 ("The apostle does not ask for the impossible. He does not ask one to be completely detached from one's own 'interests,' but to be concerned *also* for one's neighbor's"); Werner de Boor, *Die Briefe des Paulus an die Philipper und an die Kolosser* (Wuppertal: Brockhaus, 1957), 73 ("Paulus verlangt nicht, dass ich meine Sache vernachlässige und nur noch für andere bemüht bin. Damit würde ich der Gemeinde ja nur Schwierigkeiten machen"); Gerald F. Hawthorne, *Philippians* (Waco, Tex.: Word Books, 1983), 69 ("a third negative factor that must go . . . is a selfish looking out for one's own interests, or those of his special group, to the exclusion of the interests of others").

27. *The New English Bible*: "Look to each other's interest and not merely to your own." *The Expositor's Greek Testament*: "no party having an eye for its own interests alone but also for the rest." Kenneth S. Wuest, *Philippians in the Greek New Testament for the English Reader* (Grand Rapids: Eerdmans, 1945): "not consulting each one his own interests only, but also each one the interests of others." William Barclay, *The Letters to the Philippians Colossians and Thessalonians*, 2d

ed. (Edinburgh: Saint Andrew, 1960), 38: "Do not be always concentrating each on your own interests, but let each be equally concerned for the interests of others." Hawthorne, *Philippians*, 63: "Each of you must look to the interests of others as well as to the interests of yourselves." The Chicago *Complete Bible* straddles: "Do not take account of your own interests, but of the interests of others as well."

28. "Das von manchen Textzeugen ausgelassene και in v.4 hat nach K.L. Schmidt 'die Bedeutung einer steigernden Aussage: nicht auf uns selbst, sondern gerade auf die Mitmenschen sollen wir sehen'" (Werner Schmauch, Beiheft to Ernst Lohmeyer, *Die Briefe an die Philipper, an die Kolosser und an Philemon* [Göttingen: Vandenhoeck & Ruprecht, 1964], 19, with a reference to "Die Arbeit der ost-westlichen Theologenkonferenz in Novisad: Philipperbrief," *Theologische Blätter 8* [1929]:265-89). On this emphatic use of *kai,* see Walter Bauer, *A Greek-English Lexicon of the New Testament and Other Early Christian Literature,* ed. and trans. W. Arndt and F. Ginfrich, 2d ed. (Chicago: University of Chicago Press, 1979), 392.

29. Johannes Weiss, "Beiträge zür paulinischen Rhetorik," in *Theologische Studien,* Festschrift for B. Weiss (Göttingen: Vandenhoeck & Ruprecht, 1897), 175-77; Ernst Lohmeyer, *Die Briefe an die Philipper, an die Kolosser und an Philemon* (Göttingen: Vandenhoeck & Ruprecht, 1956), 88-89; Spicq, *Agapè dans le Nouveau Testament,* vol. 2, 263 ("Comme à l'ordinaire, la simultanéité de l'expression négative et positive de la même pensée en accentue la force").

30. "In the Greek here the *kai* in the second half of the sentence is perplexing. The edge would be taken off the argument if it were really to be translated: *also* that of the others. The note of absoluteness which was struck by the *hyperechontas* of v. 3, and which will presently sound again in a very different form, would be remarkably weakened thereby. Obviously we have again to do with that untranslatable *kai* that is meant to serve only to emphasize what follows. Then the whole forms a parallel to v. 3b and a closer definition of it" (Karl Barth, *The Epistle to the Philippians,* trans. J. Leitch [London: SCM, 1962], 57-58).

31. Edward M. Blaiklock, *From Prison in Rome: Letters to the Philippians and Philemon* (Grand Rapids: Zondervan, 1964), 26: "Let us not have each person or party pursuing private ends, but rather the advantage of others." Joseph Huby, *Saint Paul: les épitres de la captivité (Colossiens, Philémon, Ephésiens, Philippiens),* 14th ed. (Paris: Beauchesne, 1947), 302: "visant chacun non votre propre intérêt, mais bien celui des autres."

32. Spicq, *Agapè dans le Nouveau Testament,* vol. 2, 263. See Huby, *Saint Paul,* 302.

33. Paul Ewald, *Der Brief des Paulus an die Philipper* (Leipzig: A. Deichert, 1908), 100.

34. Pierre Bonnard, *L'Épitre de Saint Paul aux Philippiens* (Neuchatel: Delachaux & Niestlé, 1950), 40-41.

35. Jean-François Collange, *L'Épitre de Saint Paul aux Philippiens* (Neuchatel: Delachaux & Niestlé, 1973), 71, 74.

36. Ralph P. Martin, *Philippians* (London: Oliphants, 1976), 90.

37. Francis W. Beare, *A Commentary on the Epistle to the Philippians* (London: Black, 1959), 73.

38. George B. Caird, *Paul's Letters from Prison (Ephesians, Philippians, Colossians, Philemon)* (New York: Oxford University Press, 1976), 117-18.

39. Pat E. Harrell, *The Letter of Paul to the Philippians* (Austin, Tex.: R. B. Sweet, 1969), 86.

40. William Hendriksen, *Exposition of the Gospel According to Mark* (Grand Rapids: Baker, 1975), 414.

41. "This last saying is pregnant with meaning; the Son of Man concept, found in the Psalms, Ezekiel and Daniel, is linked with the Servant concept of Isaiah and both are here linked with the great ransom concept of Old Testament days (Ps. xlix.7). Even the *for many* is a memory of Isaiah liii.11,12" (Robert A. Cole, *The Gospel According to St. Mark* [Grand Rapids: Eerdmans, 1961], 171).

42. Ray Summers, *Commentary on Luke* (Waco, Tex.: Word Books, 1972), 279.

43. On the "several levels of symbolism" that converge in this formulation, see Pheme Perkins, *Love Commands in the New Testament* (New York: Paulist Press, 1982), 81-82.

44. See, e.g., Jacqueline Bernard, *Journey toward Freedom: The Story of Sojourner Truth* (New York: Norton, 1967), 31-61.

45. Spicq, *Agapè dans le Nouveau Testament,* vol. 1, 241. For similar readings of Mt 20:26-28, see Theodore H. Robinson, *The Gospel of Matthew* (New York: Harper, n.d.), 167; Paul Gaechter, *Das Matthäus-Evangelium* (Innsbruck: Tyrolia, 1964), 649 ("Jesus . . . fordert, dass man ganz auf die eigene Geltung verzichte und sich in den Dienst des nächsten stelle"); John P. Meier, *Matthew* (Wilmington, Del.: Glazier, 1980), 228.

46. Ernest de W. Burton, *A Critical and Exegetical Commentary on the Epistle to the Galatians* (Edinburgh: T. and T. Clark, 1921), 293.

47. George S. Duncan, *The Epistle of Paul to the Galatians* (New York: Harper, n.d.), 163.

48. See René Coste, *L'Amour qui change le monde: Théologie de la charité* (Paris: Éditions S.O.S., 1981), 62-63: "Une société inégalitaire engendre, d'un coté, ceux qui détiennent le pouvoir et se font 'servir,' et, de l'autre, ceux qui n'ont que des tâches d'exécution à remplir en tant que serviteurs (*diakonoi*) des premiers. Dans une société de type esclavagiste comme dans l'antiquité, la situation est encore pire pour les esclaves (*douloi*). Tout en préférant le premier terme, le vocabulaire du Nouveau Testament n'hésite pas à employer le second, comme nous venons de le voir, avec le dernier texte cité [Mt 20:26-27], où il est demandé à celui qui veut être 'le premier' de se faire l'"esclave' de tous. C'est qu'il voulait marquer avec force l'intensité de la disponibilité volontaire au service du prochain exigé par l'authenticité de l'amour fraternel."

49. C. H. Dodd, *Gospel and Law: The Relation of Faith and Ethics in Early Christianity* (New York: Columbia University Press, 1951), 55. See ibid., 73: "The terms 'paradox' and 'hyperbole' are often used in speaking of such precepts. If we take those terms to denote nothing more than figures of speech or rhetorical devices to give emphasis or stimulate reflection, we are not going deep enough. Jesus certainly intended His precepts to be taken seriously. I suggest that we may regard each of these precepts as indicating, in a dramatic picture of some actual situation, the *quality* and *direction* of action which shall conform to the standard set by the divine *agapé.*"

50. I. Howard Marshall, *The Gospel of Luke* (Grand Rapids: Eerdmans, 1978), 261.

51. Robert C. Tannehill, "The 'Focal Instance' as a Form of New Testament Speech: A Study of Matthew 5:39b-42," *Journal of Religion* 50 (1970):379.

52. Ibid., 380.

53. Ibid.

54. Ibid., 382.

55. Barth, *Ethics,* 329-30.

56. Meier, *Matthew,* 228 (emphasis added).

57. Compare William E. H. Lecky's statement that even in an earlier, more humane period, "the elder Cato, who may be regarded as a type of the Romans of the earlier period, speaks of slaves simply as instruments for obtaining wealth, and he encouraged masters, both by his precept and his example, to sell them as useless when aged and infirm" (*History of European Morals,* vol. 1, 301).

58. Hendriksen, *Exposition,* 414.

59. Josef Ernst, *Das Evangelium nach Markus* (Regensburg: Pustet, 1981), 309.

60. Cf. Marshall, *The Gospel of Luke,* 583; Joseph A. Fitzmyer, *The Gospel According to Luke (X-XXIV)* (Garden City, N.Y.: Doubleday, 1985), 1045.

61. Peter G. van Breemen, *Called by Name* (Denville, N.J.: Dimension Books, 1976), 37.

62. See Joseph-Marie Perrin, *Le mystère de la charité* (Bruges: Desclée de Brouwer, 1960), 73.

63. Ceslas Spicq, *L'Amour de Dieu révélé aux hommes dans les écrits de saint Jean* (Paris: Feu Nouveau, 1978), 55. Some see something further in the word *as.* See, e.g., Rudolf Bultmann, *Das Evangelium des Johannes* (Göttingen: Vandenhoeck & Ruprecht, 1957), 403.

64. Juan Mateos and Juan Barreto, *El Evangelio de Juan,* 2d ed. (Madrid: Ediciones Cristiandad, 1982), 615-16.

65. Robert E. Obach and Albert Kirk, *A Commentary on the Gospel of John* (New York: Paulist Press, 1979), 188.

66. John Marsh, *Saint John* (Philadelphia: Westminster Press, 1977), 496. For variant interpretations of the command's newness, see for instance C. K. Barrett, *The Gospel according to St. John,* 2d ed. (Philadelphia: Westminster Press, 1978), 452, or G.H.C. MacGregor, *The Gospel of John* (New York: Harper, n.d.), 283-84.

67. Furthermore, there is not perfect agreement concerning the Greek. See Spicq, *Agapè dans le Nouveau Testament,* vol. 2, 58 (a textual variant has given rise to the translation: "La charité ne s'occupe pas de ce qui ne la regarde pas").

68. E.g., The American Standard Bible: "does not seek its own." The Vulgate translation was similar, but Augustine initiated an interpretation compatible not only with Self-Subordination but even with Self-Preference: "Charitas enim, de qua scriptum est, quod non quaerat quae sua sunt (1 *Cor.* xiii, 5), sic intelligitur, quia communia propriis, non propria communibus anteponit" (*Regula ad servos Dei,* n. 8 [PL 32, 1382]; Epistle 211, n. 12 [PL 33, 963; CSEL 57, 366]). See, e.g., Aquinas, *Summa theologica,* II-II, q. 26, a. 4, *ad* 3; Bonaventure, *In III Sententiarum,* dist. 27, art. 2, q. 2, *ad* 1; dist. 29, art. un., q. 3, *ad* 1; Richardus de Mediavilla (Richard Middleton), *Super quatuor libros sententiarum,* book 3, dist. 29, q. 3; Denis the Carthusian, *Commentaria in tertium librum Sententiarum,* dist. 29, q. 1.

69. E.g., Hans Conzelmann, *1 Corinthians,* trans. J. Leitch (Philadelphia: Fortress, 1975), 224: "does not seek its own advantage."

70. E.g., "is not self-seeking" (Authorized Catholic, New American), "is never selfish" (New American, Jerusalem, American Bible Society), "does not insist on its rights" (Goodspeed), "does not insist on its own way" (Revised Standard).

71. Archibald Robertson and Alfred Plummer, *A Critical and Exegetical Commentary on the First Epistle of St. Paul to the Corinthians,* 2d ed. (Edinburgh: T. and T. Clark, 1914), 220. Cf. Barrett, *The First Epistle to the Corinthians,* 303.

72. C.E.B. Cranfield, *A Critical and Exegetical Commentary on the Epistle to the Romans,* vol. 2 (Edinburgh: T. and T. Clark, 1979), 731.

73. Éphrem Boularand, "Désintéressement," in *Dictionnaire de spiritualité,* dir. C. Baumgartner and M. Olphe-Galliard, vol. 3 (Paris: Beauchesne, 1957), col. 554. See John Haughey, *The Conspiracy of God: The Holy Spirit in Us* (New York: Doubleday, 1976), 104: "Where there was paralysis he released it, where there was withering of limbs he restored them; blindness became seeing; hunger was fed with bread; life returned where it had been lost. All of which is to say that every motion of the Spirit of Christ will be known by the fact that, like Jesus' own acts, it will bring wholeness to the human order, not diminishment."

74. See Völkl, *Selbstliebe,* 103-9, especially 105.

75. Reinhold Niebuhr, *Love and Justice,* ed. D. Robertson (New York: World, 1967), 31.

76. M. Lepin, *L'Idée du sacrifice dans la religion chrétienne* (Paris: Delhomme & Briguet, 1897), 306.

77. Ibid., quoting Jean-Jacques Olier.

78. Ibid. In like vein, see, e.g., José M. Aicardo, *Comentario a las Constituciones de la Compañia de Jesus,* vol. 2 (Madrid: Blass, 1920), 3 ("Así entendida la mortificación, es una virtud general que abarca la vida toda de perfección y consejos evangélicos opuesta a la vida de los sentidos y de los apetitos y a la vida de la carne, y de ella habló San Pablo, cuando dijo que así como el que vive la vida de la carne, morirá, así el que por la mortificación muriere a ella, vivirá").

79. Alois Stöger, "Flesh," in *Sacramentum Verbi,* ed. J. Bauer, vol. 1 (New York: Herder and Herder, 1970), 275.

80. Ibid., 276.

81. John L. McKenzie, *Dictionary of the Bible* (Milwaukee: Bruce, 1965), 282.

82. It is easier to show that according to the New Testament Christian love is to extend to non-Christians (see Leon Morris, *Testaments of Love: A Study of Love in the Bible* [Grand Rapids: Eerdmans, 1981], 207-24) than to show that it is to be identical toward all (e.g., is to follow the same preference-rule). However, no reason appears for supposing the contrary.

83. Augustine, *In psalmum 140,* n. 2 (PL 37, 1816; CCSL 40, 2027).

84. Readers of this chapter may wonder why I have not looked backward as well as forward and related the New Testament to the Old. Here, in retrospect, the reason can be clearly stated: The verdict for which the New Testament speaks fairly strongly can be discerned only faintly, if at all, in the Old Testament. The message is new. See, e.g., Ceslaus Spicq, *Agapè: Prolégomènes a une étude de théologie néo-testamentaire* (Louvain: E. Nauwelaerts/Leiden: E. J. Brill, 1955), 99-101.

Chapter 5

1. See Fernand Guimet, "Notes en marge d'un texte de Richard de Saint-Victor," *Archives d'histoire doctrinale et littéraire du moyen âge* 14 (1943-45):379-80.

2. Augustine, Sermon 368, chap. 5, n. 5 (PL 39, 1655).

3. See Augustine, *De doctrina christiana,* 1, chap. 28, n. 29 (PL 34, 30; CSEL 80, 23; CCSL 32, 22); *In psalmum* 56, n. 1 (PL 36, 661; CCSL 39, 694); *In psalmum* 137, n. 2 (PL 37, 1775; CCSL 40, 1979); Sermon 332, n. 3 (PL 38, 1462); *De disciplina christiana,* chap. 3 (PL 40, 670-71; CCSL 46, 209-10); *De civitate Dei,* book 14, chap. 28 (PL 41, 436; CSEL 40/2, 57; CCSL 48, 451); *De trinitate,* book 8, chap. 8 (PL 42, 959; CCSL 50, 289). "The hen, who becomes weak for the sake of her young, is full of this charity. . . . We, possessing charity for our portion, importune the Lord in regard to our brother just as that man did against his brother; but we do not use the same plea. He said: 'Master, tell my brother to divide the inheritance with me.' We say: 'Master, tell my brother that he may have my inheritance'" (*Sermons on the Liturgical Seasons,* trans. M. Muldowney [New York: Fathers of the Church, 1959], 418-19). Compare Augustine, *Commentary on the Lord's Sermon on the Mount, with Seventeen Related Sermons,* trans. D. Kavanagh (New York: Fathers of the Church, 1951), 84-86; Burnaby, *Amor Dei,* 116.

4. St. Augustine, *Christian Doctrine,* trans. J. Shaw, in *Nicene and Post-Nicene Fathers,* 1st ser., vol. 2, 528 (book 1, chap. 23, n. 22).

5. "And if God is to be loved more than any man, each man ought to love God more than himself. Likewise we ought to love another man better than our own body, because all things are to be loved in reference to God, and another man can have fellowship with us in the enjoyment of God, whereas our body cannot; for the body only lives through the soul, and it is by the soul that we enjoy God" (ibid., chap. 27, n. 28).

6. Lombard, *Libri iv sententiarum,* book 3, dist. 29, chap. 1, n. 108.

7. Earlier, such was Hugh of St. Victor's view, in *Summa sententiarum,* tr. 4, chap. 7 (PL 176, 125-26).

8. Bonaventure, *In III Sententiarum,* dist. 29, art. un., q. 1, 2. See ibid., q. 3.

9. Augustine, *Enchiridion,* chap. 20, n. 76 (PL 40, 268; CCSL 46, 91), frequently cited thereafter (by Middleton, Suarez, Van Est, Garrigou-Lagrange, etc.) in support of the same reading. Another favorite has been *Retractationes,* book 1, chap. 8, n. 3 (PL 32, 594), or (in other numbering) book 1, chap. 7, n. 3 (CSEL 36, 36).

10. Aquinas, *In III Sententiarum,* dist. 29, a. 2.

11. Ibid., a. 5.

12. Aquinas, *Summa theologica,* II-II, q. 26, a. 4. See also idem, *Opusculum* 54, chap. 3. On "Der Primat der Selbstliebe" in Aquinas, see Völkl, *Selbstliebe,* 268-82.

13. Aquinas, *In III Sententiarum,* dist. 31, a. 3, q. 3; *Soliloquium de quatuor mentalibus exercitiis,* chap. 4, n. 13.

14. See Alszeghy, *Grundformen der Liebe,* 189-90.

15. Aquinas, *Summa theologica,* II-II, q. 26, a. 13.

16. Aquinas, *In III Sententiarum,* dist. 29, a. 5, ad 3. The next two responses involve the same confusion. See also *Summa theologica,* II-II, q. 26, a. 4, *ad* 2.

17. See, e.g., Peinador, *Cursus brevior theologiae moralis,* vol. 2, 240-41.

18. See for instance Suarez, *Tractatus de charitate,* disp. 9, section 3, n. 7, and the preceding references he provides.

19. "Possemus dicere, sicut de bonis temporalibus, quod ponere vitam pro magno amico, cum ibi sit justa causa, esset laudabile. Si tamen vellet ponere vitam pro homine quocumque, puta pro latrone, esset quidem peccatum" (Francisco de Vitoria, *Comentarios a la secunda secundae de Santo Tomás,* ed. V. de Heredia, vol. 2, *De caritate et prudentia* [Salamanca: Biblioteca de Teólogos Españoles, 1932], 108-9 [on q. 26, a. 4]). "Secundum bona temporalia, quae quis & sibi & proximo tenetur velle, & aequalia etiam inter se sint, semper tenetur quis magis seipsum diligere, quam quemlibet proximum sibi parem aut se inferiorem" (Valencia, *Commentariorum theologicorum tomi quatuor,* vol. 3, col. 651).

20. See for instance ibid., col. 652; Castro Palao, *Operis moralis,* 397; and the many authors both cite.

21. In a modern disciple, this conclusion reads: "Hence, even if we have benevolent impulses, our sole final end would not be necessarily the general happiness or welfare. But, it will be said, the benevolent impulses relate to the good of all and the selfish to the good of one man only, and two such impulses would not be properly balanced unless we sought our own good as a part merely of the general happiness. Our reply is that this contention might be allowed did not the impulse for our own good outweigh all the other impulses. And that it does outweigh all others is evident from the fact that in every act we must wish our own good, whereas it is rarely that the benevolent impulses assert themselves within us. Our benevolent impulses have no part, for instance, in inducing us to eat or drink or study mathematics. Hence, the impulse for our own good is of more importance in the constitution of man than that of benevolence" (Michael Cronin, *The Science of Ethics,* vol. 1 [Dublin: Gill, 1932], 332). To learn what is better, observe what is commoner and stronger.

22. Compare Aquinas, *Summa theologica,* q. 27, a. 2, on the distinction between affective love and rational goodwill.

23. See Aquinas, *In X libros Ethicorum ad Nicomachum expositio,* book 9, l. 8 ("Et hoc ideo, quia homo maxime est amicus sibi ipsi, et sic homo maxime debet seipsum amare"), and Durandus, *In Petri Lombardi sententias,* book 3, dist. 29, q. 1, n. 9 ("Secundo potest sic argui ex altera clausula dicti Aristotelis. Unicuique est amabile bonum proprium, sed quod est bonum mihi est magis proprium quam illud quod est proximi, quia licet proximus sit alter ipse, non tamen est ego ipse, sed alter, ergo aequale bonum debeo mihi magis diligere & optare quam proximo").

24. "Dicitur *Levit.* et *Matt., Diliges proximum tuum sicut teipsum;* ex quo videtur quod dilectio hominis ad seipsum est sicut exemplar dilectionis quae habetur ad alterum. Sed exemplar potius est quam exemplatum. Ergo homo ex caritate magis debet diligere seipsum quam proximum" (II-II, q. 26, a. 4). This text and translation, like subsequent ones from questions 25 and 26, are from St. Thomas Aquinas, *Summa theologiae,* vol. 34, *Charity,* ed. and trans. R. J. Batten (New York: McGraw-Hill, 1975).

25. See J.-B. Desrosiers, *Par-dessus tout . . . la charité: Traité de la charité d'après saint Thomas* (Montreal: Éditions de l'Institut Pie-XI, 1948), 204: "Or, la règle vient nécessairement avant ce dont elle détermine la mesure, tout comme la

cause est antérieure à l'effet. Le divin Maître prescrit donc de s'aimer d'abord soi-même, le prochain ensuite."

26. See Joannes Duns Scotus, *In III Sententiarum,* dist. 29, q. un. ("Mensura est perfectior mensurato; sed dilectio sui est mensura dilectionis proximi, juxta illud Matth. 19 et 22: *Diliges proximum tuum sicut teipsum*"), and Gennaro Bucceroni, *Institutiones theologiae moralis,* vol. 1 (Rome: Forzani, 1892), 140 ("Regula autem prior est ac potior quam regulatum. Quare amor sui praecedit semper et praefertur amori proximi, ubi de bonis eiusdem ordinis agatur, et de pari necessitate").

27. "Et hoc patet ex ipsa ratione diligendi. Nam sicut supra dictum est, Deus diligitur ut principium boni super quo fundatur dilectio caritatis; homo autem seipsum diligit ex caritate secundum rationem qua est particeps praedicti boni; proximus autem diligitur secundum rationem societatis in isto bono. Consociatio autem est ratio dilectionis secundum quandam unionem in ordine ad Deum. Unde sicut unitas potior est quam unio, ita quod homo ipse participet bonum divinum est potior ratio diligendi quam quod alius associetur sibi in hac participatione. Et ideo homo ex caritate debet magis seipsum diligere quam proximum."

28. For unhelpful variations on this oft-repeated argument, see, e.g., Scotus, *In III Sententiarum,* dist. 29, q. un., 2; Luis de Torres, *Disputationes in secundam secundae D. Thomae* (Lyons: Cardon, 1617), col. 951; Carolus Thomasius, *Arbor uberrima sacrae doctrinae* (Rome: Typis Ignatii de Lazzaris, 1656), 297; Desrosiers, *Par-dessus tout,* 205; Marcel Viller and Henri Monier-Vinard, "Charité envers le prochain," in *Dictionnaire de spiritualité,* vol. 2, col. 656.

29. "Et secundum hoc dicendum est quod amicitia proprie non habetur ad seipsum, sed aliquid majus amicitia: quia amicitia unionem quandam importat, dicit enim Dionysius quod amor est *virtus unitiva,* unicuique autem ad seipsum est unitas, quae est potior unione. Unde sicut unitas est principium unionis, ita amor quo quis diligit seipsum, est forma et radix amicitiae: in hoc enim amicitiam habemus ad alios, quod ad eos nos habemus sicut ad nosipsos; dicitur enim in *Ethic.* quod *amicabilia quae sunt ad alterum veniunt ex his quae sunt ad seipsum.*"

"In Plato's *Laws* we first encounter the saying, apparently traditional, that 'every man is naturally his own friend.' This idea was to provide Aristotle with a developed theory of friendship. In the *Eudemian Ethics* he elaborates the theory that friendship is formed on the basis of self-esteem by the recognition in the friend of that rational nature which one has learned to value in himself; in the *Nichomachean Ethics* the word *philautia* is brought in to express this positive self-evaluation. . . . Within the Thomist tradition love has been used with a wide metaphysical sense to mean a movement toward, or a force maintaining, cohesion and unity, whether of the universe at one extreme or of the individual personality at the other. This will tend to yield an idea of self-love as a kind of personal ontological integrity, an 'identity with ourselves, an adherence to ourselves,' as Gilleman describes it. In this case love-of-self, so far from being the surd among loves, becomes the archetype of them all, a presupposition of all further loving relationships, which will, given the interrelatedness of all agents, necessarily lead on to other loving relationships if only it is itself complete" (O'Donovan, *The Problem of Self-Love,* 3, 6). The reference is to Gérard Gilleman, *Le primat de la charité en théologie morale* (Brussels and Paris: Desclée, 1954), 142.

30. St. Thomas, *On Aristotle's* Love and Friendship, trans. P. Conway (Providence: Providence College, 1951), 95.

31. "Ideo homo ex caritate debet magis seipsum diligere quam proximum. Et hujus signum est quod homo non debet subire aliquod malum peccati, quod contrariatur participationi beatitudinis, ut proximum liberet a peccato."

32. Willem H. Van Est, *In quatuor libros Sententiarum commentaria* (Paris: Josse etc., 1680), vol. 3, 91.

33. Scotus, *In III Sententiarum,* dist. 29, q. un.

34. See, e.g., Suarez, *Tractatus de charitate,* disp. 9, section 3, n. 6; Paul-Gabriel Antoine, *Theologia moralis universa,* vol. 3 (Naples: Sumptibus A. Cervonii, 1780), 112; Joannes P. Gury, *Compendium theologiae moralis,* vol. 1, 17th ed. (Rome: Civiltà Cattólica, 1866), 204; Desrosiers, *Par-dessus tout,* 205; Peinador, *Cursus brevior theologiae moralis,* vol. 2, 233; B. Olivier, "Charity," in *Theology Library,* ed. A. Henry, vol. 4, *The Virtues and States of Life,* trans. R. Olsen and G. Lennon (Chicago: Fides, 1957), 185. Compare St. Thomas, *On Aristotle's* Love and Friendship, 95; idem, *Summa theologica,* II-II, q. 64, a. 7; Völkl, *Selbstliebe,* 278.

35. Merkelbach, *Summa theologiae moralis,* 694.

36. Gabriel Biel, *Collectorium circa quattuor libros Sententiarum,* ed. W. Werbeck and U. Hofmann, vol. 3 (Tübingen: Mohr, 1979), 522-23 (book 3, dist. 29, qu. un., not. 3).

37. Burnaby's summary (*Amor Dei,* 274) of Scotus, *In III Sententiarum,* dist. 29, q. 1, n. 2.

38. Joseph Butler, *Works,* vol. 2, 157 (paragraph break omitted). See Charles Coppens, *Moral Philosophy* (New York: Schwartz, Kirwin and Fauss, 1920), 97-98; Paul J. Glenn, *Ethics* (St. Louis: Herder, 1941), 185-86; Louis Janssens, "Norms and Priorities in a Love Ethics," *Louvain Studies* 6 (1976-77):220.

39. Ramsey, *Basic Christian Ethics,* 163.

40. See Hugh of St. Victor, *De sacramentis,* book 2, part 13, chap. 10 (PL 176, 538-39); compare Van Est, *In quatuor libros Sententiarum commentaria,* vol. 3, 91.

41. Ibid., 90.

42. Palao, *Operis moralis,* 397. See Wöhrmüller, *The Royal Law,* 11: "Assuredly the law of charity does not exact that always and everywhere the interests of strangers should take precedence over our own—it would be a heroic thing thus to love the neighbor more than self."

43. See, e.g., St. Bonaventure, *In III Sententiarum,* dist. 29, a. un., q. 3 ("iam duos proximos deberet diligere duplo quam se ipsum, et tres in triplo, et sic ulterius ascendendo"); Denis the Carthusian, *Commentaria in tertium Sententiarum,* 486, and *Summa de vitiis et virtutibus* (Tournai: Typis Cartusiae S.M. de Pratis, 1910), 177 ("Propter quod ait Salvator: Quid proficit homo, si lucretur universum mundum, se ipsum autem perdat, et detrimentum sui faciat?"); William of Auxerre, *Summa aurea in quattuor libros Sententiarum,* book 3, tr. 6, chap. 2, q. 1: "Patet quod caritas in infinitum magis diligit Deum quam aliquem hominem et post Deum debet magis diligere se in infinitum quam alium et si infiniti homines essent magis deberet diligere se homo quam omnes illos quoniam autem diligere Deum est diligere se" (quoted in Johannes Schneider, *Das Gute und die Liebe nach der Lehre Albert des Grossen* [Munich: Schöningh, 1967], 261).

44. Völkl, *Selbstliebe,* 303-4.

45. Pomerius, *The Contemplative Life,* 137. See Erich Fromm, *Man for Himself: An Inquiry into the Psychology of Ethics* (New York: Holt, Rinehart and Winston, 1961), 128-29.

46. See John Dewey and James H. Tufts, *Ethics* (New York: Holt, 1909), 388-89; Louis Jacobs, "Greater Love Hath No Man . . . The Jewish Point of View of Self-Sacrifice," in *Contemporary Jewish Ethics,* ed. M. Kellner (New York: Sanhedrin, 1978), 175-76; Ahad Ha'am (Asher Ginzberg), *Essays, Letters, Memoirs—Ahad Ha'am,* trans. and ed. L. Simon (Oxford: East and West Library, 1946), 132; Thomas H. Green, *Prolegomena to Ethics,* 3d ed. (Oxford: Clarendon Press, 1890), 226; W. T. Stace, *The Concept of Morals* (New York: Macmillan, 1937), 167-80.

47. Gilson, *The Christian Philosophy of Saint Augustine,* 137. See Arndt, *True Christianity,* 129, 238; Maximus, *The Four Centuries of Charity,* 146-47, 158; Boniface Ramsey, "Almsgiving in the Latin Church: The Late Fourth and Early Fifth Centuries," *Theological Studies* 43 (1982):237-38 (citing Zeno of Verona, *Tractatus,* book 2, chap. 1, n. 6 [CCSL 22, 149]).

48. Janssens, "Norms and Priorities," 220.

49. Ibid., 228.

50. "In Barn. 19.5 we meet an interesting version of the command to love the neighbor 'as thyself.' Barnabas has, 'more than thy own life,' an interpretation which may also be present at Did. 2.7" (Furnish, *The Love Command,* 189-90). In the same letter, see also 1,4 and 4,6. On early appearances of Acts 20:35 ("It is more blessed to give than to receive"), see F. J. Foakes Jackson and Kirsopp Lake, *The Acts of the Apostles,* vol. 4, *English Translation and Commentary* (Grand Rapids: Baker, 1965), 264.

51. For references to these Christian authors, see the listings in chapter 1. For quotations from Fichte and Schopenhauer, see Friedrich Paulsen, *A System of Ethics,* ed. and trans. F. Tilly (New York: Scribner's, 1911), 379-80.

52. Doherty, *The Gospel without Compromise,* 13.

53. Elert, *The Christian Ethos,* 274. See F. Bourdeau and A. Danet, *Introduction to the Law of Christ,* trans. E. Gallagher (New York: Society of St. Paul, 1966), 174.

54. Fénelon, *Le gnostique de Clément d'Alexandrie,* quoted by Goré, *La notion d'indifférence,* 35.

55. Aelred of Rievaulx, *The Mirror of Charity,* 15.

56. François de la Mothe Fénelon, *Christian Perfection,* trans. M. Stillman, ed. C. Whiston (New York: Harper, 1947), 189-90.

57. Compare Spicq, *Agapè: Prolégomènes,* p. 57: "Le Stagirite enracine tout amour dans l'amour de soi, car on ne peut aimer que le bien, c'est-à-dire ce qui est bon pour soi."

58. St. Ignatius Loyola, *The Spiritual Exercises,* trans. L. Puhl (Westminster, Md.: Newman, 1951), 12.

59. Joseph de Guibert, *The Jesuits: Their Spiritual Doctrine and Practice: A Historical Study,* trans. W. Young, ed. G. Ganss (Chicago: Institute of Jesuit Sources, 1964), 534. See Ignatius's *Spiritual Exercises,* n. 169, and Juan Rovira, "La indiferencia," *Manresa* 8 (1932):328: "La indiferencia que se requiere no es una indiferencia afectiva, esto es, una especie de frialdad e insensibilidad, que excluya las aficiones o inclinaciones a las cosas criadas, sino que basta la indiferencia racional o apreciativa, que no se deja vencer ni dominar de esas pasiones e in-

clinaciones, antes, a pesar de ellas, se mantiene como el fiel de la balanca, dispuesta a inclinarse según la mayor moción racional, y no según moción alguna sensual." Ignatius's preference for Self-Denial as an ideal (see below, and chapter 1) does not argue against this interpretation of his "First Principle and Foundation," proposed to all retreatants.

60. Loyola, *Spiritual Exercises*, n. 234.

61. Luther, *The Freedom of a Christian*, 367.

62. Luther, *Letters of Spiritual Counsel*, 196.

63. Bucer connects this first reason with the fourth: "Our nature is so attached and subservient to worldly goods, and is always so anxious to get enough of them, that it has no free will to help others unless it has first helped itself with what it imagines to be indispensable. But our nature will never rest from helping itself and never believe that it has gained enough. Only the certainty of being children and heirs of God can give the security of already possessing what is necessary for both the present and the future" (*Instruction in Christian Love*, 45).

64. Clark, *The Christian Method of Ethics*, 188.

65. Arndt, *True Christianity*, 239.

66. Burnaby, *Amor Dei*, 293.

67. Paul Althaus, *Grundriss der Ethik*, 2d ed. (Gütersloh: C. Bertelsmann, 1953), 93.

68. Austin Fagothey, *Right and Reason: Ethics in Theory and Practice*, 6th ed. (St. Louis: Mosby, 1976), 164.

69. Arnaldo Pigna, "Vivere per gli altri," in *La carità: Dinamismo di comunione nella chiesa* (Rome: Teresianum, 1971), 143. See Morris, *Testaments of Love*, 202-3.

70. Pigna, "Vivere per gli altri," 122.

71. I grant the point for argument's sake, without conceding it. The denial belongs to a class which repudiates common usage, on the ground of supposedly superior insight. See Garth L. Hallett, *Language and Truth* (New Haven: Yale University Press, 1988), 113-15.

72. C. S. Lewis, *The Four Loves* (New York: Harcourt Brace Jovanovich, 1960), 167. On this strain in Augustine's thinking, see Boularand, "Désintéressement," col. 567.

73. Book 2, chap. 1. See, e.g., *The Conferences of St. Vincent de Paul to the Sisters of Charity*, trans. J. Leonard, vol. 4 (London: Burns Oates and Washbourne, 1940), 296-97 ("Learn from this that the sole means of preserving peace of mind is to desire nothing").

74. Lewis, *The Four Loves*, 168-69.

75. O'Donovan, *The Problem of Self-Love*, 23.

76. See Burnaby, *Amor Dei*, 274-75; C.A.J. Van Ouwerkerk, *Caritas et Ratio: Étude sur le double principe de la vie morale chrétienne d'après S. Thomas D'Aquin* (Nijmegen: Janssen, 1956), 81; St. Peter of Damaskos, in *The Philokalia*, trans. and ed. G. Palmer, P. Sherrard, and K. Ware, vol. 3 (London: Faber and Faber, 1984), 155; Louis Bouyer, Jean Leclercq, and François Vandenbroucke, *The Spirituality of the Middle Ages* (New York: Desclée, 1968), 12; Hugh of St. Victor, *The Divine Love*, 10-12; Tauler, *The Inner Way*, 26-27, 248-49; idem, *Sermons and Conferences*, 11-12; Luthardt, *History of Christian Ethics*, vol. 1, 357; William of St. Thierry, *The Golden Epistle*, trans. W. Shewring, ed. J. McCann (London: Sheed and

Ward, 1930), 66-68; Ruysbroeck, *The Seven Steps,* 40, 47; Girolamo Savonarola, *De simplicitate christianae vitae,* ed. P. Ricci (Rome: A. Belardetti, 1959), 17; Goré, *La notion d'indifférence,* 67; St. Alphonsus de Liguori, *Letters,* ed. E. Grimm, vol. 2 (New York: Benziger, 1892), 259-60; idem, *The Great Means of Salvation and of Perfection,* ed. E. Grimm (Brooklyn: Redemptorist Fathers, 1927), 437; Arndt, *True Christianity,* 31, 142; Albert Raffelt, "Interesse und Selbstlosigkeit," in *Christlicher Glaube in moderner Gesellschaft,* vol. 16 of *Enzyklopädische Bibliothek,* ed. Franz Böckle et al. (Freiburg: Herder, 1982), 144.

77. Aquinas, *Summa theologica,* I-II, q. 108, a. 4. See de Sales, *Oeuvres complètes,* vol. 5, 293.

78. Aquinas, *In duo praecepta caritatis,* prol. Concerning love for human beings, see idem, *Summa theologica,* II-II, q. 24, a. 8, c.

79. Eckhart, "About Disinterest," in *Meister Eckhart,* 85.

80. John Baptist Scaramelli, *The Directorium Asceticum,* vol. 3, rev. ed. (London: Washbourne, 1879), 113.

81. St. Ignatius Loyola, *The Constitutions of the Society of Jesus,* trans. G. Ganss (St. Louis: Institute of Jesuit Sources, 1970), 109 (n. 103). As chapter 2 explains, Ignatius's frequent references to "one's own salvation" do not offer grounds for interpreting his words in the sense of Self-Subordination. Other evidence may, but the commentators I have consulted see no reason to temper the words' rigor. See Aicardo, *Comentario,* vol. 2, p. 4 ("Después, para concluir la doctrina, se le encarga que tome como 'su mayor y más intenso oficio' buscar continuamente contrariarse, perseguirse, atormentarse"); Arthur Vermeersch, *Miles Christi Jesu: Meditations on the Summary of the Constitutions,* authorized translation, 3d ed. (El Paso, Tex.: Revista Católica Press, 1951), 158-59.

82. Bultmann, *Theology of the New Testament,* vol. 1, 344. See E. W. Trueman Dicken, *Loving on Principle* (London: Darton, Longman and Todd, 1969), 138-39.

83. Uhlhorn, *Christian Charity,* 59.

84. DuRoy, *La réciprocité,* 49.

85. Nygren, *Agape and Eros,* 217.

86. "The love of self being totally opposed
   To the holy fire of the love of God,
   Everything is to be suffered, everything done,
   To rid ourselves of its subtle poison."

Louis-Marie Grignion de Montfort, *Oeuvres complètes* (Paris: Seuil, 1966), 886.

87. Lillie, *Studies in New Testament Ethics,* 156.

88. Dewey and Tufts, *Ethics,* 367.

89. See Fénelon, *Christian Perfection,* 147: "As nothing is more dangerous than to go beyond the limits of our state, nothing would be more harmful to a soul who needs to be upheld by feelings of gratitude than to deprive itself of this nourishment suited to it, and to run after ideas of a higher perfection, for which it is not ready."

90. "Le vice d'une hiérarchie unilinéaire des valeurs," writes René Le Senne, "est de déprécier les valeurs inférieures et de susciter le fanatisme de la valeur mise à la tête de la liste. Or toute valeur est absolument respectable et aimable; et chacune doit se tempérer du respect des autres si elle n'est pas destinée à susciter l'entraînement d'une passion. Si mince que paraisse une valeur, en tant que valeur elle enveloppe l'absolu et exige pour sa part l'estime qui lui est due" (*Traité*

de morale générale, 5th ed. [Paris: Presses Universitaires de France, 1967], 678).

91. "When we speak of denying the self, we do not mean a negation of the self as such but a negation of the self *as evil.* Christianity is sharply contrasted with Hinduism and Buddhism at this point. These great Oriental religions regard as evil the natural self and its desires for things in the world of space and time. Consequently, they insist upon self-negation and world-negation in a sense quite different from that of Christianity, i.e., an absolute renunciation of self and the world as a whole. On the other hand, Christianity regards the self and the world as essentially good, since they constitute the creation of a good God, and condemns only the perversion of the self by sin and its idolatry of things in the world. As a result, it calls for negation, not of the self and the world, but of the egoism of the self and its tendency to find its highest good in the world" (Thomas, *Christian Ethics and Moral Philosophy,* 514). "Neo-Platonism came more and more to treat the body and the entire visible creation as an intrinsic obstacle to spirit, to be eliminated by the latter as completely as possible; at least this very prominent strain within it was undoubtedly pushed on to this extreme by the Gnostic sects. But Christianity has ever to come back to its central pre-supposition—the substantial goodness and spiritual utility and transfigurableness of body and matter; and to its final end,— the actual transformation of them by the spirit into ever more adequate instruments, materials, and expressions of abiding ethical and religious values and realities" (Friedrich von Hügel, *The Mystical Element of Religion as Studied in Saint Catherine of Genoa and Her Friends,* vol. 2 [London: Dent, 1923], 127).

92. Dietrich von Hildebrand, *Gesammelte Werken,* vol. 3, *Das Wesen der Liebe* (Regensburg: Josef Habbel, 1971), 341.

93. See Hallett, *Christian Moral Reasoning,* 129-37.

94. Luthardt, *History of Christian Ethics,* vol. 1, 314. See Burnaby, *Amor Dei,* 113.

95. Tertullian, *Apology,* chap. 42, quoted in Martin Hengel, *Property and Riches in the Early Church,* trans. J. Bowden (Philadelphia: Fortress, 1974), 61.

96. De Sales, *Oeuvres complètes,* vol. 5, 293.

97. Pittenger, *Love Looks Deep,* 57.

98. For instance, a central New Testament value is community, which cannot be sought without desiring others' presence and their reciprocated love. "Could you not watch with me one hour?" asked Jesus (Mt 26:40). "Open your hearts to us," wrote Paul (2 Cor 7:2).

99. Ivo of Chartres, *Decretum,* Introduction, in *The Library of Christian Classics,* vol. 10, *A Scholastic Miscellany: Anselm to Ockham,* ed. and trans. E. Fairweather (Philadelphia: Westminster Press, 1956), 239.

100. Alszeghy, *Grundformen der Liebe,* 190.

101. Sister Nazarene Morando, *The Characteristics of Charity* (Boston: St. Paul, 1963), 52, 55.

102. Thomas Barrosse, *Christianity: Mystery of Love: An Essay in Biblical Theology* (Notre Dame: Fides, 1964), 92. Exactly comparable is Wolfgang Schrage, *Die konkreten Einzelgebote in der paulinischen Paränese: Ein Beitrag zur neutestamentlichen Ethik* (Gütersloh: Gerd Mohn, 1961), 252.

103. Emmerich R. von Frentz, "Drei Typen der Liebe. Eine psychologische Analyse," *Scholastik* 6 (1931):10.

104. Boularand, "Désintéressement," col. 556 (emphasis added; column number corrected).

105. Bourdaloue, *Oeuvres complètes,* vol. 3, 435, 437; vol. 4, 25.

106. Fénelon, *Christian Perfection,* 145.

107. Kenneth E. Kirk, *Vision of God: The Christian Doctrine of the* Summum Bonum (New York: Longmans, Green, 1931), 460-61. Kirk adds: "This was the truth which Fénelon asserted in the controversial letters following upon the publication of the 'Maxims'." In like vein, see ibid., 554; Radoslav A. Tsanoff, *The Moral Ideals of Our Civilization* (New York: Dutton, 1942), 259; Joseph L. Allen, *Love and Conflict: A Covenantal Model of Christian Ethics* (Nashville: Abingdon, 1984), 119.

Chapter 6

1. Birch and Rasmussen, *Bible and Ethics,* 143-44, 148-51.

2. Ibid., 150.

3. See Adam Smith, *The Theory of Moral Sentiments,* in *Adam Smith's Moral and Political Philosophy,* ed. H. Schneider (New York: Harper, 1970), 38-39 (e.g.: "Though the standard by which casuists frequently determine what is right or wrong in human conduct, be its tendency to the welfare or disorder of society, it does not follow that a regard to the welfare of society should be the sole virtuous motive of action, but only that in any competition it ought to cast the balance against all other motives"); Palmer, *Altruism,* 12 ("When a man is charged with selfishness it is usually because he is thought to have obtained some advantage. But why should he not? He is blamable only when he detaches the thought of his own advantage from advantage to others. My good must not be had at another's expense. When a plate of apples is passed and I pick out the best one, the wrong is not in my obtaining a good apple but in my depriving somebody else of one. That is selfishness. Whenever my gain is not inconsistent with his or, as is usually the case, actually contributes to it, the larger the gain made by me the better").

4. See, e.g., Hallett, *Reason and Right,* 12-14, or C.D. Broad, *Five Types of Ethical Theory* (London: Kegan Paul, 1930), 63-66.

5. John G. Milhaven, "Love: Giving of Self or Meeting the Self's Needs?" *America* 136 (1977):502.

6. C.D. Broad, *Ethics and the History of Philosophy: Selected Essays* (New York: Humanities, 1952), 65-66. In Sidgwick's *The Methods of Ethics,* see, e.g., xviii.

7. For an effective critique of Richard Price's self-preferential intuition, see W. D. Hudson, *Reason and Right: A Critical Examination of Richard Price's Moral Philosophy* (San Francisco: Freeman, Cooper, 1970), 107-8.

8. Max Hocutt, "Toward an Ethic of Mutual Accommodation," in *Humanist Ethics: Dialogue on Basics,* ed. M. Storer (Buffalo: Prometheus Books, 1980), 144.

9. Such naive egoism, equating rationality with self-interest, is widespread. It appears, for instance, in attempts to "justify" morality: "The traditional philosophical problems of morality and politics are incomprehensible if they are not seen to involve the attempt to show how it is the particular individual's interest to conform his life to the moral order, an attempt to show why one should be moral"

(John Charvet, *A Critique of Freedom and Equality* [Cambridge: Cambridge University Press, 1981], 5).

10. Ayn Rand, *The Virtue of Selfishness: A New Concept of Egoism* (New York: New American Library, 1964), 22-23.

11. Dewey and Tufts, *Ethics,* 387. In like vein, see David Hume, *An Enquiry concerning the Principles of Morals,* section 2, part 2; Herbert Spencer, *The Data of Ethics* (New York: Rand, McNally, 1879), 226-27; Percival M. Symonds, *The Dynamics of Human Adjustment* (New York: Appleton Century, 1946), 551. In partial confirmation, see Keith F. Nickle, *The Collection: A Study in Paul's Strategy* (Naperville, Ill.: Allenson, 1966), 95.

12. Ewing, *Ethics,* 32-33.

13. See Law, *A Serious Call,* 83: "You will perhaps say that, by this means, I encourage people to be beggars. But the same thoughtless objection may be made against all kinds of charities, for they may encourage people to depend upon them. The same may be said against forgiving our enemies, for it may encourage people to do us hurt. The same may be said even against the goodness of God, that, by pouring his blessing on the evil and on the good, on the just and on the unjust, evil and unjust men are encouraged in their wicked ways. The same may be said against clothing the naked, or giving medicines to the sick, for they may encourage people to neglect themselves, and be careless of their health. But when the love of God dwelleth in you, when it has enlarged your heart, and filled you with bowels of mercy and compassion, you will make no more such objections as these."

14. Spencer, *The Data of Ethics,* 220.

15. Ibid., 220-21. Compare Rand, *The Virtue of Selfishness,* viii: "Observe what this beneficiary-criterion of morality does to a man's life. The first thing he learns is that morality is his enemy: he has nothing to gain from it, he can only lose; self-inflicted loss, self-inflicted pain and the gray, debilitating pall of an incomprehensible duty is all that he can expect."

16. Spencer, *The Data of Ethics,* 221.

17. Ibid., 218.

18. Ibid., 219. "When the ablest are honored and promoted," Walter Rauschenbusch concurs, "it benefits all. A superior type is thereby placed in a conspicuous position, and the rest are more or less modeled after it" (*Christianizing the Social Order* [New York: Macmillan, 1913], 174).

19. "Perhaps some will think that the person with greater natural endowments deserves those assets and the superior character that made their development possible. Because he is more worthy in this sense, he deserves the greater advantages that he could achieve with them. This view, however, is surely incorrect. It seems to be one of the fixed points of our considered judgments that no one deserves his place in the distribution of native endowments, any more than one deserves one's initial starting place in society" (John Rawls, *A Theory of Justice* [Cambridge, Mass.: Harvard University Press, 1971], 103-4).

20. Charles H. Patterson, *Moral Standards: An Introduction to Ethics* (New York: Ronald, 1949), 308-9.

21. Paulsen, *A System of Ethics,* 393.

22. Dewey and Tufts, *Ethics,* 380-81.

23. Paulsen, *A System of Ethics,* 388.

24. Maisie Ward, *Gilbert Keith Chesterton* (London: Sheed and Ward, 1944), 11.

25. See Ewing, *Ethics,* 38; Westermarck, *Christianity and Morals,* 279-80.

26. James S. Fishkin, *The Limits of Obligation* (New Haven: Yale University Press, 1982), 21. Virginia M. Chudgar remarks (in "Feedback" to John Mahoney, "Let's Junk the Profit Motive," *U.S. Catholic,* June 1972, 16): "Somehow I can't bring myself to feel guilty when my husband and I enjoy an occasional dinner in a good restaurant. The money saved could have been donated to charity, but—and what about the children's music lessons, the family camping trips? Hardly the necessities of life to which Mr. Mahoney would limit us. All these are what my mother always called 'hyacinths for the soul.' Is it wrong to enjoy them?"

27. See chapter 3.

28. Peter Singer, *Practical Ethics* (Cambridge: Cambridge University Press, 1979), 163.

29. Peter Singer, "Famine, Affluence and Morality," in *Philosophy, Politics and Society,* 5th ser., ed. P. Laslett and J. Fishkin (New Haven: Yale University Press, 1979), 33.

30. Fishkin, *The Limits of Obligation,* 5.

31. Hallett, *Christian Moral Reasoning,* 76.

32. Neil Cooper, *The Diversity of Moral Thinking* (New York: Oxford University Press, 1981), 183.

33. Kierkegaard, *Works of Love,* 61.

34. Cooper, *The Diversity of Moral Thinking,* 183.

35. Alexander D. Lindsay, *The Moral Teaching of Jesus: An Examination of the Sermon on the Mount* (London: Hodder and Stoughton, 1937), 18-19. See J. L. Mackie, *Ethics: Inventing Right and Wrong* (Harmondsworth: Penguin, 1977), 131-32; Knox, *The Ethic of Jesus,* 31-32; C. G. Montefiore, *The Synoptic Gospels,* vol. 2 (London: Macmillan, 1927), 86; Joseph Klausner, *Jesus of Nazareth* (New York: Macmillan, 1925), 392-93.

36. Kuppermann, *The Foundations of Morality,* 142.

37. Singer, *Practical Ethics,* 180. See idem, "Famine, Affluence and Morality," 29-30.

38. Singer, *Practical Ethics,* 180.

39. Marshall, *The Challenge of New Testament Ethics,* 108.

40. Sigmund Freud, *Civilization and Its Discontents,* trans. and ed. J. Strachey (New York: Norton, 1961), 89-90.

41. Green, *Prolegomena to Ethics,* 295-96. See Derek Parfit, *Reasons and Persons* (Oxford: Clarendon Press, 1984), 27-29 ("There are many ways in which, if we were all pure do-gooders, this might have bad effects").

42. For "some of the different ways we can encounter the obligation to look after interests of the self as a means to serving the interests of others," see Allen, *Love and Conflict,* 122-26.

43. Richard T. Nolan and Frank G. Kirkpatrick, *Living Issues in Ethics* (Belmont, Calif.: Wadsworth, 1982), 116.

44. *The Little Flowers of St. Francis and Other Franciscan Writings,* trans. S. Hughes (New York: New American Library, 1964), 218.

45. Henry Fehren, "Meriam Lux," *U.S. Catholic,* August 1977, 39.

46. Ibid., 39-40.

47. Gilbert Highet, *The Art of Teaching* (New York: Random House, 1950), 12-13.

48. Green, *Prolegomena to Ethics,* 291-92.

49. Viktor E. Frankl, *Man's Search for Meaning: An Introduction to Logotherapy* (New York: Simon and Schuster, 1963), 154-59.

50. Ibid., 161-62, 164-65, 178-79, 184-86. See 175 ("Self-actualization cannot be attained if it is made an end in itself, but only as a side effect of self-transcendence").

51. Stephen D. Ross, *Moral Decision—An Introduction to Ethics* (San Francisco: Freeman, Cooper, 1972), 174.

52. Parfit, *Reasons and Persons,* 31.

53. See ibid.

54. Ernest Wallwork, "Thou Shalt Love Thy Neighbor as Thyself: The Freudian Critique," *Journal of Religious Ethics* 10 (1982):297.

55. Dodd, *Gospel and Law,* 61. See Knox, *The Ethic of Jesus,* 22-23, 34-52.

56. Niebuhr, *An Interpretation of Christian Ethics,* 131.

57. Dodd, *Gospel and Law,* 61-62. See Knox, *The Ethic of Jesus,* 23, 53-55, 73-74.

58. Whether Christians are tormented by their failures and their limitations depends as well on their sense of their own importance. The link between humility and peace of mind can be seen in the remark of Brother Lawrence, St. Francis's companion, "that when he had failed in his duty, he only confessed his fault, saying to God, 'I shall never do otherwise, if you leave me to myself; 'tis you must hinder my falling, and mind what is amiss.' That after that he gave himself no further uneasiness about it" (quoted by C. H. Dodd, *The Johannine Epistles* [New York: Harper, 1946], 92-93).

59. Ha'am, *Essays, Letters, Memoirs,* 132. See Green, *Prolegomena to Ethics,* 226; Janssens, "Norms and Priorities," 228.

60. Charles Hartshorne, "Some Thoughts on 'Souls' and Neighbor Love," *Anglican Theological Review* 55 (1973):146. On Buddha's view, see Parfit, *Reasons and Persons,* 502-3.

61. Hartshorne, "Some Thoughts," 147.

62. On the incoherence of such Cartesian talk about selves, see for instance Norman Malcolm, *Problems of Mind: Descartes to Wittgenstein* (New York: Harper and Row, 1971), 24-28.

63. See John Laird, *A Study in Moral Theory* (New York: Macmillan, 1926), 218-19: "I, who think now, am the same person who remembers how he began to ponder these things. If I show signs of being educated, it is *I* who was trained. If I come to a conclusion for certain reasons, *I* must hold the reasons together in my mind in order to be able to infer from them. If I am disappointed at my indifferent success, *I* must have hoped for better things." For a full discussion of personal identity and morality, see Parfit, *Reasons and Persons,* Part Three.

64. Cooper, *The Diversity of Moral Thinking,* 263.

65. Kurt Baier, "Ethical Egoism and Interpersonal Compatibility," *Philosophical Studies* 24 (1973):358 (italics omitted).

66. Ibid., 357; idem, *The Moral Point of View,* 189-90. See David Pugmire, "Altruism and Ethics," *American Philosophical Quarterly* 15 (1978):77: "Suppose altruism always to be virtuous and sometimes the sole or highest moral option: and suppose acting with the highest moral rectitude to be always the overriding good; then the altruist, who logically bars sacrifice by another, has curtailed that person's greatest interest in caring for a lesser one and has thus done him a disservice." The same distinction that meets Baier's objection answers Pugmire's too.

67. Baier, "Ethical Egoism and Interpersonal Compatibility," 358.

68. Ibid., 359.

69. E.g., Richard B. Brandt, *Ethical Theory: The Problems of Normative and Critical Ethics* (Englewood Cliffs, N.J.: Prentice-Hall, 1959), 374.

70. Brian Medlin, "Ultimate Principles and Ethical Egoism," in *Morality and Rational Self-Interest,* ed. D. Gauthier (Englewood Cliffs, N.J.: Prentice-Hall, 1970), 63 ("It may be worth pointing out that objections similar to those I have brought against the egoist can be made to the altruist").

71. See Geisler, *Ethics,* 140-41; Pugmire, "Altruism and Ethics," 76-77, 79; Harris, "Can Agape Be Universalized?," 25-26; Jacobs, "Greater Love Hath No Man," 176 (quoting J. H. Hartz); Ayn Rand, *For the New Intellectual* (New York: New American Library, 1961), 144; Arno Plack, *Die Gesellschaft und das Böse* (Munich: Paul List, 1967), 318; and perhaps Immanuel Kant, Preface to *The Metaphysical Elements of Ethics,* trans. T. Abbott, in *Kant's Theory of Ethics* (London: Longmans, 1909), 304 ("That one should sacrifice his own happiness, his true wants, in order to promote that of others, would be a self-contradictory maxim if made a universal law").

72. Spencer, *The Data of Ethics,* 270. See L. Harold deWolf, *Responsible Freedom: Guidelines to Christian Action* (New York: Harper and Row, 1971), 105-6.

73. John Hospers, "Baier and Medlin on Ethical Egoism," *Philosophical Studies* 12 (1961):11.

74. John Hospers, *Human Conduct: Problems of Ethics,* 2d ed. (New York: Harcourt Brace Jovanovich, 1982), 135.

75. See Ewing, *Ethics,* 31-32; Hazlitt, *The Foundations of Morality,* 103; Lecky, *History of European Morals,* vol. 2, 157 (St. Anthony's visit to St. Paul the hermit); Cooper, *The Diversity of Moral Thinking,* 274-75; Dorothy Emmet, *The Moral Prism* (New York: St. Martin's, 1979), 122; Michael Scriven, *Primary Philosophy* (New York: McGraw-Hill, 1966), 260.

76. P. 224.

77. Hastings Rashdall, *The Theory of Good and Evil: A Treatise on Moral Philosophy,* vol. 2 (Oxford: Clarendon Press, 1907), 128. See Bentham's *Deontology,* quoted in Hazlitt, *The Foundations of Morality,* 82; Francis Hutcheson, "Inquiry concerning Moral Good and Evil," in *A Guide to the British Moralists,* ed. D. Monro (London: Fontana/Collins, 1972), 154-55; Charles A. Baylis, *Ethics: The Principles of Wise Choice* (New York: Holt, 1958), 99-100; John Laird, *An Enquiry into Moral Notions* (New York: Columbia University Press, 1936), 272-73; Patterson, *Moral Standards,* 305, 317-18; Christopher New, "Saints, Heroes and Utilitarians," *Philosophy* 49 (1974):185; Ewing, *Ethics,* 32.

78. Thomas Nagel, *The Possibility of Altruism* (Oxford: Clarendon Press, 1970), 92. See Stace, *The Concept of Morals,* 164-67.

79. Hallett, *Christian Moral Reasoning,* 128. See ibid., 96-102, 127-28.

80. Broad, *Five Types of Ethical Theory,* 242. See ibid., 241.

81. Ibid., 240.

82. Paulsen, *A System of Ethics,* 391.

83. Rescher, *Unselfishness,* 33.

84. Ibid., 42.

85. Ibid., 43.

86. Bourdaloue, *Oeuvres complètes,* vol. 3, 448-49.

87. Contemporary ethicians distinguish between a norm whose *practice* would be best and one whose *acceptance* would be best. See William K. Frankena, *Ethics,* 2d ed. (Englewood Cliffs, N.J.: Prentice-Hall, 1973), 40.

88. E.g., Broad, *Five Types of Ethical Theory,* 241.

89. J. Philip Wogaman, *A Christian Method of Moral Judgment* (Philadelphia: Westminster Press, 1976), 40-41.

Chapter 7

1. Stace, *The Concept of Morals,* 168-69.

2. Nygren, *Agape and Eros,* 47-48. For comparable statements, see Spicq, *Agapè dans le Nouveau Testament,* vol. 2, 7; C. H. Dodd, *The Interpretation of the Fourth Gospel* (Cambridge: Cambridge University Press, 1953), 200.

3. Herbert Waddams, "Ascetical Theology," in *Dictionary of Christian Ethics,* ed. Macquarrie, 18-19.

4. Kierkegaard, *Works of Love,* 28-29. See David Little and Sumner B. Twiss, *Comparative Religious Ethics* (San Francisco: Harper and Row, 1978), 101; Bernard Gert, *The Moral Rules: A New Rational Foundation for Morality* (New York: Harper, 1966), chap. 8; G. J. Warnock, *The Object of Morality* (London: Methuen, 1971), chap. 6; Frankena, *Ethics,* chap. 4; Outka, *Agape,* chap. 5.

5. Patterson, *Moral Standards,* 303. Chapter 2 took issue with this sort of terminological imperialism; *good* is used, frequently and legitimately, to describe objectively moral conduct, abstracting from motive or intention.

6. Joseph H. Fichter, "Jesuit Involvement with the Poor and Needy," in *The Creighton Symposium: Justice Education for Social Concern* (Omaha: Creighton University, 1978), 29-30.

7. Herbert Hendin, *The Age of Sensation* (New York: Norton, 1975), 13, quoted in Paul C. Vitz, *Psychology as Religion: The Cult of Self-Worship* (Grand Rapids: Eerdmans, 1977), 121. More recently, in *Habits of the Heart: Individualism and Commitment in American Life* (Berkeley: University of California Press, 1985), 109, Robert N. Bellah et al. write of a widespread attitude toward love and marriage: "Since the only measure of the good is what is good for the self, something that is really a burden to the self cannot be part of love. Rather, if one is in touch with one's true feelings, one will do something for one's beloved only if one really wants to, and then, by definition, it cannot be sacrifice."

8. Massillon, "On Charity," 412. On the basis of his experience in a Japanese concentration camp, where theologically trained missionaries showed themselves adept at perceiving the will of God in their egoistic preferences, Langdon Gilkey learned the sad truth that "teaching high ideals to men will not in itself produce better men and women. It may merely provide the taught with new ways of justifying their devotion to their own security." *Shantung Compound* (New York: Harper and Row, 1966), 112. See Garrett Hardin, *The Limits of Altruism: An Ecologist's View of Survival* (Bloomington, Ind.: Indiana University Press, 1977), 21.

9. See Ludwig Wittgenstein, *Culture and Value,* ed. G. H. von Wright, trans. P. Winch (Chicago: University of Chicago Press, 1980), 53; Niebuhr, *An Interpretation of Christian Ethics,* 115, 230; idem, "Love and Law," in *20 Centuries of*

Great Preaching, ed. Fant and Pinson, vol. 10, *Luccock to Niebuhr,* 371; Joseph Katz, "On the Nature of Selfishness," *Journal of Philosophy* 45 (1948):102.

10. Dodd, *Gospel and Law,* 60-61.

11. Paulsen, *A System of Ethics,* 390. See Alasdair MacIntyre, "Egoism and Altruism," in *The Encyclopedia of Philosophy,* ed. P. Edwards (New York: Macmillan, 1967), vol. 2, 466.

12. Paulsen, *A System of Ethics,* 387.

13. Gilleman, *The Primacy of Charity,* xxix.

14. Ibid., xxviii-xxix.

15. Thomas E. Jessop, *The Christian Morality* (London: Epworth, 1960), 77.

16. Hallett, *Christian Moral Reasoning,* 173.

17. See ibid., 187.

18. Jessop, *The Christian Morality,* 71.

19. Richard S. Peters, *Reason and Compassion* (London: Routledge and Kegan Paul, 1973), 119.

20. Stephen C. Mott, *Biblical Ethics and Social Change* (New York: Oxford University Press, 1982), 58. See Francis X. Meehan, *A Contemporary Social Spirituality* (Maryknoll, N.Y.: Orbis, 1982), 51-54.

21. Konstantinos Delikostantis, *Der moderne Humanitarismus* (Mainz: Matthias-Grünewald-Verlag, 1982), 187, citing A. Auer, *Autonome Moral und christlicher Glaube,* Düsseldorf, 1971, 82. See Lionel S. Thornton, *Conduct and the Supernatural* (New York: Longmans, Green, 1915), 191: "The problems of personal relationship between individuals are unchanging and absolutely determinative, for upon them, in the last resort, the whole structure of society rests."

22. Rauschenbusch, *Christianizing the Social Order,* 275-76.

23. Ibid., 272.

24. Hospers, *Human Conduct* (1st ed.), 170.

25. On the split in the Lutheran tradition, between personal and social ethics, see N. H. Søe, *Christliche Ethik* (Munich: Chr. Kaiser, 1965), 162-64. "In another way both Emil Brunner and William Temple have given love and justice separate and different relevances, holding that 'love' is an imperative in interpersonal relations and 'justice' in intergroup relations—Brunner speaking of 'systems' and Temple of 'organizations'" (Joseph Fletcher, *Moral Responsibility: Situation Ethics at Work* [Philadelphia: Westminster Press, 1967], 44). See Emil Brunner, *Justice and the Social Order,* trans. M. Hottinger (New York: Harper, 1945), 114-18, 125-29; and William Temple, *Christianity and Social Order* (New York: Seabury, 1977), 78-79.

26. Schweitzer, "He That Loses His Life," 678. See Fishkin, *The Limits of Obligation,* 3 ("Our common ethical assumptions, which work well at the small scale, break down when they are applied to large enough numbers") and 7-9.

27. Schweitzer, "He That Loses His Life," 679.

28. Rawls, *A Theory of Justice,* 3.

29. There is widespread agreement that charity and justice differ, but little agreement as to how they differ. Missing from any discussion I have read is clarification of the kind that might come from a prior determination of agape's precise norm. See, for instance, Jean-Yves Calvez and Jacques Perrin, *The Church and Social Justice: The Social Teaching of the Popes from Leo XIII to Pius XII,*

trans. J. Kirwan (Chicago: Regnery, 1961), chap. 7. "Charity," it is said, "incites men to do more for each other than justice demands" (ibid., 173). Self-Subordination helps specify the "more."

30. Rawls, *A Theory of Justice,* 303.

31. Ibid., 3.

32. See Hardin, *The Limits of Altruism,* 117; Robert G. Olson, *The Morality of Self-Interest* (New York: Harcourt, Brace, and World, 1965), 10 ("The disinterested altruist who preaches the sacrifice of the individual in the name of society allows little, if any, place for efforts at social reform").

33. Lindsay Dewar, *An Outline of Anglican Moral Theology* (London: Mowbray, 1968), 168-69.

34. Thomas F. Higgins, *Man as Man: The Science and Art of Ethics,* rev. ed. (Milwaukee: Bruce, 1958), 556.

35. Edgar S. Brightman, *Moral Laws* (New York: Abingdon, 1933), 238-39.

36. Niebuhr, *An Interpretation of Christian Ethics,* 139.

37. Johannes Messner, *Social Ethics: Natural Law in the Western World,* trans. J. Doherty, rev. ed. (St. Louis: Herder, 1965), 336 (italics omitted). "A small community, similarly, may sacrifice its own advantage, power and utility for the needs of an empire" (Laird, *A Study in Moral Theory,* 227).

38. Ha'am, *Essays, Letters, Memoirs,* 137. See Hardin, *The Limits of Altruism,* 27.

39. Reinhold Niebuhr, *Man's Nature and His Communities* (New York: Scribner's, 1965), 42.

40. Idem, *An Interpretation of Christian Ethics,* 133-34. See ibid., 136-37.

41. John C. Bennett, *Christian Ethics and Social Policy* (New York: Scribner's, 1956), 65.

42. A. Macbeath, *Experiments in Living* (London: Macmillan, 1952), 434.

43. If agape's norm applies to societies, the same problem reappears for them (e.g., for an individual corporation within a nation, and its relations to corporations within the same nation and those in others nations).

44. For extensive (but unsatisfactory) discussion of the analogies between persons and corporations (not nations), see Peter A. French, "The Corporation as a Moral Person," *American Philosophical Quarterly* 16 (1979):207-15, and Thomas Donaldson, *Corporations and Morality* (Englewood Cliffs, N.J.: Prentice-Hall, 1982), e.g., chap. 2.

45. I here paraphrase statements concerning "every individual," in Peters, *Reason and Compassion,* 122. See Howard L. Harrod, *The Human Center: Moral Agency in the Social World* (Philadelphia: Fortress, 1981), 82 ("At a concrete level, the social past is the coexperienced story of predecessors and their larger social meaning; and the social future is the image of shared projects which we, along with our contemporaries, hope to realize"), 116 ("The identity and distinctiveness, as well as the temporal duration of moral communities are made possible by shared paradigms of value meaning").

46. Donaldson, *Corporations and Morality,* 19 (of corporations).

47. Roger Mehl, *Pour une éthique social chrétienne* (Neuchatel: Delachaux & Niestlé, 1967), 59.

48. Andre Donner, *The Christian and the Nations* (Grand Rapids: Eerdmans, 1968), 13-14.

49. Jeremy Bentham, *The Principles of Morals and Legislation,* chap. 1, iv (his italics), quoted in Allen, *Love and Conflict,* 266.

50. Harrod, *The Human Center,* 82.

51. Donner, *The Christian and the Nations,* 34.

52. W. G. Maclagan, *The Theological Frontier of Ethics* (New York: Macmillan, 1961), 39.

53. Allen, *Love and Conflict,* 267. See Laird, *A Study of Moral Theory,* 241-44.

54. Ernest Gellner, "Explanations in History," *Proceedings of the Aristotelian Society,* suppl. vol. 30 (1956):163.

55. Ibid., 172-73.

56. Hallett, *Christian Moral Reasoning,* 91.

57. Gerald Runkle, *Ethics: An Examination of Contemporary Moral Problems* (New York: Holt, Rinehart and Winston, 1982), 296. See Peter L. Berger and Brigitte Berger, *Sociology: A Biographical Approach* (New York: Basic Books, 1972), 172-73; Edward LeRoy Long, Jr., *The Role of the Self in Conflicts and Struggle* (Philadelphia: Westminster Press, 1962), 14-18, 67-69; Charles Cooley, *Human Nature and the Social Order,* rev. ed. (New York: Scribner's, 1922), 308-9.

58. Michel Bouet, *Les motivations des sportifs* (Paris: Éditions Universitaires, 1969), 97 (paragraph break omitted).

59. Darrell Puls, "Kathy: A Holiday Remembrance," *Teacher's Voice,* 22 Dec., 1980, 1, is as revealing about the author as about his subject, and about the society they both represent.

60. Quoted in Garrett Hardin, *Promethean Ethics: Living with Death, Competition, and Triage* (Seattle: University of Washington Press, 1980), 35.

61. James W. Keating, quoted in Runkle, *Ethics,* 296.

62. Aquinas, *Summa theologica,* I-II, q. 32, a. 6, *ad* 3.

63. See Frank H. Knight, *The Ethics of Competition and Other Essays,* 2d ed. (New York: Harper, 1936), 72-73.

64. Nagel, *The Possibility of Altruism,* 131.

65. Ernest Van Den Haag, *Passion and Social Constraint* (New York: Dell, 1965), 133, quoted by James W. Keating, "The Ethics of Competition and Its Relation to Some Moral Problems in Athletics," in *The Philosophy of Sport: A Collection of Original Essays,* ed. R. Osterhoudt (Springfield, Ill.: Charles C. Thomas, 1973), 161.

66. Viktor E. Frankl, *The Unheard Cry for Meaning: Psychotherapy and Humanism* (New York: Simon and Schuster, 1978), 98.

67. Bruce C. Ogilvie and Thomas A. Tutko, "Sport: If You Want to Build Character, Try Something Else," *Psychology Today,* October 1971, 63.

68. Bouet, *Les motivations des sportifs,* 107.

69. Robert J. Higgs, *Sports: A Reference Guide* (Westport, Conn.: Greenwood, 1982), 197.

70. Bouet, *Les motivations des sportifs,* 110.

71. William J. McGucken, *The Jesuits and Education* (New York: Bruce, 1932), 36.

72. Robert Schwickerath, *Jesuit Education: Its History and Principles* (St. Louis: Herder, 1904), 514-15.

73. Ibid., 512-13.

74. Hardin, *Promethean Ethics,* 36-37. See Donald W. Shriver, Jr., *Rich Man Poor Man: Christian Ethics for Modern Man* (Richmond, Va.: John Knox, 1972), 59.

75. Albert T. Lauterbach, *Man, Motives, and Money: Psychological Frontiers of Economics* (Ithaca, N.Y.: Cornell University Press, 1954), 40.

76. Ruth F. Benedict, "An Anthropologist's View of Values and Morality," in *The Problems of Philosophy,* ed. W. Alston and R. Brandt, 2d ed. (Boston: Allyn and Bacon, 1974), 133.

77. Rauschenbusch, *Christianizing the Social Order,* 312-13. See ibid., 165.

78. Richard H. Tawney, *Religion and the Rise of Capitalism* (London: J. Murray, 1926), 286, quoted in Westermarck, *Christianity and Morals,* 281.

79. See Hallett, *Christian Moral Reasoning,* 10; Antony Flew, "The Profit Motive," *Ethics* 86 (1975-76):312-22. As Laurent Dechesne remarks, "the moral value of the individuals concerned makes for tremendous differences in the actual effects of the profit-seeking motive. Whereas some persons give free expansion to their greed, with no scruple whatsoever, others are detained by praiseworthy moral considerations and try hard to contribute to the welfare of their fellow men" ("The Factors of Altruism," in *Explorations in Altruistic Love and Behavior,* ed. P. Sorokin [Boston: Beacon, 1950], 231).

80. Mahoney, "Let's Junk the Profit Motive," 14. See Arthur O. Lovejoy, "Christian Ethics and Economic Competition," *The Hibbert Journal* 9 (1910-11):327-30.

81. See Dechesne, "The Factors of Altruism," 233-34; Long, *The Role of the Self,* 45-46.

82. George Palmer's phrase. See *Altruism,* 87.

83. Thomas Tutko and William Bruns, *Winning Is Everything and Other American Myths* (New York: Macmillan, 1976), xi. See Stuart H. Walker, *Winning: the Psychology of Competition* (New York: Norton, 1980), 4, 17-18 ("Competition is a satisfying demonstration of creativity, mastery, and courage").

84. *America,* 21 June, 1980, 528.

85. See Francis J. Sheed, *Society and Sanity* (New York: Sheed and Ward, 1953), 96-97.

86. Knight, *The Ethics of Competition,* 47.

87. William James, *Principles of Psychology,* vol. 2 (New York: Holt, 1939), 409. See idem, *Talks to Teachers on Psychology,* new ed. (New York: Holt, 1939), 51-54.

88. Bertrand Russell, *Authority and the Individual* (New York: Simon and Schuster, 1949), 8.

89. Cooley, *Human Nature and the Social Order,* 309.

90. See Harry Kaufmann, *Aggression and Altruism: A Psychological Analysis* (New York: Holt, 1970), 140; Ogilvie and Tutko, "Sport," e.g., 61-62; Frankl, *The Unheard Cry for Meaning,* 98-101.

91. Lovejoy, "Christian Ethics and Economic Competition," 336-38; Keating, "The Ethics of Competition," 163.

92. Knight, *The Ethics of Competition,* 74. See Robert G. Osterhoudt, "On Keating on the Competitive Motif in Athletics and Playful Activity," in *The Philosophy of Sport,* ed. idem, 194.

93. The title I presently conceive for this planned inquiry—*Nearest versus Neediest*—suggests its motivation and its focus.

94. Quoted in van Breemen, *Called by Name,* 39.

INDEX